THE GRIEF LETTER
The Adventure of Grief Finds Joy Again

Fran Buhler

Fran Buhler

... to comfort all who mourn.

Titus 3:4-6

TGL QR Code

Scan QR Code using favorite smartphone App to direct to TGL Website

www.TheGriefLetter.com

www.Facebook.com/TheGriefLetter

Copyright © 2018 Fran Buhler

All rights reserved.

ISBN: 978-1-981978-13-7

DEDICATION

Dedicated to Nancy, my favorite cheerleader, exceptional wife, mother and grandmother - soon to be great grandmother - known as "Mom B" to the Buhler families, and our "Teacher of the Year"!

And also to the 776 families with whom I have walked in their grief ... whether for funerals and memorial services, at graveside or cremations.

ENDORSEMENTS AND TESTIMONIALS

"I found so much comfort in the manuscript, it was a healing experience for me. TGL connected with me. I cannot think of any issue, feeling or thought associated with grief which I experienced that is not addressed in TGL. I would rate TGL as excellent! It is comprehensive, easy-to-read and very well researched."

Ms. Kathryn L. Funchess - Environmental Attorney, Florida Department of Environmental Protection; Sanctuary Choir, First Baptist Church of Tallahassee

"Your concern and passion for helping those in grief comes through loud and clear and establishes a personal relationship between the reader and you, the author. This makes the book personal---written just for me."

Dr. Ken Boutwell - Founder, Capital Health Plan; Former President & CEO of MGT of America

"A great grief-read book. The thing I loved most about TGL is the short chapters and individual topics many books don't deal with. One thing I intend to use myself is Nancy's comment, 'I hurt with you'... I love it---it says so much."

Mrs. Beverly Baines - Retired, Production Department, The Carthage Courier; Pastor's wife; Loudon, Tennessee

"I really enjoyed your illustrations from lives of people. I would give TGL high marks because it is written with sincere empathy and tells many stories of people who grieve. I will give it to friends, encouraging them to read it a little at a time."

Mrs. Janice Cruce - Third Grade Teacher, Moore Elementary School; Pastor's wife; Tallahassee, Florida

"TGL addresses a difficult topic with a remarkable blend of compassion and practicality. You offer a host of helpful suggestion, each with an appropriate measure of substantive theological truth. TGL will be a blessing to so many in their season of need."

Dr. Doug Dortch - Pastor, Mountain Brook Baptist Church; Birmingham, AL; Moderator, Cooperative Baptist Fellowship 2016-17

"Several chapters reminded me of the grief that I have experienced as Pastor counseling those in grief. Other chapters spoke to me personally of my own grief process, especially the grief I felt for many years of the deaths of those I personally knew…who died in Vietnam."

Rev. Thomas Baines - Vietnam Veteran; Former Pastor; Director of Missions; Interim Pastor, Piney Grove Baptist Church; Midtown Community / Harriman, Tennessee

"TGL offers us profound insights, helpful strategies and a realistic portrayal of grief and its many issues. Every pastor needs a copy of TGL."

William D. Shiell, Ph D. - President & Professor of Pastoral Theology and Preaching, Northern Seminary; Lombard, Illinois (Chicago)

"Your insight about 'grieving without faith' spoke to me. I have witnessed so many people down through the years who have tried to travel down a faith-less road, only to find it a dead end."

"I found the scripture references, the chapter take-away, and the action steps to be very constructive. As a grief read, I would rate TGL as relevant, comforting, challenging, creative, inclusive and many times inspiring."

Rev. Joel S. Hawthorne - Pastor, Montgomery Hills Baptist Church; Silver Spring, Maryland

CONTENTS

INTRODUCTION		i
PREFACE		iii
HOW YOU READ THE GRIEF LETTER IS YOUR CHOICE		vii
PART 1: "THE GRIEF LETTER"		1
Chapter 1	HOW "THE GRIEF LETTER" BEGAN	3
Chapter 2	CONFRONTING THE OCTOPUS OF GRIEF	9
Chapter 3	THE DARK AND WINDING, OFTEN CONFUSING, HALLWAYS OF GRIEF	15
Chapter 4	"HOW WILL I GET THROUGH TODAY?"	23
Chapter 5	LEARNING TO HANDLE THE "BODY BLOWS" OF GRIEF	28
Chapter 6	OWN YOUR GRIEF	37
Chapter 7	GRIEVING IN THE WILDERNESS OF "WHY?"	47
Chapter 8	PERSONAL WILDERNESS DISCOVERIES	59
Chapter 9	HAVE YOU TRIED THE "ANGER BUCKET"?	68
Chapter 10	"WILL I EVER LAUGH AGAIN?"	76
Chapter 11	GRIEVING ALONE IN THE "PAIN CLUB"	88
Chapter 12	"A GRIEF LIKE NO OTHER": GRANDPARENT GRIEF	98
Chapter 13	"GRIEF IS A SACRED TIME"	103
Chapter 14	"IS TRANSFORMATIONAL GRIEF POSSIBLE?"	113

| Chapter 15 | GETTING OVER GRIEF: "IS CLOSURE THE BEST OBJECTIVE?" | 123 |

PART 2: GRIEF ADVENTURE IS A LIFE CHOICE — 133

Chapter 16	THE SOULFUL JOURNEY OF GRIEF: "FEELING YOUR WAY OUT OF GRIEF"	137
Chapter 17	GRIEF ADVENTURE LEADS TO PERSONAL GROWTH: BEYOND THE "WADDLE-WADDLE" STAGE	146
Chapter 18	THE SOUL SIDE OF GRIEF: THE ADVENTURE OF GRIEF FINDS JOY AGAIN!	157
Chapter 19	THE PERSONAL BENEFIT OF GRIEF-FAITH; "A COMFORT…ONLY FROM GOD"	164
Chapter 20	THE ADVENTURE OF FAITH: THE PROMISE OF A PRESENCE	172

PART 3: THE TEN COMMANDMENTS OF GRIEF — 179

Chapter 21	THE TEN COMMANDMENTS OF GRIEF	183
Chapter 22	WHY TWELVE STEPS FROM GRIEF TO HEALING?	190
Chapter 23	THE GRIEF TEXT AND THE SOCIAL MEDIA EPITAPH	198
Chapter 24	REDEMPTIVE STEPS FOR GRIEVING FAMILIES	205
Chapter 25	THE "WOE-IS-ME" DISEASE	213
Chapter 26	"ARE GRIEF AND FAITH ENEMIES OR FRIENDS?"	223
Chapter 27	GRIEF AND GUILT Q & A: "IS THERE SUCH A THING AS 'GUILT REMOVAL'?"	231
Chapter 28	"HOW DO I KNOW I'M GETTING BETTER?"	236

	PART 4: WHAT TO SAY AND DO WHEN SOMEONE DIES	245
Chapter 29	"WHAT DO I SAY WHEN SOMEONE DIES?"	249
Chapter 30	THE ELEVENTH COMMANDMENT OF GRIEF	258
Chapter 31	HELPING A CHILD WITH THE CHALLENGE OF GRIEF	263
Chapter 32	THE BEST PART OF GRIEVING IS BELIEVING!	271
Chapter 33	THE ADVENTURE OF LISTENING TO THOSE WHO MOURN	276
	APPENDICES	283
	APPRECIATION FOR PREPUBLICATION READERS AND FOR PERSONAL ASSISTANCE	284
	APPRECATION FOR GRIEFSHARE AND HOSPICE	287
	CHAPTER NOTES	289

THE GRIEF LETTER

INTRODUCTION

Grief invades our lives. Even when we know grief is at the door, it is a complete "take over"---jerking us through a heart-breaking sadness. The most frequent comment I hear about grief is the soft declaration "**You have no idea what I'm going through!**" We have no Road Map for Grief. In our emotional tumult and tears, grief is our response to what another life meant to us.

When I was nine, my uncle died. I sat through the funeral and graveside with a little boy's curiosity but with little emotion. Grief did not grab me. When my fifth grade teacher's husband died, I saw her grief erupt in the midst of our classroom. I saw how overpowering grief can be! But I never experienced such grief, until my Mother died, a grief I share in Chapter 5.

For over two decades, as associate pastor/director of ministry, I wrote an annual letter to every church member who experienced a death that year. Congregants called it "the grief letter". In 2006, I began chapter drafts that over the next ten years became a 90,000 word nonfiction book to comfort and encourage grieving individuals and families, titled: **"The Grief Letter" (TGL)**.

I'm guessing you're no stranger to grief, or you wouldn't be reading TGL. Check the grief themes I write about. See how they relate to your grief experience. Give *The Grief Letter* a chance. Open your grieving heart to the Holy One. You may feel differently several months down the road of grief. I stake my faith here: The griever who lives by faith with a heart of courage plus the God-given strength of perseverance finds joy again![1]

The Grief Letter (TGL) reflects my journey, my seminary education and my professional grief experience. I write out of my own personal grief as well as my pastoral grief ministry. What I write also reflects my considerable research into the grief experience of others.

If you come to these pages in grief, you are already in my prayers. I am interested in your personal grief progress. I hope and pray your grief will mean something to you and do something for you. In the power and love of the Holy One, I pray His providential care will comfort you in your grief, nurturing new courage and enthusiasm for life---every day you live. Given the way you may feel today, this could seem like grief pie in the sky!

Having personally gone through the experience of soul-shaking grief, I write from my own grief challenges. In my pastoral grief ministry experience, I have walked the painful path of grief with hundreds of grieving souls. Now, I want to share with you my faith and offer my findings.

While we have no roadmap for grief---no guided tour to soften our sorrow---we do have an inspired guidebook. The Bible, as evidenced by texts throughout the pages of TGL, says far more about grief than most people think. We also have a "personal guide" the Bible calls "the Holy One." The Most High God leads us gently through our sorrow. In the depth of our grief pain, there is a faith experience for daily help and encouragement. Each TGL chapter is my personal letter to you in your grief. Allow it to become a springboard for your grief-faith exploration, a personal venture shaping the future God has for you.

Welcome to *The Grief Letter*. Pull up a chair and be comfortable. You will be glad you did.

PREFACE

We have a school for grieving, an academy for facing the death and loss of a loved one. We call it "life"! When we mourn a death, we represent a significant portion of our population. **The magnitude of grief in the US is simply mind-boggling**.

Grief in the U.S. Today

Since 2014 we have been at the 2.5 million deaths per year benchmark in the US, according to the National Center for Health Statistics in the Center for Disease Control and Prevention.

In the US, an estimated eight million people grieved the death of someone in their immediate family in 2014 and the years following. We expect the deaths of grandparents and parents, but what about the following examples?

- One million grieved the death of a spouse. (Harvard Family Health Guide)
- 400,000 people under age 25 grieved the death of a loved one. (National Mental Health Association)
- 228,000 children die every year. (Theravive Grief Counseling website)
- 36% of the US population grieves the death of a son, daughter, brother or sister. (Theravive Grief Counseling website)
- 169,000 grandparents grieve the death of a grandchild each year.

Death and grief are growth industries, a shocking assertion, yet a true reality! We all experience grief due to the death of someone in our lives. "The Grief Letter" (TGL) addresses this staggering need in the US today.

No one by-passes life's grief journey. There are no escape hatches. We do not choose the experience. We do not sign up for it. In the course of our lives, we become acquainted with both sorrow and joy. We each live through our own grief and sadness.

Why This Matters

For many individuals and families, grief is a life passage to acknowledge briefly, accept passively, put behind us quickly and then move on rapidly.

As we each face the death and grief challenges in our lives and families, I invite you, regardless of your personal faith or family views, to engage *The Grief Letter* as a grief support resource in your life in the community where you live.

We are bound together by what F. Forrester Church calls, "this mortar of mortality."[2] In my professional grief ministry experience, I have been invited into people's lives at the time of their greatest sorrow and pain, and I will not sell their experience for selfish gain. At the request and with the permission of many people with whom I have walked in their individual and collective grief, I will draw from their grief experience while guarding their privacy, using fictitious names and references

If you consider yourself a non-believer, if you are agnostic or an avowed atheist, I respect you and your point of view. You will also experience the death of family and friends. While I believe I must write out of my faith tradition, my personal grief and ministry experience, I do not wish to shove my faith "down your throat." I will express my faith in the course of writing *The Grief Letter*, but I will not use these pages to bully or demean those holding other views. I welcome your readership. I hope we can meet on the pages of "The Grief Letter".

What This Means

While I'm duty bound to keep the faith to which I have been called, I am also compelled to be as inclusive as possible. "The shrapnel of sorrow" is no respecter of persons and represents a divisive danger point.

The quantum ache of grief and sorrow distributed across America at any point in time is palpable. We surely can stand together in our grief in the face of death even though so much of life seeks to tear us apart and splinter us into so many divisive "isms".

The Banquet Table of Faith

There is more at stake here than being sensitive to other faith traditions and being inclusive with non-believers. While I write from a Christian faith point of view, I come to the "banquet table of faith" with a vast number of persons from other faith traditions whose desire to follow the Most High God in the journey of grief and sorrow is just as sincere and genuine as mine.

The most important aspect of "the banquet table of faith" is that it is not my table or your table or the table of any particular faith group. No, the banquet table of faith is the table of the Most High God. The Most High controls the "open" invitation policy.

I do not intend my words in *The Grief Letter* to be limited to fellow Christians. My hope is that readers of the Jewish, Islamic, and other faiths will not read my words in opposition to "your" faith tradition as I write from a Christian perspective. At the same time, I surely hope Christian readers will understand why I write inclusively.

By the very nature of the incarnation---the belief that God was in Christ---when we Christians point to Jesus, or when we make reference to the Holy Spirit, we do not intend a second god, a third god, or another god. We point to the Holy One, to the Most High God, in whom we trust. We do not intend the expression to be a slap in your face or at your faith. When we speak the name Jesus, we do so because it is our way of affirming the ONE TRUE GOD.

For agnostics, atheists and other non-believers, when I make reference to the Most High God, or to Jesus, would you ask yourself: "If I could believe in a God, what would that God be like?" Then see how what you come up with squares with the views, beliefs and concepts I use. In everything I write, I never question that you care.

The Preface "Take-Away": "God's comfort is as sure as the sunrise!"

As planet earth revolves, the high level of human grief represents one of life's givens—as certain as the sunset—the most painful of life's challenges and losses. I pray *The Grief Letter* narrative gives you comfort and gentle understanding in your sorrow. I hope *The Grief Letter*—the counsel it offers and the help it provides—will now be set loose in the universe, connecting with those who are heart-deep in their pain, offering solace to those who live out their sorrow, giving comfort to those who mourn.

In our grief, if we leave the door of our heart open, we find God's comfort is as sure as the sunrise.

We find our hope in a higher power, the Holy One, the God of Abraham, Isaac, and Jacob: the God of Sarah, Rebekah, Leah, and Rachel. In the words of Isaiah, "For the Lord comforts His people, and will have compassion on His afflicted ones." (Isaiah 49:13) We are His people, and the sheep of His pasture—all of us!

I offer "The Grief Letter" to all who mourn, and remind us: Even a Preface needs a blessing:

"May the God of life and death throughout all space and time be a Comforting Presence with each of us in our lives, in our grief—throughout our grief---and beyond.

In the Name of the Most High God, the Holy One, Amen.

THE GRIEF LETTER

HOW YOU READ THE GRIEF LETTER IS YOUR CHOICE

Every chapter of "The Grief Letter" is my personal letter to you in your time of grief, with my salutation and a personal close.

The Table of Contents provides a "self-guided tour" for *The Grief Letter*. You may read sequentially, chapter by chapter, or exercise your choice and read topically according to your grief experience or according to your need.

Part 1: Chapters 1 thru 15 of *The Grief Letter* address the staggering grief need in the US today, speaking to hurting hearts, offering comfort, reflection, challenge and guidance for the grief we face---no matter who we are or what our faith may be.

Part 2: Chapters 16 thru 20, "Grief Adventure is a Life Choice", address grief at both a faith and a feeling level, offering solace and building griever strength for the healing journey ahead. Good grief adventure choices result in transformative outcomes.

Part 3: Chapters 21 thru 28, "The Ten Commandments of Grief", help avoid the pitfalls of the grief recovery challenge, taking us beyond a potentially stagnant grief into the new life of purposeful grief and personal growth---evidence of a transformative quality.

Part 4: Chapters 29 thru 33, "What to Say and Do When Someone Dies", equips the reader to become more effective at comforting those who mourn. When we grieved, someone cared, giving us comfort. We have an opportunity now to be a comfort for someone else. Months may pass, even a year, before we are able to comfort others.

My Suggestion:
- Read the Introduction plus Chapters 1 through 6 of Part 1.
- Then go to chapters that address your immediate grief need.
- After your initial grief, read Part 2 in sequence, Chapters 16 – 20.
- Part 3, Chapters 21 – 28, is ready when you are.
- If you are grieving hard, it could be a while before you want to read Part 4, Chapters 29 – 33. This is normal.

Select your chapter reading order according to your personal grief circumstance. I hope you find "The Grief Letter" helpful. On the pages to follow, I pray you experience the peace of God as you discover a life beyond your grief.

In the Name of the One Who Comforts, and Gives New Strength, Amen.

PART 1

"THE GRIEF LETTER"

PART 1 - CHAPTER 1

CHAPTER 1

HOW "THE GRIEF LETTER" BEGAN

Dear Reader,

Grief is difficult! When we have tears in our eyes and sorrow in our hearts, crying harder won't help. Trying harder won't fix it.

When a loved one dies, grief shatters our lives and scatters our attention. Whether death is anticipated or comes as a shocking surprise, grief is life's heaviest burden! Whatever we may think, feel or wish, when grief has us in its grip it is painfully slow about letting go.

In the face of grief's challenge, no matter how heavy our grief, God's grace will free us from the overwhelming burden of grief, lifting us to a higher level of living. The grace of the Most High God is ever present, never expires. If you are serving time in the prison of broken hearts, allow the Holy One to fortify your spirit, bring sunshine to your days and laughter to your life.

Grief is always difficult, but grief does not have the final say. God's grace and comfort turn our tears into fuel for grief's challenges. If you bought, borrowed, or were gifted *The Grief Letter* because you grieve the death of someone important in your life, my heart goes out to you. I know how it feels to grieve, and I have already prayed for you. This is how "the grief letter" began, as a personal letter to those in grief---long before it ever found life via this book.

How "the grief letter" Became The Grief Letter

In 1993, immediately after Thanksgiving, as associate pastor and director of ministry of a flagship church in Florida's capital city, Tallahassee, I began sending a letter to everyone in our church who had a death in their immediate family during that year. Recipients started calling it "the grief letter". You may read the original "grief letter" at the end of this chapter.

Over the years I've had more comments, notes and appreciation for "the grief letter" than any single thing I've done in ministry---except a short sermon!

PART 1 - CHAPTER 1

I began "the grief letter" without a grand plan, simply to comfort those members who mourned. In the life of our church, the actual number of member deaths in a given year, at that point in time, was typically two to three dozen. Immediate family member deaths, including persons who may not be members of our church, moved the number to 75 to 100, plus hundreds more in the extended circle of family and friends. Anecdotal evidence indicates a high pass-it-on circulation factor for each "grief letter", ranging from three to eight additional people.

The grief letter has reached a sizeable universe of grievers. During my 21-year tenure, I have conducted or assisted in 776 funerals. From this platform of grief ministry, I write *The Grief Letter: The Adventure of Grief Finds Joy Again*. Let's take this soulful journey of grief together!

Why The Grief Letter Matters

The Grief Letter as a book speaks to the life-sized sorrow we experience when someone dies. The soul-deep pain of an irrevocable loss of someone near and dear---due to death---is rigorous and raw and unlike any other loss. As "the grief letter" has spoken over the years to people suffering in grief, I surely hope and pray "The Grief Letter" as a book will speak to hurting hearts and comfort every soul in sorrow who comes to this volume for help and healing.

Having faced the challenge of "the grief avalanche" in our church for 21 years, I wanted to do something for individuals beyond our doors, persons I shall never be able to reach or touch except via the proven pathway of a volume accessible to anyone who wants to buy a grief book and grow as you grieve, or one who wants to "comfort those who mourn."

Many have asked for a book to help with their grief, as one person said, "something griever-readable". So I write in response to spoken need, having seen the human hunger for a "read" companion addressing life's deepest pain. Every work week of my career I have witnessed the cry for a resource to comfort and challenge those who mourn. We each live out of our own experience of grief and gladness. In the course of life, we become acquainted with both sorrow and joy. We may in God's grace and comfort discover new purpose as we live forward toward new possibilities.

"Shall we agree on a definition of grief?"

Let's keep it simple, keyed to an acceptable source for our task of clarification. I suggest we use the definition offered by Siri on our Smart

Phones, the straightforward dictionary definition: "Grief is a deep sorrow caused by someone's death."

The Grief Letter Connects with "the Griever in Each of us".

One of our biggest life challenges is how we handle grief. "The Grief Letter" as a book speaks to what Isaiah calls "the day of grief and desperate sorrow." (Isaiah 17:11) Our human experience with death and grief is as old as humanity and as new as the Smart Phone. Just as my IPhone addresses daily communication needs, "The Grief Letter" approaches an age-old "need to grieve" in new and thoughtful ways.

If you feel alone or abandoned in your grief, help is near. In our personal experience, can we say with the psalmist: "This I know, that God is for me" (Psalm 56:9)? This has been the faith attitude of hundreds and hundreds of individuals and families I have known. Grief is God's sacred time. Whenever grief comes, be open to His Presence.

The Chapter "Take-Away": How to Use The Grief Letter

Engage *The Grief Letter* according to your "need" agenda. The narrative walks and talks with the reader who grieves while offering insight to the grief helper. The reader who wants a better understanding of grief may follow the topical structure. One who comes in sorrow may be drawn to a chapter here, a sub-section there, in short snatches, according to one's grief-attention span.

As you grieve, allow the chapter format and sequence to take you by the hand and lead you into a time of healing and soul-deep help, a process of reflection and potential transformation, a place where tears are welcome and heart-break works its way toward new life and joy. Whether you come to *The Grief Letter* as a reader who grieves or as a grief professional, you receive a thoughtful, helpful reward.

- Brief chapter lengths average six and a half pages. They are "grief length", not standard publishing or academic length. The narrative is designed to connect within a griever's "attention scope".
- Remember to spot read what interests you immediately, by scanning the Table of Contents, reading according to your sorrow and your "grief attention span".
- Each chapter is my personal "grief letter" to you, in your particular time of grief.

PART 1 - CHAPTER 1

My author bias is intentionally biblical; my faith is simply Christian. As my friend Joel Hawthorne, Pastor of Montgomery Hills Baptist Church, Silver Spring, Maryland, says, "Whatever tomb we may be standing by, there is good news to share." I believe grief, when approached with a heart of faith and practiced with sincerity, is potentially transformative and, if pursued faithfully, has the power to become transformational.

In this first chapter, I want to express my personal regard for readers of other faith traditions and also welcome grieving non-believers. In the deep pain of our grief, we each in our own way look to the Most High God in faith, wondering along with the writer of "The Lamentations"…"if there is any sorrow like my sorrow"? (The Lamentations of Jeremiah, Chapter 1, verse 12b)

Your partner in grief,

Fran Buhler

A Grief PS: Don't try to avoid your grief! Grief is something to think, ponder and pray about…

1. Ask God for help with your grief. Pray the all-sufficient grief prayer: "God, help me." I have prayed that prayer myself---it works! Remember the words of Robert Browning. Take them to heart. Allow them to steady you:
"I tread no path in life to Him unknown;
I lift no burden, bear no pain, alone…"

2. Write down two of your grief concerns. Pray what's on your heart…because you mean it!

3. Remember, you do not grieve alone. As we noted in the Preface, numerically grief is much larger and involves many more people than we may be aware. The message here is not the national statistic, but the awareness of death and grief swirling all around us within our borders, wherever we may live, including our own grief and our own community.

THE GRIEF LETTER

AN ORIGINAL DRAFT of "the grief letter"

Date: Thanksgiving, 1993

Dear Reader and Partner in Grief,

I am writing out of my own experience with grief to say something I hope will be helpful during the holidays. After a loved one dies, the holidays can be challenging and difficult. The absence of our loved one makes the holiday time very different. In my experience, I have found it helps to give some thought to this matter before the time arrives.

Some try to act as if nothing has changed. Others decide to ignore the holidays completely as if the pain can be pushed aside. A spiritually and emotionally healthy approach is to acknowledge the loss, recognize the pain of our continuing grief and think about ways to approach this time--- confident that God's grace will get us through.

Here are just a few suggestions:

1. Be aware you will have mixed emotions. Christmas and other holidays may reawaken your grief and intensify your feelings of loss. Your memories of previous times together may cause you to feel incomplete and sad. Permit yourself to cry if you need to, embrace your pain. But be sure to give thanks for the life and the years you had together. The pain of grief is very real but the Grace of God will bring healing.

2. Be honest and open with family and friends about your feelings. This will help you and other members of your family come to terms with the death. Cry when you have to, laugh when you can, and don't give up on God.

3. Be realistic about your expectations. The fairy-tale fantasy of how Christmas "should   be" fails to recognize that the death and absence of a loved one is a **natural** and **normal** thing for individuals and families to experience as a part of their Christmas celebration. "Coping with grief during the holidays," writes grief specialist Joe Gross, "has the potential of creating even greater stress upon oneself or the family system. The expectation of other family members and friends… can be a problem. Their plans for you may conflict with your plans and thus create confusion or disappointment between you."

4. Plan to be with someone on the actual holiday if possible. Because your

grief is deep and painful, you may want to avoid others. But sitting alone during these days can be miserable. Staying alone will only increase your sense of isolation. This is a time to motivate yourself to do something for someone else. If you need your "alone" time, the holidays will allow times for that other than Christmas day.

5. Be gentle to yourself. If your emotions bubble up unexpectedly, take a break, don't be embarrassed, and **be glad you are a person who has the capacity for such healthy human feelings**. Claim the life that God has given you. Feel good without feeling guilty. Feel sadness without totally blocking out the joy of Christmas. Certain sights and sounds may trigger your emotions and cause you to be hard on yourself or, in severe instances, cause you to question your sanity. Remember God created the grief process as an outlet and as a way of healing.

6. Don't forget the power of God and His faithfulness. Let prayer be an ever-present resource for you. Yet don't push yourself, if you "don't feel like praying." That's a very normal reaction. Claim the promises of God's presence and care. God will honor that. Or simply pray the Prayer of Serenity: "God grant me the serenity to accept the things I cannot change, courage to change the things I can, and wisdom to know the difference."

7. Allow God's word to speak to you. Consider overlooked passages such as Psalm 34:18: "God is near to the broken hearted and delivers the crushed in spirit." Turn to your favorite texts. Grief is an opportunity to expand our spiritual experience of God. If you believe anything in the Bible, believe God will never leave you nor forsake you.

Trust God's grace with your grief. Trust God's power with your pain. Have a blessed Christmas and a happy New Year!

In Christ's Love,

Franchot Buhler
Associate Pastor/Director of Ministry

CHAPTER 2

CONFRONTING THE OCTOPUS OF GRIEF: THE FIRST THING WE LEARN!

Dear Reader,

"I have never hurt like this before in my life," the gentlemen said, following the death of someone close and dear. Over the course of my personal life and professional experience in ministry, I have heard this assertion from numerous grieving individuals. At the deaths of each of my parents, I felt the same way.

Following my mother's death, our family entered the sanctuary where our father had once served as pastor. For our celebration of her life, the gathered congregation was singing "Amazing Grace." It felt like the day I was swimming when an octopus grabbed my ankle, pulling me where I didn't want to go.

Memories tangled with my tears as the thought flashed across my grieving brain: "Grief is like putting an octopus to bed while someone sings 'Amazing Grace.'"

Grief grabs us, pulling us where we don't want to go. Like an octopus, grief has a will and a schedule of its own. Try keeping your grief under control and you find it is so squiggly wiggly strong there is little you can do to subdue it. You never know when the octopus will put the squeeze on you, grabbing you tightly, wrestling you into submission and tears. From two Greek words that mean "eight feet", "octopus" even sounds biblical!

When someone important in our life dies, the more we try to strong-arm our grief, the more belligerent our grief becomes, the more relentless our grief remains and the less life benefit our grief provides.

The First Thing We Learn

The first time I used the octopus metaphor, I was with a grieving gentleman whose wife died suddenly, unexpectedly. I went by to visit him the week after his wife's funeral.

He was exhausted, and even apologized that he was so tired.

"You should be tired," I asserted. "Grief is like wrestling an octopus!"

"You know, that is exactly where I am," he said, "wrestling that octopus every day!"

Several months later, I used the octopus again, this time with a lady whose father died following a lengthy illness. Death's arrival is always intrusive, and exhausting. "I've been searching for words to describe what I'm experiencing," she confessed. "I feel like I've been in a wrestling match. And there's never any time to rest. Grief is almost non-stop", she announced.

"Like wrestling an octopus," I asked? "Yes!" she shot back. "Where did you get that?---that's it," she said.

This may be the first thing we learn when we grieve. "Grief is almost non-stop"---like wrestling an octopus!

Why This Matters

Grief, with its bitter taste, is difficult to swallow. Grief hurts because everything in life is connected. Never underestimate the power of grief. There is no way we can push our grief aside, stuff it in a closet or hide it out of sight, any more than we could hope to put an octopus to bed.

Grief is like a reverse massage. While a massage helps us relax, grief makes us tense, bringing us to tears. After a 50-minute massage, we are reinvigorated. After an hour of grief, we are tense, tight and full of turbulence.

I recently stumbled upon an "on-line" example of what the grief experience is actually like when we find ourselves wrestling the octopus in frustration and tears. Grief is like the person who wrote the following online plea: "My friend just died. I don't know what to do?"

Grief is also like the generous response to the above online request, coming from a responder who merely identified himself as "old". I would consider him "experienced". The self-identified "old man"---who no doubt is about my age---wrote about the "scar tissue" of grief and the deep meaning behind our sorrow before turning to his personal grief description which...[3]

THE GRIEF LETTER

Sounds like an Octopus to Me!

Here is what the "old man" had to say:

> "As for grief, you'll find it comes in waves. When the ship is first wrecked, you're drowning, with wreckage all around you. Everything floating around you reminds you of the beauty and the magnificence of the ship that was, and is no more... You find some piece of the wreckage and you hang on... Maybe it's a happy memory or a photograph. Maybe it's a person who is also floating. For a while, all you can do is float. Stay alive."

Then the "experienced" responder ventures into the "waves of grief" that follow with their turbulent impact, as if we were wrestling a stubborn octopus on steroids:

> "In the beginning, the waves are 100 feet tall and crash over you without mercy. They come ten seconds apart and don't even give you time to catch your breath... After a while, maybe weeks, maybe months, the waves come farther apart...they still crash all over you and wipe you out... You never know what's going to trigger the grief. It might be a song, a picture, a street intersection, the smell of a cup of coffee. It can be just about anything...and the wave comes crashing."

The "old" man's description is accurate, faithful and complete, capturing grief's early bombing raids, as well as its ongoing impacts:

> "Somewhere down the line, and it's different for everybody, you find that the waves are only 80 feet tall. Or 50 feet. And...they come farther apart. You can see them coming. An anniversary, a birthday... And when it washes over you, you know that somehow you will, again, come out the other side. Soaking wet, sputtering, still hanging on to some tiny piece of the wreckage..."

Then the gentleman concludes, "Take it from an old guy, the waves never stop coming. But you learn...you'll survive them." In contrast to some strong opinion, grief is never a weakness, but the inevitable "pay-back" of love and strong relationships.

Why allow the octopus-nature of grief to hold sway in our lives? Grief pain cries out for a grief Presence. We surely need the Presence of the Holy One who "comforts all who mourn".

PART 1 - CHAPTER 2

"Does the Bible Know How I Feel?"

Her daddy had died. She was ten years old when she asked the question above. When we grieve, we appreciate the respect others have for our grief. Yet in today's world, many do not expect to hear anything matching their grief experience---especially from scripture.

The prophet Jeremiah captures our grief pain with words we might never expect to find in the Bible, words even a ten year old can understand. "My joy is gone, grief is upon me, my heart is sick." (Jeremiah 8:18 ESV)

Before our very eyes, we find evidence from God's Word: The Holy One knows our sorrow. But, we wonder, does the God of all space and time stand ready to comfort us as we mourn?

Yes, according to scripture and personal experience, He does!

Grief and Sabbath Rest

In Matthew 11, Jesus answers the question from John, sent from prison via one of his associates: "Are You the Expected One, or shall we look for someone else?" For myself, I have always been drawn to Jesus's response near the end of Matthew 11.

First, the words as they appear in a modern, widely accepted, translation: "Come to Me, all who are weary and heavy laden, and I will give you rest. Take my yoke upon you, and learn from Me, for I am gentle and humble in heart; and you shall find rest for your souls." (Matthew 11:28-29 NAS) Why turn to these words in sorrow?

Because Jesus's response to grief-filled circumstance or sorrow-heavy situations may be understood as follows in verse 28: "Come to Me, all who are weary in sorrow and burdened with grief, and I will lift you, giving rest to your spirit and peace to your soul."

This is promise and comfort. The Holy One of the universe made known through His self-revelation and via His revelation in the one called "Jesus" is specifically concerned about our grief. His purpose is to refresh and renew us. Every time I have grieved, I have needed this promise of rest for my soul.

Verse 29 offers a promise we may read as follows: "Take my school of life and faith and follow it, and you will find rest, you will find wholeness and peace for your soul." Interestingly, here the Hebrew word for "rest" is used elsewhere and refers to the Jewish "shabbat" or Sabbath rest. What is described here is the promise and the divine assurance that in our grief the Holy One offers what every grieving heart needs---Sabbath rest.

When we grieve the death of someone dear to us, God in Christ Jesus offers us Sabbath rest---any moment of the day, any time of the year.

Verses for the Valley: "The Lord is my Light and my salvation: whom shall I fear? The Lord is the strength of my life; of whom shall I be afraid?" (Psalm 27:1).

Also: "...you will be sorrowful, but your sorrow will turn to joy." (John 16:20).

Can Grief Become a Friend?

Why not view grief as a friend? Why not welcome grief as a natural part of life and get to know grief as one of life's learning and growing experiences?

Writing about grief differs from writing about other topics because grief has its own "hooks". Yet grief has a similarity. One has to have grieved in this life before writing about it. Grief commands our attention and keeps it. None of us recall the first time we cried, but we remember the first time we grieved. And all the grief times after that.

So, why does our grief matter? Because we are creatures who love, who care; because we are spiritual beings. We grieve to deepen, widen and enlarge our experience of death and loss. In the redemptive power of a loving God, even in our grief and especially in our grief, we are blessed. Even if in that moment we cannot grasp it!

The Chapter "Take-Away"

In my grief following the death of my mother, and, again, when a few years later my father died, I discovered the comfort of Sabbath Rest (both immediately, and over time), the life-giving comfort of the Most High God who---when we need it most---gives strength for our lives.

In the grip of the octopus, in spite of its non-stop strength, the Holy One reaches out to us in ways that calm our spirit and heal our sorrow. Like the Hebrew saying, "No matter how dark the tapestry God weaves for us, there's always a thread of grace." In times of sorrow, the Holy One stills us

PART 1 - CHAPTER 2

as He frees us from the octopus. His Presence comforts us. His Grace sustains us, if we give Him the chance.

This is why I started "the grief letter". Over the years "the grief letter" took on a life and pursued a purpose all its own. After responses from numerous "grief letter" recipients, I prayed about an appropriate non-invasive way to follow up "the grief letter" in a manner that would continue and expand its original mission and ministry. Why?

In the spirit of shared humanity and common grace I wanted to speak comfort and healing for our grief-saturated lives, especially when the octopus gives us fits.

In the midst of our grief, I wanted to focus where we hurt, become aware of how we are healing, and remain alert to how we might in turn comfort others.

Each chapter of "The Grief Letter" concludes with a grief PS, a combination of challenge thoughts and action steps, placed strategically at the close of each chapter-letter.

As we share sorrow and heart break, we walk the hallowed halls of grief together, partners in grief, benefactors of grace, sharing a soul-deep pain, opening our hearts and minds to the Holy One who comforts all who mourn.

Your grief partner and friend,

Fran Buhler

A Grief PS: You may ask: Why use this strange octopus metaphor for grief?

1. Well, have you ever tried to control or manage an octopus?

2. And, have you ever tried to manage, subdue or control your grief?

3. I rest my case.

CHAPTER 3

THE DARK AND WINDING, OFTEN CONFUSING, HALLWAYS OF GRIEF

Dear Reader and Partner in Grief,

Grief can be confusing. If you opened this book because your heart is broken with grief, if you feel the weight of sorrow today, or if you carry sorrow's burden from weeks gone by, then follow your grief onto the pages of "The Grief Letter" and into the presence of God. Let's share some grief perspective.

Grief can be like falling through a trap door. Instantly, we are thrust into a new world and forced to adjust. There is no negotiation. Our loss is final and forever. We find ourselves in a different zone from everyone else. They seem to be above us, living life, enjoying life. We suddenly feel we have dropped out of life. We find ourselves in a darker, lower level, mourning death and suffering life.

I do not write "The Grief Letter" from Mt. Olympus or Mt. Sinai. I have been a griever too. I know what the mourning experience is like. As I remember the grief scattered across my life, when I walked the dark and winding, often confusing, hallways of grief, I count it a privilege to walk with you in your grief.

As a personal and also a family matter, grief over the death of a loved one singles out the most painful part of our universal human circumstance. If you opened this volume because your heart is broken with grief, if you feel the weight of sorrow in recent days or if you carry sorrow's burden from weeks gone by, then follow your grief onto the pages of *The Grief Letter* and into the presence of God.

Why This Matters

Following the death of someone near and dear, our lives are flooded with sorrow. We do not look for sorrow. We do not want sorrow. But inevitably sorrow comes. A life ends. The one we thought would be here is gone. What we thought would hold comes apart. Life becomes a tidal wave of tears, whether flowing visibly or churning deep inside---sometimes taking our breath away---leaving us in "the valley of the shadow of death."

The one thing the octopus of grief cannot subdue and dominate in our lives is the welcomed presence of God. As a minister, required to know the theology of the Bible, I find it forever significant and earth-shaking to note: "God does not remember our sin" (Jeremiah 31:34) but He "keeps track of all our sorrows" (Psalm 56:8). This matters because each of us needs a positive grief perspective for life's journey.

Grief is "the Unexpected Guest"

"To be honest, I never, ever thought about it," Walter said, referring to the death of his college-age daughter months ago. "I had no idea her death would come out of nowhere, totally unexpected, 'zapping' me with pain like I've never felt before."

We grieve from the same place we love, from the deepest part of ourselves.

Plus grief often operates by "sneak attack". Grief is "the unexpected guest" who invades our lives, moves in---and stays. We are fully occupied with life's daily demands. Grief interrupts us anyway. The thing about grief we never expected is the "pain point", the grief hurt, the way in which it infiltrates our defenses and interferes with our plans. Whenever our grief arrives, it will have no concern about our work schedule or our personal agenda.

Grief grabs our attention! It may be an abrupt interruption or a long vigil. Grief is invasive. Jumps to the top of our "To do" list. Grief is relentless. When are we going to recognize the prevailing reality of grief?

The evidence is powerful. No matter one's prior experience with death and loss, grief visits each of us as an unexpected guest. No matter our name, where we live, what we do, grief finds us. We each have what Longfellow called our "secret sorrows."

Grief can be "Unknown" Territory

"I have never been here before," she said, referring to her grief following her husband's unexpected death. "Our parents are still living. Our grandparents died before we were born. So I haven't had a lot of experience with this, and my husband's death wasn't even on my radar screen."

In spite of grief's universal nature, grief may feel like walking through unknown territory. Grief produces in us a sense of bewilderment, leading us into a zone of uncertainty about ourselves, about life. Our individual grief reactions do not follow a formula---we each grieve in our own way.

One of the first encounters for me personally was the discovery, without any advance notice, I could not negotiate the length or the depth of my grief. The maze of my grief was my own. Yet I could not prescribe it. The unknown often creates a helpless feeling.

Grief is Personal and Relational

Obviously grief is universal. Yet in our grief we do not share the exact same grief experience. One primary reason is the fact we each, as "mourners", grieve our individual losses. Sorrow is always an emotional package reflecting the relationship we have with the deceased.

Because our connections with the deceased persons in our lives are altogether different, we therefore experience grief in ways that are both personal and relational, and often quite different. A child never grieves the death of a distant cousin in the same way one might mourn the death of a close parent. We do not grieve the death of our favorite uncle in the same manner we might mourn the death---expected or unexpected---of our own child.

"Grief is about broken hearts, even broken faith!"

When I arrived at the gentleman's home following the death of a family member, he was surrounded by friends. He asked them to excuse him as he led me to the deck along the back of his house. "I've heard of broken hearts," he began, "and even broken lives; but I'm afraid I'm dealing with a broken faith!"

His child had been the mid-night auto accident victim of a drunk driver. A child of only 18, she had such great promise. Now her life had been crushed and blotted out in the darkness of night. "How could a good God allow such a thing?" the father screamed, leaving the whole bloody matter up to me. In such circumstances, I never try to defend God. He doesn't need a defense attorney, much less an associate pastor, to polish his reputation.

As the silence gave me time to think, naturally I thought of some gentle reminders. We each have the human capacity to make choices, to decide for ourselves how we live and conduct our lives. Our choices have both intended results as well as unintended consequences. There is the possibility "my" choice or decision will inflict damage to "you", maybe even end your life, as the driver did to my friend's daughter.

We blame God for a human choice when that bad choice is not God's fault. But I did not speak those thoughts. I called the father by name and said "I'm sorry".

In the silence, I thought of the sign outside an auto repair shop in south Georgia which captures the challenge: "We can mend everything but a broken heart." Then I thought of Jesus's words from his sermon on the hill, second on his list. "Blessed are those who mourn, for they shall be comforted."

Grief is always about broken hearts. Often grief is about broken lives, broken families, even broken futures---when the circumstances of death may be unusually disturbing. Examples come to mind like the families grieving the mysterious disappearance of Flight 17 somewhere in the distant Pacific Ocean. In our grief, we need God's assurance of His comfort.

There is One Who Knows Our Pain

In the darkness of our grief, we have a divine stake-holder who knows our pain. We are never alone in our grief, unless in our stubbornness we want to be. We read in sacred scripture there is One who "comforts all who mourn." I am a "comfort recipient". In my pain and heartbreak, I have tasted the grace of the Holy One.

A Verse for the Valley: "The Lord is near to all who call upon Him, to all who call upon Him in truth." (Psalm 145:18).

Is this promise from the Psalm book one we forget?

When Jesus' own disciples were shocked at his references to the time when he would leave them, due to his death, as we read in John 16:16-22, he offered comfort and explanation in verse 20.

A Verse for Grief's Challenge: "Truly, I say to you, that you will weep and lament…you will be sorrowful, but your sorrow will be turned to joy." (John 16:20)

Jesus compares grief pain to the universal pain women experience in child birth. In verse 21, a woman giving birth to a child has pain, but when her baby is born she forgets the anguish because of her joy. The consistent testimony of sacred scripture is that in due time our sorrow will be turned to joy.

Can we embrace and really believe this truth? Is it possible?

In my experience and in the grief experience of hundreds and hundreds of grieving folks with whom I have walked, it is possible. It is absolutely possible!

Grief is a Divine-human process

No matter the circumstance of death, our theology shapes our grief as we grieve out of who we are. Death can sometimes fracture our faith. I've never tried to clean up the grief experience or make it more attractive. When a lady told me following her husband's death, "I feel like I have been in hell for a year," I accepted her expression. I respected her grief feelings because in the depths of our grief we are blunt about everything. I would never say, "Oh no, you shouldn't say that!" Or "How can you say that about God?"

But there is a matter here of far more importance, having immediate and lasting consequence, than what our grief sounds like or how it may come across to others. I have seen people grieve without the bedrock comfort of faith and I have seen people grieve in the comfort and peace of God's sustaining, uplifting grace. There is a colossal difference.

We grieve the way we grieve, not necessarily the way we should grieve. We grieve what we feel in **this** very moment---not what we are supposed to feel, and not according to someone else's formula. We grieve as individuals, on an "as needed" basis, often as amateurs, and sometimes all alone. We grieve unexpectedly, spontaneously, haphazardly, painfully---all over the place---not in a grief closet hidden away in a back corner of our lives. And we grieve at a soul-deep level regardless of how we appear on the surface. We grieve as a function of our faith or our unfaith. This is a statement of fact, not a pejorative notion. Our grief is always demarcated and defined by the presence of faith, or by the absence of faith.

"by faith": The Holy God...the Supreme Grief Counselor

When one grieves by faith, then the Holy God of the universe in His divine Presence is our supreme Grief Counselor. In Isaiah 9:2, we read of the people "who walk in darkness" and do not consider this verse might have a dual meaning beyond Israel's exodus journey in the Old Testament, a meaning related to the worst of all human darkness, that of death itself and the grief that follows.

Later in verse 6, this "Prince of Peace" who is to come is called "Wonderful Counselor", "Mighty God" and we of the Christian community should relate this truth to God's Comforting Presence. The book we call "the Bible" makes it abundantly clear: Grief is God's sacred time with us. Jesus' famous sermon on the hill in Matthew 5, verse 4, reminds us the God who comforts those who mourn always shows up. He is available in our time of need, no matter how long it may take to get us back on track again. Jesus is saying: "Comforting those who mourn is an everyday commitment---a top priority!" God is on our side!

"without faith": "tears…but nothing more"

When one grieves without faith, there is a solitary confinement as final wishes are carried out with hugs and condolences from friends. Since the hope of faith and the assurance of resurrection faith are neither valued nor believed, then grief is a solitary time of tears and an appreciation of the life lived, but nothing more. Life ends. There is nothing else but the life in front of you. So get back to work, back to life. Forget about your questions and your deep hurt. Deal with today and tomorrow. Remind yourself you are strong and don't need any grief help…from close by…or from "on High'.

Grief Privacy is Our Habit

Most of us acquire the lifelong habit of keeping our grief to ourselves. It is a "learned behavior." Typically we do not share our grief the way we share where we work, what we did last weekend or where we're going on vacation.

There is an American proclivity to keep our grief private. The language of grief includes the syntax of sorrow, punctuated with tears. Grief's language is personal and private, accompanied by soul-deep mourning. Yet grief needs to be personally acknowledged, accepted, and processed so that we grow through our grief and gather strength even in our sorrow.

How we view death, how we grieve, how we cope with death and how we process our subsequent grief, are matters confronting each of us.

The giant grief vortex encircles us unexpectedly, strings us out inexplicably, leaving us on the edge, precariously. As everyone goes scrambling by, we feel alone. We are surrounded by people, encircled by activity, yet we feel alone. Grief sentences us to live in this strained isolation. People enter and

THE GRIEF LETTER

exit our lives day to day and they don't seem to have a clue how deeply we hurt. Still, how we view death, how we grieve, how we cope with death and how we process our subsequent grief, are matters confronting each of us.

"The Dreaded Question"

"How are you doing?' is the dreaded question," says a man whose wife died six months ago.

"What should be the simplest things get so complicated," observes a wife whose husband died before his time.

"I'm doing pretty good," a college student told me, referring to his Father's death, "until someone asks, 'How are you doing?' and then I come completely apart," he said. "From one moment to the next," he added, "you wouldn't know I'm any better than I was a month after he died. And it has been over a year or more!" he noted in frustration.

This is one of the reasons I write about grief. "How are you doing?" is an instant reminder: Grief carries a big "because", because grief is challenging, consuming and always totally exhausting.

"There is Sacredness in Tears..."

Standing by those who are hurting, giving time to those who grieve after our cultural "grief permission slip" has expired---these have been every day passions for me. The longer I live the more certain I am Washington Irving got it right when he wrote:

> "There is sacredness in tears. They are not the mark of weakness, but of power. They speak more eloquently than ten thousand tongues. They are the messengers of overwhelming grief, of deep contrition, and unspeakable love."[4]

The Chapter "Take-Away"

I do not write from Mt. Olympus or Mt. Sinai. I write from the valleys of my own grief, and for all the individuals and families with whom I have walked in "the valley of the shadow of death".

Yes, grief can be confusing. Grief is a real valley. The shadows are dark and long. We need not walk this valley alone. I have walked through "the valley" with hundreds of grieving individuals and families, always surrounded and comforted by a Holy Presence, plus their "faith family" and "believing" friends. I wish the same for you.

If "the dreaded question" has you by the throat, remember this: The dark and winding, often confusing, hallways of grief lead eventually to "the hallowed ground of grief"---if we learn to handle the "body-blows" of grief. Yet the good news is the Most High God does not remember our sin, but keeps track of all our sorrow.

Your partner in grief,

Fran Buhler

A Grief PS: You may need to spend some time to internalize the truth of this chapter...

1. God does not remember my sin, but he tracks my sorrow. Can you believe it? Wow!

2. Have you allowed the Most High God into your grief? Invite the Most High into your life---allow God entry--- and give thanks for His Comfort and Peace.

3. Use Mary R. Bittner's words to voice your prayer:

"In my times of sorrow, when I dread tomorrow, I will turn to You."
"In each time of grieving, strengthen my believing, lift my spirit, too."[5]

CHAPTER 4

"HOW WILL I GET THROUGH TODAY?"

Dear Reader and Partner in Grief,

Grief is invasive. It will not wait until we are ready to grieve. After each of my parent's deaths, I can remember thinking, "Can I make it through today?"

"I never expected this. I'm completely overwhelmed," said a 26-year-old mother, following her own mother's death. She had experienced the deaths of a friend's parents, and an aunt, but never someone this close.

"Our family is in deep grief right now. It's a very difficult time for us," said a father whose 15-year-old son was killed in an auto accident two weeks prior.

Hear a grand daughter's tribute to her grandfather: "We knew his death was soon. Yet even when you know death is coming, it still hurts when it arrives. We could never have had him long enough. He was such a sweet man."

Whoever it may be, whenever they may die, no matter where or how death may come, a loved-one's death brings a soul-shaking question. I shall never forget the husband's question following his wife's death---the universal grief question: "How will I get through today?"

Grief always begins with today! Tomorrow is not our concern. Who cares about next week? The only question is the raw question: "How will I get through today?"

Why This Matters

Part of life is dealing with death. We have to go on living following the death of those who are dear to us. And the very first thing we have to deal with in our grief is "today." It is the first thing we face. It's the first time we've had this challenge. Even if we have experienced grief before, this is the first day we've grieved for this person.

During many of our "todays" we find ourselves wondering about the answer to Max Lucado's question: "Why won't the sorrow leave me alone?"

"Because you buried more than a person," writes Lucado, "you buried some of yourself."[6]

Grief is always hard work and takes more time than we ever think it should.

When everything in our lives is coming undone, changing painfully before our eyes, the most important thing we can do is to live in our grief with a personal reliance upon God's Grace and Comfort.

Why? Because: God's grace is stronger than all our sin, and greater than all our grief.

We have to start somewhere, sometime. Choose to start the process of grief and healing today…right now. It will not be any easier tomorrow, next week or next month.

Exhibit A for Starting Now

A TGL prepublication reader wrestled with the "how will I get through today?" issue. Read below her honest, descriptive and accurate depiction of her grief. In a letter dated May 20, 2016, Kathy Funchess expressed her experience as follows:

> "I grieved the death of my grandparents, but their deaths were not unexpected due to their ages and health issues, and the grief did not overwhelm me as it did later. My father's death was the first time I had ever felt the "body blows" of grief and it was a difficult time. But, my siblings and I had our mother to help us, and despite her own grief, she offered amazing comfort to her four children. I remember her telling me after my father's death that now she understood what the hymn-writer meant when he penned the words, 'when sorrows like sea billows roll…' And now, I, too, understand exactly what he meant."

Kathy's experience is typical. Many of us have grief experience and think we know about grief but then are blind-sided by a grief that clobbers us emotionally and physically. Kathy explains:

> "Despite my earlier experiences with the loss of loved-ones, the death of my mother, (and tears spring to my eyes even now as I type those words), was a deep, haunting, wrenching grief like I had never before experienced. I cried great, gulping sobs that I had never before

experienced, but I could not help myself. I thought I knew everything there was to know about grief until my mother died! It's not that I loved my father any less, I guess it was because of a number of factors; she was my last surviving parent, she had lived with me for the last year of her life, and I was older than when my father died, and Mama's death made me more cognizant of my own mortality. And, I was now alone."

Kathy used the original "grief letter" to help her through the first Christmas after her mother's death. Is this random coincidence or a God thing?

"My mother died in October, 2013, just two months prior to Christmas. I had spent EVERY Christmas of my life with her, even when we lived in different towns/states. I have always loved Christmas, the music, the decorations, the gift-giving, but Christmas 2013 was just another date to 'get through.' Then, a week or two before Christmas, 'the grief letter' arrived. At first, I didn't want to read it, but curiosity got the better of me. What a blessing it was! Finally, I felt like I wasn't a terrible Christian, that someone understood what I was going through, and that others in my situation felt and acted the same way! Christmas was still difficult, but not as difficult as I had expected. My feelings were normal, I wasn't some fallen-from-grace sinner that God had forgotten! I passed the letter on to my siblings, and kept it in the drawer in the kitchen, where I would pull it out and read it from time to time."

Verses for the Valley: A Psalm for Today

If God's grace is greater than all our grief, then act on this truth, beginning today. Place your faith in the reality of the Most High God. You won't find a better way to do that than following some key verses from Psalm 118, an "O Give Thanks to the Lord" psalm. From my study of the Psalm book, this is one of those "faith" moments where God always meets his people. I have never felt abandoned at this intersection of grief and faith.

I could select this psalm because of its history in the life and worship of Israel or for the fact it was a favorite of Martin Luther. Instead, I choose this psalm because it speaks to my personal grief. I pray the same for you.

Psalm 118:5-6; 14; 29 (NAS)

Verse 5: "From my distress I called upon the Lord; the Lord answered me...

Verse 6: "The Lord is for me; I will not fear; what can man do to me?"

When my primary source of distress is my personal grief following the death of one who meant so much to me, these words take aim directly at my heart, giving me encouragement for the day ahead.

Verse 14: "The Lord is my strength and my song, and He has become my salvation."

Personally, I have learned I cannot combat the grief and sorrow that penetrate my life. I have not found a handy, effective action on my part to make the hurt go away.

What I have found is One who becomes my strength, my grief salvation. The Holy One has never made my grief go away like magic. Instead, the God of All Space and Time not only brings salvation from my sin but also speaks encouragement to me in my grief.

Verse 29: "Give thanks to the Lord, for He is good; for His lovingkindness is everlasting."

Many times in my life I have prayed this verse as a prayer of thanksgiving to God for His deliverance and comfort in the deep hurt of grief.

A Song for Today

Psalm 27 is a song of fearless trust in God, a psalm for today even if grief has invaded our day, even if sorrow presses upon our heart.

Verse 1: "The Lord is my light and my salvation; whom shall I fear?"

Verse 11: "Teach me Your way, O Lord, and lead me in a level path."

In 1956 I memorized a powerful lyric from Psalm 27, words James Montgomery gave us in 1822: "God is my strong salvation; what foe have I to fear? In darkness and temptation, my Light, my Help, is near"

The Chapter "Take-away"

We never experience a darkness like the darkness of grief. And we will not find a presence in our times of grief like the comfort and strength of the Most High to help us through today!

THE GRIEF LETTER

So when our grief time arrives, a good way to "get through today" is to use the focus of Psalm 118 and the assurance of Psalm 27.

Another way is to become like Nahum, that little known contributor to the Old Testament canon. Apart from his three-chapter, 47-verse, testament to God's sovereignty, justice and faithfulness to His promises, little is known of Nahum apart from his brief book.

Yet the name "Nahum" means "consolation", "full of comfort". And on that day of grief and mourning when our heart-felt cry is "How will I get through today?" may we have the physical capacity and mental competence to find refuge in the Most High God…in such a way that our circle of family and friends will know the Lord God is awesome and good:

"The Lord is good, a stronghold in the day of challenge, and He knows those who take refuge in Him." (Nahum 1:7)

In the Name of the Father, the Son, and the Holy Spirit, Amen.

Your grief partner and friend,

Fran Buhler

A Grief PS:

1. We never experience a darkness like the darkness of grief.

2. Be honest. How are you getting through today?

3. We will not find a Presence in our time of grief like the comfort and strength of the Most High to help us through today! When you are unsure, lean on the Most High God.

CHAPTER 5

LEARNING TO HANDLE THE "BODY BLOWS" OF GRIEF

Dear Reader and Partner in Grief,

For my mother's funeral, I was walking with my siblings and our families into our home church sanctuary where our father had been the Pastor years ago and we had become members when we each came of age and came to Christ through faith.

For the drive home to Tennessee and the family interaction before the funeral, I had done well, keeping my composure and comforting those around me. In the short walk from the prayer room to the sanctuary for Mother's celebration service, something hit me in my throat and chest---pounding my body---bringing me to tears.

I was Exhibit A for the "body-blows" of grief! As Dean Koontz wrote in *Odd Hours*, "Grief can destroy you---or focus you."[7]

Ever find yourself thinking: "Grief pain, grief pain, go away; come again another day"?

Why This Matters

At the start, grief pain never stays away very long. And even when it returns, we are always caught off guard---no matter how many times we have received this intruder.

Along the way, we each find ourselves walking what Louisa May Alcott called "the rough and thorny way" of grief.

Personal destruction or a better focus on life, which will it be? For a period of time, and no one can define the time precisely, our grief pain will not go away; it will come again every day. It becomes a personal question: "Will grief destroy me, or focus me?"

The Body-Blows of Grief

After the death of his wife in her early 40s, the husband who in his 20s had been an amateur boxer, said to his brother: "You know, grief slipped up on me. I knew when Katie died I would grieve. But I didn't expect it to feel like those body-blows when I was boxing."

In her memoir, *The Long Good-bye*, Meghan O'Rourke writes about "the jagged darkness of loss" when she describes her own grief.

> "In the months that followed my mother's death, I managed to look like a normal person. I walked down the street; I answered my phone; I brushed my teeth, most of the time. But I was not ok. I was in grief. Nothing seemed important. Daily tasks were exhausting. Dishes piled in the sink, knives crusted with strawberry jam. At one point I did not wash my hair for ten days."[8]

Someone I'll call Rita is memorable because of her vivid, home-made metaphors. A month after the death of her husband, she told a guest: "I feel like someone hit me all over and left me battered and bruised by the side of the road."

"Grief slams us in the face" was the way my seminary professor, Dr. Wayne Oates, described the impact of grief, like a body-blow in boxing. Former Texas pastor Herschel Hobbs' metaphor for dealing with life's "body-blows" was "the shock absorbers of faith." Faith helps us handle the heavy blows of shock and grief.

We need a grief faith that deals with present losses, responds to the challenges of death and sorrow, but welcomes and embraces the future

My Lady of Challenge

No sooner had I graduated from seminary when I got a call to do a graveside service. The deceased lady was a retired friend I had visited on several occasions over a two-year period. In our chats, reading Bible texts and praying together, we bonded in a spiritual way.

This person I choose to call "My Lady of Challenge," taught me---through her life challenges---about the "walk of faith", a more sustaining lesson than the "talk of faith".

Every person experiences profound grief pain via nights and days of bitter sweet sorrow and challenge. Walking "through the valley of the shadow of death" may darken your days. Nights of sickness and silence may be part of your grief.

You may experience grief and deep sorrow, days of disappointment and great difficulty,

My "lady of challenge" had suffered and endured more than her share of difficult life experiences. Another lesson she taught me was that "not crying has a cost", an especially good lesson for me.

"Not crying has a cost"

Our tears contribute to our healing. Our tears also give others permission to cry. We are learning professionally that crying is helpful both physiologically and psychologically. Tears contain an exocrine substance, like sweat, that helps cleanse the body of stress-related substances that accumulate under stress.

When we cry, the work of healing in our bodies has already begun. Crying is like singing in the dark. The great British preacher, Charles H. Spurgeon, preached a sermon on Job 35:10: "Where is God my maker, who gives songs in the night?" Only a person of faith can sing in the darkness of death---in spite of grief's body blows.

Singing in the Dark

In our grief, following the death of a significant someone in our lives, we have to "learn" to sing in the dark. It's not something we naturally know how to do. Plus, in our grief we may not feel like singing. I have found when I think of how the life of this special person touched my life and made life better, I just naturally begin to hum a tune. It's usually a song that connects with my memories. Sometimes it's a hymn with lyrics that speak to my personal grief in some way.

Remembering the words of my father, Allen Buhler, preaching long ago in Lebanon, Tennessee, at Fairview Baptist Church, has helped me in the darkness of my personal grief: "If we sit and mourn our loss, we will remain in the valley of the shadow of death. But if we get up and walk by faith when we cannot walk by sight, we will emerge stronger and more joyful because God has brought us through the valley."

A Verse for the Valley: "The Lord is my shepherd…" (Psalm 23:1).

In the storehouse of faith, we don't have to look far to find helpful grief connections. Each of us will find ourselves living through the valley, in what Isaiah called "troubled waters" as we are "walking through the fire of life." (Isaiah 43:1-3)

We need a grief faith that deals with present losses, responds to the challenges of death and sorrow, serves a shock absorber function with our pain, but welcomes and embraces the future.

Learning to Handle Grief

In my own personal experience with soul-deep sorrow and God-sized grief, I have come to believe that in Dr. John Claypool's words, it is possible to "learn to handle grief."

Some talk about grief as if it were no more than a universal "toothache of the soul" experience. That is simply not true. Every personal loss-thru-death experience I have had threw me for a loop of grief and pain bathed in tears. That's why I have been drawn over the years to Claypool's words on this matter.

When John Claypool's ten-year old daughter died following an 18-month battle against leukemia in Louisville, Kentucky, my wife and I were living in Louisville. I had finished seminary and was campus minister at a local college. Dr. Claypool did chapel services with us twice a year. We who were aware of his daughter's illness, experienced what Dr. Wayne Oates described as "the dark mysteries of the shrouds of grief."

One thing I never try to do when death occurs under tragic or difficult circumstances is explain what is essentially unexplainable. "It is always futile and unproductive," to borrow Claypool's words, "to try to explain tragedy in some comprehensive way."

In his bestselling book, *Tracks of a Fellow Struggler: How to Handle Grief*, Dr. John Claypool, then pastor of Louisville's Crescent Hill Baptist Church, offered four sermons from his experience with his daughter's illness and death. Three sermons were preached in Louisville – the first after the initial diagnosis, the second after his daughter's first relapse nine months later, the third several weeks after his daughter's death. The fourth sermon was preached three years later at Broadway Baptist Church in Fort Worth, Texas, shedding light on the whole grief process.[9]

Bitterness vs. an Adventure with God

In the final sermon, Claypool outlined the clear alternatives of what the experience of loss and its resultant grief can do to us, what we might call the experience of bitterness versus the experience of life adventure with God.

Claypool makes it clear when he writes: "The experience of loss can embitter a person forever." As Claypool describes, people may become "resentful against God," may live in "defiant rage," becoming "hardened and isolated."

"I have known people," Claypool writes, "who have experienced the pain of loss who say: 'Never again. I will not make myself vulnerable to this kind of agony.'"

Claypool's testimony from first-hand observation and experience matches my observation and experience when he writes: "Closing themselves off from everyone and everything, they become shriveled and lifeless."

I shall never forget John Claypool's description of three paths available to grievers, based upon his personal grief experience. Again, I am prompted by his sermons and by "Tracks of a Fellow Struggler", plus a college chapel service he led.

Some travel the "road of unquestioning resignation", said Claypool, which suggests "we must not question God". Others, he said, follow the "road of total intellectual understanding", what he called "the way of explaining everything completely or tying up all loose ends in a tidy answer". Claypool's testimony was that he tried each of those options and found they were "dead ends".

The Road of Gratitude

According to Claypool only the third option, "the road of gratitude," enabled him to navigate the darkness of death. The lesson came from his childhood family experience.[10]

John's parents had a washing machine borrowed from a generous neighbor. His family had used the washing machine so long he had forgotten how the family came to have the washing machine. Therefore when the neighbors took the washing machine back, Claypool was mad and upset until his mother gave him a proper perspective.

"You must remember", his mother said, "that machine never belonged to us in the first place. That we even got to use it at all was a gift. So, instead of being mad at its being taken away, let's use this occasion to be grateful that we had it at all."[11]

The Gift of Life

Dr. Claypool told our chapel of students that such gratitude "seems to me to be the best way down from the Mountain of Loss."

"Laura Lue was a gift, pure and simple," John said, "something I neither earned nor deserved nor had a right to. And when I remember that the response to a gift, even when it is taken away, is gratitude, then I am better able to try and thank God that I was ever given her in the first place."

Such truth breeds joy and jubilation even in the tough territory of grief. Following chapel that day, students and faculty gave Dr. Claypool a standing, extended ovation.

During his life, John Claypool was also faithful to outline and describe the alternative grief experience of life adventure with God:

> "But if we are willing, the experience of grief can deepen and widen our ability to participate in life. We can become more grateful for the gifts we have been given, more open-handed in our handling of the events of life, more sensitive to the whole mysterious process of life, and more trusting in our adventure with God."[12]

Personally, I shall always remember Dr. Claypool's closing argument, so to speak, from his last chapter on learning to handle grief, when he asked: "If yesterday was so full of meaning, why not tomorrow? All the days come from the same source!"[13]

The Unmentionable!

Another grief lesson worth learning might surprise us. Have you known people who in their grief hardly ever mention the name of a loved one who died?

This habit or tendency is unfortunate and unnecessary.

After his wife's death, a member of our church said, "I've been reluctant to mention her name again." Then he added, "I've learned the hard way that doesn't work."

His next comment was unforgettable: "Her absence in body does not eliminate my sense of her presence in memory. Remembering her and speaking her name is a source of continuing joy."

One of the readers of an early draft of *The Grief Letter* scribbled the following in the margin at this point in reference to her deceased husband: "He is always walking beside me, just as in life. I actually talk to him (out loud), discussing things, asking Qs, sharing experiences with the grandkids---always asking his advice."

Don't ever deny yourself the joy and comfort of remembering your loved one by speaking his or her name, by recounting what has special significance for you now. It takes courage to mourn. People around us may get impatient with our mourning, wondering why we can't snap out of it and get on with life. Mourning requires a certain amount of determination, and endurance, if it is to have meaning.

Yet, if we mourn in the arms of God, we are comforted. We are strengthened. We are encouraged. Mourning is like holding your breath and then accepting air by breathing in deeply. God wraps His arms around us and says, "I am with you. You will be all right."

The "hallowed ground of grief"

Martha Whitmore Hickman has authored more than twenty books for adults and children. As a wife, mother, and grandmother, she is acquainted with grief.

> "After the loss of a loved one there is, at first, a great buzz of activity as we make arrangements. There is comfort in the close press of friends, in shared tears and hugs, in remembering. But then the religious services are over, relatives and friends go home, and we are left to enter a new and strange land – a land where one of the persons who has given meaning to our life is gone."

From her life experience with the death of loved ones, Martha writes:

> "The process of bereavement goes on for a very long time. For years, not for days or months, if the loved one has been close. But if we are wise and fortunate and have the courage and support to tread the hallowed ground again and again, the loss will begin to lose its controlling power. Eventually there will come a sense of our own inner strength and our ability to rejoice in the life we have shared, and to look toward the future in which the loved one, though not

physically present, continues to bless us."¹⁴

Hickman is another voice with a resume of grief experience who offers excellent grief-based advice when she drafts a viable prayer-line for each of us: "May I honor – and trust – the process of grief and healing, knowing that, in time, a new day will come."

"An Anchor of the Soul"

In the early darkness of a long ago Tennessee morning, my father and I were fishing on Center Hill Lake. A stormy wind came upon us, making it difficult and challenging for us to fish. Our custom was to float within casting distance of the shore line, floating along with the boat motor off so we could quietly cast for fish in their early morning feeding cycle.

The strong wind whipping across the lake, blowing us into the shoreline, was defeating and disrupting our morning---very much like the waves of daily grief greeting a grieving soul. This is why the octopus metaphor for grief is important in helping us understand what we are up against. If left alone, grief will never turn us loose.

My father reached behind him, grabbing an anchor, lowering it into the dark tomb of Center Hill Lake. The stormy wind did not subside, but – anchored in the boat – we continued to fish another hour until we caught our legal limit of fish.

Grief is like those stormy Tennessee winds on Center Hill Lake. When grief storms ruffle our days, we need an anchor for the soul, so that even grief's heavy hits--- with the power to blow our lives off course---are unable to overpower us if we are anchored in the welcoming waters of the One who comforts all who mourn.

We may receive strong encouragement, we who have fled for refuge from our grief, by laying hold of the steady hope set before us. "This hope we have as an anchor of the soul, a hope both sure and steadfast", according to Hebrews 6:19, is part of God's unchangeable purpose to comfort His Grieving Ones who mourn.

Grief pain refuses to go away completely, forever, it seems. Yet there comes a time when our grief pain subsides and the sun, believe it or not, shines again.

PART 1 - CHAPTER 5

The Chapter "Take-Away"

Yes, it is possible to learn how to handle the "body-blows" of grief.

Each of us will experience the ever so human desire expressed in our chapter opening:

"Grief pain, grief pain, go away, come again another day." If we could wish the pain away, we would surely do so. But we cannot. No one can.

The "body-blows" of grief represent grief's signature emotional experience with pain. The "thru-line" of grief is always pain, soul-deep pain. We make a huge step toward recovery when we learn to handle the "body-blows" of grief. Because Dean Koontz is right – grief can destroy us, or focus us!

Your partner in grief,

Fran Buhler

A Grief PS: Remember, we're on the "hallowed ground of grief..."

1. If you feel like a punching bag for the Grief Universe, check out the road of gratitude. List four reasons you have for gratitude.

2. Why not thank God right now for the one for whom you grieve.

3. Trust God with your grief. Pray: "God, I am trusting You, as the anchor of my soul and as my Shepherd, the guardian of my grief!"

THE GRIEF LETTER

CHAPTER 6

OWN YOUR GRIEF

Dear Reader and Partner in Grief,

"Why in the world," you may be thinking, "should I want to 'own' my grief?" You may never have thought about grief ownership. Yet when we grieve, it's a matter we need to face. We have to come to terms with it for an important reason: Grief ownership signals our attitude and makes better outcomes possible.

Helen felt the best response to her grief was to ignore it and move on with life. "Yet the more I tried to ignore it," Helen sobbed, "the more it overpowered me. I was at the mercy of my grief."

Joe said: "I looked at my grief like a stray dog. 'If I don't take it in,' I thought, 'then maybe it will go away.' But it did not."

Grief pounces, savage and relentless, clawing at every aspect of our lives. (And we thought the octopus was bad!) Grief has a super-abundance of stamina. We expect the fog of grief to lift in a few days or a few weeks, and before we know it we find ourselves still grieving months, sometimes years, later.

Why This Matters

Every griever knows the sting of "I regret…" and "I wish I had…" Yet to own our grief, we need to start from where we are---not where we were or even where we ought to be. Who knows where we ought to be? Often we reacted and grieved the best we knew how. In the future, we may learn to grieve better. At some point we must turn in the Book of Life to the chapter called "Grief" with an intentional attitude that we are going to get to know our grief and treat it as a special guest. So, instead of ignoring our grief and hoping it will go away, why not make grief our friend?

Why not own our grief?

Let's take some "grief givens", experiences and feelings we may expect to be part of our grief, and see what's involved in grief ownership.

1. Generic grief does not exist. All grief is personal. It is your grief, my grief, or someone else's grief.

2. You will not grieve in general or on the "average" but "on demand". You will grieve because you have to grieve, because your head and body make you grieve, demand that you grieve---whether you want to grieve or not. Your pain and grief are uniquely yours because you will hurt deeply and differently from anyone else.

3. Grief is very much a "do it yourself" process because you cannot recruit or hire someone to do your grieving for you.

4. Communities, cities, entire nations may grieve. Yet even our communal grief experiences vary person to person, place to place.

5. Grief is more easily "felt" than "finished", more likely to be remembered than researched. Therefore, my treatment of grief in "The Grief Letter", while including considerable research over a twenty year span, is driven by my "felt" grief, by my personal grief experience and my extensive professional experience with the grief and sorrow of hundreds of individuals and families over the same time frame.

"The Comments I Hear Most"

"When is there time to grieve? I have to make a living."

"I flat out don't have time to grieve. The only way I could grieve as much as I need to would be to retire. And that's out of the question."

"You take time off from work to grieve and first thing you know you're on the periphery, and that's not a secure place to be."

There is also the "disconnect factor". The pervasive question is always "why do you need more time?" As if grief followed the flat tire model. You have a flat tire. You get it fixed. You don't need more time. So perhaps we should address the "grief time" issue up front.

"No time to grieve!"

In my experience, people often literally have "no time to grieve" – not because they are in denial, not because of a lack of faith, not because of any personal reason, but because of the way things happen.

Notice, I did not say "schedule", because we have some control over our calendar and our schedule. But sometimes the time demands in our lives are not of our own choosing or of our own making.

Someone I'll call Jonathan had his own financial firm focused in a market with high demand. Jonathan was married, his wife worked with a successful consulting firm. He was in a good marriage, with three daughters. Jonathan's wife died in June following a decade-long bout with cancer. So Jonathan had already had ten years of heavy schedules and long-term exhaustion. His oldest daughter's wedding was set for July. His second daughter was leaving for her senior year in college in mid-August.

I did Jonathan's wife's funeral, followed up with Jonathan after the service, then again a week or so later. I knew his calendar was jammed after that so I waited till early November to follow up again.

Here's the first unvarnished, verbal summary report I received:

"I'm just now getting to where I can work all day without becoming emotionally exhausted. I had the summer flu before she died, then the wedding, then I had to move (his daughter) back to (college) for the Fall term of her senior year. When was there a chance to grieve?"

"On top of that," he said, "what I need most are space and time, and uninterrupted mornings."

Jonathan really needs "bill-able" work time for his clients. Yet friends don't seem to understand and often drop by his office unannounced, ripping a big hole in his work schedule when he needs to be productive. Jonathan is not a male with a stubborn resistance to grief. He wept openly at graveside, and grieved openly during the family visitation time. He just had an impossible family schedule already in place, dates born of good intention and backed by considerable financial and family commitment. There was not a time when he could arbitrarily clear his calendar and give himself to his grief.

This is precisely when and where grief ownership should occur. When there is "no time to grieve", we have to make time. We have to make room in our lives to own our grief. Owning our grief is absolutely necessary and extremely important. We must set an appointment with our grief, as if grief was an important, high priority client.

"Do You Really Want to Heal?"

In *Life after Loss*, Bob Deits expresses the strategic notion that "grief is something I do" if I really want to heal.[15]

"Grief doesn't have to be a passive thing that happens to you", says Deits. "Grieving is first and foremost something you do to heal your wounds after experiencing a terrible loss in your life."[16]

In my experience, I would say my grief healing is something I have experienced as a God-process that needs my cooperation and collaboration. I cannot pull it off by myself without God. Yet God cannot bring about solace in my grief and comfort in my mourning without my participation, even my ownership! If you are unclear about "how" to own your grief, we will explore the "how's" shortly.

Grieving is "Unknown Territory". Grief introduces us to a strange land. Even if we have been there before, the experience is always intimidating. In her poem "When a Loved One Dies," Dolores Dahl gently guides us to this foreign territory:

> "It comes to all. We know not when,
> or how, or why. It's always been
> a mystery, a frightening thing,
> enshrouded in the silencing.
> When suddenly a loved one dies
> we seem to sort of paralyze,
> to just stop still within our track.
> And oh, how much we want them back."[17]

"Let's Be Clear"

Diane Baggett, professional counselor, wife of a Methodist Pastor and author of her own blog, wrote on March 23, 2012 at 4:27 pm:

> "It is a mistake to believe grief can be avoided if we have enough strength of character, or enough faith. When we suffer a loss, whether we are among the strong or weak, whether our faith is small or great, it is natural for us to experience grief. It is not a sign of weakness, but a manifestation of our humanity."[18]

THE GRIEF LETTER

"The Best Thing We Can Do…"

We are persons who grieve. God created grief. Grief, in the created order, is intended for the purpose of recovering from loss. We are persons who grieve our losses. This is the way we are wired. When we own our grief, grief is no longer a stranger. Grief becomes our friend.

So… how do we own our grief? Follow the "How's?"

We get to know our grief as we make an effort to become familiar with our grief. How? "I had to introduce myself to my very own grief", Jonathan said.

We process our grief with a positive attitude, learning the nuances of grief. How? "I had to get familiar with my own grief", Margaret said, "by spending time with it."

We embrace our grief. It becomes our grief. We own it when we want to own it. How? George told me he decided embracing his grief was like going fishing. He could zip around the lake, casting here and there, waiting for something to happen. Or he could fish when the fish feed, early in the morning and late in the afternoon. "Fishing has a rhythm", he said, "so does grieving."

Because we own our grief, we may begin the healing process. How? Healing cannot happen when we view grief as an opposing force, as someone else's grief, or as the big Grief Cloud in the room.

Welcome your grief. Embrace it. Feel it. Allow it to reside at your address. "I guess I thought if I ignored my mother's death, life would go on," Virginia said. "But the problem was I couldn't go on," she explained, "I couldn't function the way I needed to." Grieving the death of a loved one leaves us wondering if we can carry on. We can. We must. The unavoidable dynamic is: Until I own my grief, I cannot cope with it.

A Verse for the Valley: "He leads me beside still waters. He restores my soul" (Psalm 23).

"Four Helpful Grief Actions"

Treat grief like a special guest – invite grief inside.

View grief as your ally – not your enemy.

Allow room for laughter in your grief. For example, when I was growing up in Tennessee, I had a high school summer job in the city cemetery, and I never could understand how a cemetery could raise "burial charges" – and blame it on "the cost of living".

Approach grief as if it is a safety valve, not a huge wall. Approach it as an important part of God's design to help us let off steam, reduce the pressure, and move forward.

Owning our grief, recognizing it, verbalizing it, finding outlets for it will definitely help. Remember, it's ok to ask for or seek help. When we share our grief honestly, when we recognize we must give ourselves permission to grieve, to hurt and to get better, then healing begins to slowly move into our lives. Until I own my grief, I am not really grieving. I am resisting the healing process. In the wake of loss and death, call on God's Mercy, recall God's Faithfulness, turn to God and acknowledge Him as Your Redeemer. You will be glad you did.

Now, consider the following seven statements of grief ownership. Believe it or not, the pain heals. This is where your ownership begins. Think of the following seven statements as expressions or "nuances" of grief ownership. Follow the pain.

Seven Statements of Grief Ownership

1. The pain of personal grief hurts, hurts deeply, and is different from any other pain.

2. When you own your grief, the pain of grief means you are alive with feelings.

3. Your grief pain reflects the "appreciation quotient", "the love relationship", in the loss.

4. Your grief accurately measures the depth and the extent of your loss.

5. Grief charts your path toward healing and recovery. Meaning? You're on schedule.

6. The pain of your grief triggers insight into the grief experience and pain of others. Grief ownership contributes to grief fellowship, linking us with other grieving souls.

7. The pain of your grief is not automatically the same as everyone else's pain. Stated another way, the grief and pain of others are not necessarily the same as your particular pain and grief. Similar, in many ways, but not necessarily the same.

Remember, your grief experience is unique and personal. You grieve best when you give yourself permission to grieve and grieve your way. Your decision to read "The Grief Letter" reflects where you are in your grief. It says you want to know more, and perhaps grieve in more meaningful, more helpful ways.

Evidently you reached for "The Grief Letter" at the book store or accepted it as a loan or gift from someone who cares about you. Either way, receiving the book was your choice. What does that tell you?

I believe it means you "want to" own your grief! You want to better understand your grief, cope with it, maybe even grow because of it.

Use "the Empty Chair" Approach

Family Life Consultant and Grief Counselor, Dr. Britton Wood, writes and speaks about *The Experience of Grief*.[19] Dr. Wood testifies to the dramatic changes seen in the lives of survivors when they give themselves permission to grieve. In cases where anger and other strong emotions are present after the death of a loved one or friend, the griever may feel frustration because the unresolved matter won't go away. Each day seems clogged with regrets. Thoughts filled with "I wish..." abound. Painful estrangements fill our minds. For such challenges, Dr. Wood gives wise, helpful advice.

Dr. Wood helped a student whose mother died, when the student complained, "I can't do anything about my anger toward my mother because she is dead. I can never resolve my feelings." In her helpful little booklet, The Experience of Grief, Dr. Wood recounts how she suggested the student use the "empty chair" approach. Label the chair "Mom", Dr. Wood suggested, "And talk out loud to that chair as if Mom were present. Say everything with no limitations of words or feelings. Nothing said will hurt Mom's feelings. Get all the feelings out."[20]

When we own our grief we can actually have such conversations. They are liberating. They free us to do what we ought. Two days later, Dr. Wood received a thank you note from the student who had followed Dr. Wood's advice.

"She said that she talked to the chair for a solid hour. She could not believe all she had to say to her mother. When she got through, she felt as if a heavy load had lifted off her back. She said 'Now I can get on with my life.'"[21]

If you carry unresolved issues that need to be voiced and resolved, this can happen for you as well. Verbally expressing our feelings helps get those feelings out of our system.

"Get Up and Go On"

Helen tried to ignore her grief, but the more she tried the more her grief over-powered her.

Joe learned grief is a bigger challenge than a stray dog. "I finally realized," Joe said, "I have to take ownership of my grief. I've got to bring this dog inside and deal with it."

How? Joe decided to put his grief front and center and face it, deal with it every day. He adopted a daily grief agenda in which he committed to meet his grief "head on". He stopped playing grief "dodge ball" and willed himself to engage his grief. Instead of shoving his grief aside or pushing it out of "feeling" range, he faced it, dealt with it, anytime, every time, grief reared it's emotional head.

Grief's Life Connections

Marjorie Holmes became known for writing about human hurting. She was a columnist for the *Washington Star* and *Woman's Day Magazine*, and author of numerous best-selling books. Holmes wrote about "the greatest hurt of all," "losing someone you love."

Having been through that hurt herself, Holmes "shared the terrible hurting of others." In *To Help You Through the Hurting*, her collection of things she had written about human hurting, Holmes wrote the following: "We all need comfort. We all need hope. We all need to realize 'this too will pass.' This is not the end for us. So long as there is life in our bodies, God wants us to get up and go on. When we do, he often has wonderful things in store for us.

Beyond our family ties, grief has strong life connections. Holmes' little book was published in 1983, from columns she had published earlier in the 70s. I purchased it in a used book store in Micanopy, Florida in 1993. I'm

THE GRIEF LETTER

quoting from it in 2013. Such is the arc and the archive of grief.

The last time Nancy and I drove to Winter Park, Florida, to visit a son and daughter-in-law, we made our usual Micanopy, Florida "bookstore stop". Our "used book" friend, the owner, was not there, having recently died. Friends were removing the remaining books for disposal.

I have had to "own" my grief for my "bookstore-owner" friend, a special "book lover" relationship gone from my life, a grief I will "own" by acknowledging missed conversations and his book recommendations on every future trip that takes me by that I-75 Micanopy Exit!

Trying not to grieve, resisting our natural inclination to grieve, refusing to grieve---any of these responses is counterproductive. Yet neither grief's time nor its intensity are primary. The most important aspect of grief is for it to be genuine.

The Chapter "Take-Away"

Ask yourself the tough "self-check" question: "Am I grieving my best grief?" Get acquainted with your grief. Invite grief inside, make grief your alley and friend.

Own your grief and move forward. Ask the Most High to help you. Don't put it off any longer. Becoming a qualified "grief owner" will give you peace, leading to a time when you are fully at peace in the absence of the one gone from your life.

I pray this chapter and your "empty chair conversations" will enable you to get up and live forward in the future God has for you.

Your grief partner and "empty chair conversationalist" friend,

Fran Buhler

A Grief PS: Are you ready to own your grief?

1. Ask yourself: "Do I really want to heal?" Then become a grief owner and grieve your best grief.

2. Find your "empty chair", and talk to your designated person in the empty chair. Say everything you need to say. Don't hold back. Do it now, there isn't a better time.

3. Allow the Most High God to dwell in the "empty chair", and talk to Him in prayer.

"For You are with me, You comfort me…" (Psalm 23).

THE GRIEF LETTER

CHAPTER 7

GRIEVING IN THE WILDERNESS OF "WHY?"

Dear Reader and Partner in Grief,

If you have ever wrestled the octopus, you have probably been there. Many of us have done time in the wilderness of "why?" **Grief produces an abundance of "why" questions.**

When "Gran-Pa" Buhler, my paternal grandfather, died, I wrestled the octopus, unsure from whence it came, uncertain about what it meant, unable to see clearly the octopus I wrestled was the octopus of grief. "Gran-Pa" Buhler had taught me how to grow strawberries in his garden, saddle a horse in his barn, catch fish in his pond. As a grieving grandchild, a high school kid, I wondered, "why?" Why now? Why couldn't he live a little longer?

When my maternal grandfather, "Gran-daddy Graves", came to his death, I was perplexed. With a touch of anger, I wondered "Why did he have to die?" Then it dawned on me, I had assumed he would live longer so my children would know him---the way I knew him.

In the wilderness of "why", I began to think about deaths earlier in my life. When a high school basketball team mate died, and, later, a college football team mate died, one after a big game, the other during Spring practice, I wondered "why?" Part of it was frustration grief. I knew our team would not be as good without them. The bigger part was friendship grief. I really missed them. I hurt deep inside.

When "Granny" Buhler and "Gran-granny" Graves died, I was older, a more experienced griever, more aware of life and death, more aware of the nuances of grief and the expectation of death after a loved one's long and useful life. Yet I wanted them to live long enough for our sons to know them. So I still wondered, "why"?

Why This Matters

I was almost 40 when I read a 1977 volume *Living When A Loved One Has Died*, published by Beacon Press in Boston, and found a sentence on page 8, a sentence I will never forget: "Unanswered 'whys' are part of life."[22]

Chuck Swindoll says it is "the question that hits first and lingers longest." Why?" Why me? Why now? Why this?"

In Kathe Wunnenberg's devotional companion, titled *Grieving the Loss of a Loved One*, devotional number 11 is "Wandering Through The Wilderness of 'Why.'"[23]

I don't know anyone who hasn't grieved in "the wilderness of 'Why?'"

Grieving in the Wilderness of "Why?"

Inevitably, in the circle of death and grief, we may doubt something, or someone. We may doubt the doctor. We may doubt the cause of death. We may doubt ourselves, our response, our care. We may doubt God.

In her book *Why? Trusting God When You Don't Understand*, Anne Graham Lotz captures the grief question we all ask in the wilderness of "why?" "Can you keep on trusting God," asks Lotz, "when the pain is sharp and the doubt is deep?"[24]

Is this where you are? Could you be wandering, alone, in your particular wilderness? Asking, "why?" Left to itself without an intervening point of view, the Wilderness of "Why?" becomes a Wilderness of Despair.

Kathe Wunnenberg knows the terrible pain of losing a loved one. She writes from her personal "why" experience when she states "the bottom has dropped out of your life." She speaks from her personal pain when she asks: "Will the ache ever cease, the tears ever stop?" When she asks further: "How can you go on in the face of a grief so profound?" The questions are not academic. The questions come from her heart, because of her life experience.

Kathe endured three miscarriages and the death of an infant son. She understands from her personal experience "the sense of loss never really goes away." Yet as surely as God is faithful, she reminds us, "there is hope for your broken heart to mend." Then Wunnenberg drives home a comforting conclusion when she asserts:

> "There is life beyond the sorrow. And as hard as it might be to believe right now, there is even the promise of joy – joy in due season, as you live through your grief one day at a time."[25]

How does Kathe answer her own question: "Are you wandering through the wilderness of why?" "God understands," Kathe writes. "He is there. Sometimes that's the only answer there is."

After honest persistent prayer, the most significant parts of the grief process are the actions we may take to help our grieving selves. Remember, the grief is ours, the loss is ours, the heartbreak and pain are ours. The "Whys" are ours as well.

"Why?" Questions – Backward or Forward?

"Why?" questions do not mean I have no faith. They mean my faith is challenged, stretched to the breaking point. Soul-deep grief following the death of a loved one flies under the banner "Why?" In his book, *Naked Spirituality*, Brian D. McLaren, author of *A New Kind of Christianity*, writes "everything is possible again when you have fought and struggled and been defeated, when you have come to zero."[26]

The "whys" begin when we "come to zero". But all "whys" are not the same. Consider McLaren's distinction as you wrestle with your own "whys".

- "The 'why' that seeks an explanation or a plan looks backward;
- "The 'why' that seeks meaning by bringing some future good out of this agony looks forward.

Very good counsel, advice I have followed in my own wilderness of "why?" Yet the important matter here is the radical difference in the two questions?

The "why" question looks backward, longing for answers and explanations.

The "what now?" question looks forward, not merely wondering what lies ahead but actively seeking to engage life with meaning, looking to participate in life for a positive purpose.

Focused totally on the "why?" question, I bog down, enter a self-centered orbit, and stop living forward.

When I am more interested in "what now" I may grieve just as hard with as much intensity. Yet I grieve as I'm living forward. I grieve with the positive purpose of moving forward in my life rather than the negative habit of always looking in life's rear view mirror, chasing the unending "whys" that pile up along the road already traveled.

PART 1 - CHAPTER 7

"What now?"

A friend of mind said "he learned long ago not to ask God 'Why?' but to ask 'what now?'" When "Where do we go from here?" is the question, keep going forward. When "why?" is the question, a better alternative is "what now?" Over the past two decades I have witnessed any number of family members ask "why?" And I have come to know a significant number who have chosen to move on to "what now?"

I commend it. I cannot think of a better grief response when we find ourselves wandering in the wilderness of "why?"

"When the 'Why?' is pointed at me"

Often, the age-old grief question, "Why?" has a flip side. We have noted the "Why God, why?" question directed at God. Yet, when compound grief surrounds us, the "whys?" may be pointed at ourselves.

In a parent-child or a child-parent relationship, the burning question following the death of one or the other may be "Why did I botch the relationship?"

The "whys" are not "why did my child or my parent die?" The question is a self-incriminating: "Why did I blow the opportunity I had to be a good parent, to be a good child?"

Often our grief centers on a narrow slice of the relationship spiked with bitterness – and regret.

When a child dies and the parent has a long list of "whys": "Why wasn't I a better parent?" "Why didn't I use the opportunities I had?" Then the parent experiences deep grief fueled by regret.

When a parent dies and a child has a long list of "whys": "Why wasn't I a better child?" "Why didn't I provide better care?" "Why was I always too busy to stop and spend the time I should?" Likewise, the child experiences deep grief fueled by regret.

Deep regret is the emotion that hurts the worst when a parent or a child dies and the surviving child or parent has a long list of "whys?"

One person poured out his heart: "I was alone when I got the call. There are no words to describe what that moment was like, the feeling of deep regret, knowing in an instant it was too late to do what I should have done long ago", he said, choking back the tears.

"It was a massive stroke, and he was gone. And all the things I should have said, and all the things I should have done, to express my love for him... but the door was slammed shut. Now I will never have the opportunity." After a pause, he went on: "The pain was so sudden, so swift, I dropped to my knees."

I listened. He added: "I don't know which is worse, my anger at myself, or my anguish over the loss of my dad---forever!"

"What do I do?"

"So what do I do?" Ellen asked, a daughter in her late 30s whose mother died at age 56 just hours after they had an argument.

"Practice forgiveness", I said, "and begin with yourself." "Talk to God as you pray. He'll understand", I added. Then I tried the following words: "Ellen, pretend your mother is here right now, tell her how sorry you are, and ask her to forgive you. What do you think your mother's response would be?"

"Beneficial Actions...to Help Us Heal"

When a loved one dies, pills can't stop our pain. Medication can't heal our hearts or mend our minds. But there are several beneficial actions we can take to help us heal over time.

Ask yourself a simple question: How would my loved one or special friend want me to live after his or her death? You may dismiss my challenge, ignore my instruction, and go right on grieving full speed ahead. Yet consider this: What would this special person in your life want you to do?

When we approach the challenge from the "point of view" of what our loved one or special friend would want, we change the slant. We alter the perspective. We don't change the deep pain. We don't alter how much we miss them. But we do change the grief posture from which we view our great loss and by which we feel our loss.

A Loved One's Point of View

When my Mother began to decline in her health, I asked our church for "staff time away" so I could visit her. I had seen too many children wait until the parent died to go home, then live their lives in regret, asking "Why didn't I go?" "Why didn't I go?" So I went.

The visit was very difficult. I felt guilty the total "care-giving" load was on my three sisters, who had a rotation schedule with each taking turns, providing the best care possible for our Mother. Thinking about the "turns" I missed was another agony. But one thing happened to make me forever grateful I made the time to go home.

At one point in my visit, my mother seemed to reach for clarity, when she said: "Fran, when I die…don't…focus on me…and the past. I gave you…life…and I want you to… enjoy life. Don't…spend your time…grieving…that I'm gone. The life you have…after I'm gone…is…life I want you to enjoy."

Considering the other person's "point of view" gives us a powerful perspective, a release from guilt, a better angle from which to process our grief. It also gives us help… and approval… to live forward. Because it raises a simple question: Is it possible for me to live as my loved one wishes?

Yes, over time, it **is** possible. Maybe not immediately. Maybe not by next week, next month, or even by next year, in some cases. But it is possible. We begin to discover that if we want to please our loved one or friend, it is possible – we have the ability – to live as our loved one would want us to live after his or her death.

Your loved one neither expects nor wants you to live with life-crushing grief. Take your loved one's advice. Abide by his or her wishes.

Now, consider seriously, even prayerfully, the following eight beneficial actions you can take to help you grieve as you move beyond the wilderness of "why"?

Eight Actions to Escape the Wilderness of "Why?"

1. Don't ask "why"? Ask "how"? "What now?"

Asking "why did this happen?" will get you nowhere. Asking why a death happens sends us into a never ending spiral of questions without answers. We have to overcome the "why" question and focus instead on our coping challenge. I have deleted this 'why'?"[27]

THE GRIEF LETTER

Asking "how am I going to cope with my loss?" begins a positive process with a potentially life-affirming, grief-enhancing outcome. Asking "how?" is an excellent way to follow up on "what now?"

Be sure to ask the "who?" question. Who may become the recipient of divine help: "Who may ascend into the hill of the Lord? Or who may stand in His Holy place?" (Psalm 46:3).

Get beyond the question, "why?" "Why" is beyond my ability, beyond the scope of my control. Ask "how am I going to deal with my loss?" and begin the healing process of recovery.

- How will I handle the hole in my life?
- How am I going to adjust?
- How am I going to be with other people who are enjoying life?
- How am I going to help my broken heart begin the process of healing?
- How am I going to respond? And "who" will help me?

You see, all the "how" questions are within your ability to respond, within your scope of control. Make it your first prayer, "God help me learn **how** to handle this jagged hole left by the one ripped from my life."

One of the best treatments available for asking "How?" versus "Why?" comes from Bob Deits, organizer of the "Growing through Loss" conference series, himself a superb pastoral counselor. "The worst thing about 'Why' questions," Deits writes, "is that they have no satisfactory answers. Questions that begin with 'why' reflect a desperate yearning for meaning and purpose in your loss. It seems so unfair. You are sure there is some reason for what happened. You think you might feel better and hurt less if only you could discover the reason 'why?'."

And no one, no one, can tell you "why?"

"Questions that begin with 'how', Deits says, "indicate you are ready to face the reality of your loss." And what a life-changing "readiness" that is! "Questions that begin with 'how'," Deits writes, "also express your search for ways to put together a life after loss."[28]

2. Focus on "now", not "then".

The death has already happened. The death is a done deal. Take a moment. Grab a piece of perspective. The death was yesterday, last week, last month, last year, ten years ago. Focus on now – not then. Feel yourself in the "now". Take all the time you want or need to recall the special relationship, the love, the life you shared. Reminisce, remember, as often as you need to. Feel the "then", as you feel yourself in the "now". But focus on now.

Live life now, today. Live this moment. Recall "then". Cherish "then". Remember everything that meant so much to you "then". But focus on now.

Deal with now. Pay the bills. Fill out the required forms. Meet the challenges of now. Love then. But don't let "then" keep you from loving and enjoying "now". Living compulsively in the "then" will leave you wandering in the wilderness of "why?"

3. Live in the present – not the past.

Grief is redundant. In the typical grief pattern, we naturally grieve over and over and over again. So a little redundancy helps us deal with a redundant grief. We cannot change the past. We cannot make the past come out any differently than it did or than it has. But we can control more than we may realize about the present, and we can do it over and over.

How we respond to the death of someone who is special to us is totally – 100% - within our control. We control how we feel about the person in the present. We can recall the person's strengths. We can remember their contributions to life around them. We know the person's impact on our lives, the legacy of benefit the person left behind.

4. Look toward the future, plan for the future, yet treasure the past.

Three of the most important things in life are:

- The way we live today.
- The way we plan for tomorrow. And…
- The way we remember yesterday.

Living in the past is a recipe for a wasted life. We want to live today, make the most of today, look toward the future and plan for the future. Failure to plan for tomorrow assures our tomorrows will be less than they could be, less than we dreamed.

Yet when we never remember yesterday, we guarantee ourselves a one dimensional existence.

A healthy approach to life is to: Grieve every day, if we need to, but grieve so that grief makes the day worthwhile. How? Recall how the one gone from our lives made an ordinary day special, unusual or perhaps even unforgettable! Grieve every day, if we need to, but grieve so that our grief enhances our plans for tomorrow. How? Think about an event or activity you could plan for a future tomorrow that remembers the one physically gone from your life, that recalls a special contribution or honors a personal accomplishment. Grieve every day, if we need to, but grieve so that our grief never removes our remembrance of yesterday and always improves our embrace of today.

5. Anticipate a grief "break-through" when you least expect it.

What is a grief "break-through"?

Sally knew first hand the depths of grief. She experienced the deep, dark pit of despair. She had rearranged the furniture in the room called remorse more times than she could remember. "What would a day without the dark pain be like?" she wondered. Then one day without any advance notice, a ray of sunshine broke through the gloom, actually filled the room, where life placed her that day. She felt joy that "they" had those years together. She felt the warmth of his thoughtfulness, the softness of his kindness. She felt love... again. She could hear her own laughter... again. A tiny breakthrough after an unrelenting string of long gray days, a testament to her healing, a sign she was on schedule to embrace life again.

6. Don't be embarrassed when your grief surprises you.

Grief is natural, but 75% of the time we don't expect it. After his wife's death, Jim quickly developed a series of rote responses to use in life's most common situations: at work, in the community, at the supermarket or public events. Jim pre-packaged his reactions for social settings so that he kept concealed his feelings of heartbreak, his moods of despair, his personal times of pervasive grief.

Jim viewed grief as a personal weakness, especially for men, so he never, ever wanted to be seen grieving in public. He wasn't prepared for how grief will slip up on us. He never anticipated the ways grief bubbles up in conversation, for example. He would be giving directions, explaining something, or describing somewhere he went, when out of the clear blue, his grief would spill out– without any warning – without any chance to subdue it or conceal it. He would utter a blurt-like "grief-choke" of broken words and scrambled syntax. "Oh, if I had only stayed home," he thought. "Now", he feared, "they know how weak I am." One of the best days in Jim's life of grief was when he had a surprise "grief-choke" and then went on with the story, punctuating his story appropriately with sobs and smiles, even laughter. What a release, he felt, doing what comes naturally.

Feel good about your grief. **Don't ever be embarrassed about it.**

7. Don't apologize for your grief – grief is natural, human and healthy.

Grief is as healthy as proper exercise, brushing your teeth, or eating a proper diet. Grief is very healthy when we grieve the right way for the right reasons. We never need to make apology for when grief sneaks up on us. Others who have experienced grief will understand. Those who have not experienced grief will experience it in a matter of time.

Consider grief your friend---not your enemy. Don't run from your grief. Don't hide from your grief. Don't try to avoid grief like a difficult person. View grief as your friend. Get acquainted with your grief. Spend time with it. Get to know and appreciate your grief as you would a good friend. Our grief isn't out to get us and bring us down. Like a good friend, we can trust our grief, we can believe our grief is good for us, and we can accept the blessing of our grief – because grief is our friend.

Our cultural expectation for "brief grief" hurts our ability to experience healthy grief. Grief is like fermenting vinegar. You can't rush it. You can't "fast forward" it. You can't zip through it full speed ahead and come out the other side a healthy individual.

Grief is not a habit or a commodity we acquire. Grief is how we feel when we are totally numb, devoid of our normal capacity to "feel", living most moments in soul-deep sorrow. Honest grief is healthy. Good grief is essential for our well-being. Each takes time.

8. Give thanks for your grief.

It took me a long time to understand it---several years, actually---but I came one day to the realization I had benefitted from my personal grief. Let me stress this realization was over a period of time. A huge help to me was the gradual but ever stronger realization grief is part of the created order. Grief was not created by human sin, although our grief may sometimes result from sin. Grief emerges because of our human design as creatures capable of feeling, loving and appreciating another individual.

But just as humans were created with the capacity of choice and decision-making, grief choices may bring healing and help into our lives. When my grandparents died, four of the most special people in my life, wrestling the octopus was a confusing, confounding experience each and every time. Yet I was able to grieve each of their deaths and grow from each of those grief experiences. I give thanks---call it a grief thanksgiving---for what I have learned in my grief.

The Chapter "Take-Away"

Our grief isn't out to get us and bring us down. As Robin Williams expresses it, "Death is life's way of saying, 'Your table is ready'."

We actually open the door for a radical life change when we move beyond "why?" and start asking "how?" and "What now?" Each of the eight beneficial actions noted above lend themselves to prayerful approaches. Each includes an element of personal prayer. A sip of prayer with each action helps the grief medicine go down. When grieving, one of the best things we can do is to give thanks for our grief. Let's do that now.

>God, our Father,
>We give You thanks for our grief,
>for our ability to grieve,
>for the ways in which
>grief enhances and enriches our lives.
>We don't understand grief,
>but we ask You to help us grieve
>in healthy and life-affirming ways.
>May we grieve and cope
>in ways that honor You
>and bring help to ourselves
>and to our families.
>May we be honest about our grief,
>open about our need for healing,
>and always ready to experience
>your healing grace.
>In Your Holy Name we pray, Amen.

Your prayerful grief partner and wilderness friend,

Fran Buhler

A Grief PS: The Wilderness of "why?" is more than a metaphor, it is "everyday" real---a dark and wild wilderness!

1. Write down your two or three biggest "Why?" questions.

2. Convert them into "how", "what now" questions. Dig deep inside. Take time to focus.

3. List three ways you may give yourself a "helping" of God's healing Grace. Practice forgiveness, and begin with yourself.

CHAPTER 8

PERSONAL WILDERNESS DISCOVERIES

Dear Reader, my Grief Partner,

If you're anything like me, living life with a clear vision isn't as easy as it might seem. What I am about to say may be hard for you to believe, yet it is true: **Death and grief help us see.**

Why This Matters

Like a walk in a park where we have never walked before helps us see the pathway design, the layout and special features of the park, so death and grief help us see the one who is gone from our midst. They help us see ourselves... our family... our past... our present... even our future.

Yet everything we see represents the subtraction of one from our lives. Our loved one or special friend is gone from our midst yet remaining in our thoughts and our grief.

No matter our place and time in the long story of humanity, we experience death "head-on" in the lives of those around us – and one day we experience death ourselves. Along the way, if we are alert to the Holy One, we entertain personal wilderness discoveries for ourselves.

Death – Yesterday and Today

I just returned from a walk through the Tallahassee, Florida, City Cemetery, the earliest of several local cemeteries – though not the oldest in the region.

Births ranged from the early 1800s to the mid and late 1800s; and early 1900s.

Deaths covered a similar time frame, from the early 1800s – with many infant deaths – to the late 1800s and the early to mid 1900s.

For the surviving friends and family of those interred there, the cemetery is hallowed ground. But – like any cemetery – it is also a historical "snap-shot in time".

In the serenity of the cemetery, giant live oaks parade throughout, punctuated by sunshine and shade. A walk-thru evokes reflections of a century to a century and a half ago. Today's peaceful setting does not capture the stress and strain of life "then" nor the total grief impact of death experienced then.

An FSU journalism student doing a paper on the history of the cemetery stopped me to inquire if I was maintaining a family burial plot. Disappointment covered his face when he learned I was taking a walk, gathering impressions for a book about grief.

He began to talk about how simple life was then and how complicated and advanced life is today, as if there was some existential advantage to living in a prior era of supposed simplicity.

I gently challenged the notion life was always simpler in by gone days. In the life-span of the cemetery, major wars were waged---including a nasty, divisive civil war plus two deadly, devastating world wars, and even more.

Post-war recovery was always slow. Families suffered profound grief. Death was distributed everywhere and no less difficult than today. Life was not easy. For those living then, life was just as complicated, just as challenging, as it is for us today.

In every historical era, individuals and families experience personal wilderness challenges – trials and difficulties unappreciated by those who come after. Every person, including each of us living today, experiences personal grief to which others are oblivious.

Death Examples We Never Think About

Missy Buchanan is a daily caregiver for her mother who lives in a senior care residence in Rockwell, Texas. In her book Living With Purpose in a Worn-out Body, she captures the life a significant portion of our population has experienced. Buchanan writes about "Life and Death":[29]

"There are daily announcements in the dining room."

"You can read them on bulletin boards and oversized calendars, too."

"At a senior center, ambulances come and go, stirring questions about who and what.

"Here one cannot deny death. It cannot be glossed over or ignored."

"It is a part of everyday life and sometimes the announcements serve as sobering reminders of our mortality."

"Here at the center, life and death ebb and flow in a strangely natural way."

Then Missy Buchanan shares her personal faith in the midst of death announcements: "But because of the Cross, I live with reassurance that my future is secure. Eternity is mine. I rejoice in the promise."[30]

Personal Wilderness Discoveries

When Isaiah announces in chapter 61 "the year of the Lord's favor" he turns attention to the primary tasks at hand, "to bind up the brokenhearted", "to comfort all who mourn", indeed "to provide for those who grieve in Zion" – or anywhere else. For the Holy One brings "the oil of gladness instead of mourning" and more – "a garment of praise instead of a spirit of despair". Isaiah 61:1-3 displays the grief-sensitive "splendor" of the Holy One who visits us where ever life may place us and offers gifts of grace when we are blindsided by death's invasive misery.

I was still a young adult when I discovered the following…

A Verse for the Valley: "For the Lord comforts His people and will have compassion on His afflicted ones." (Isaiah 49:13c and d).

My discovery came because of a hard-to-accept death in the family. An aunt and uncle were killed instantly when a loaded truck plowed into their car. Grieving in the Wilderness of "Why?" often leads to such personal discoveries. Now, that text speaks to me in all times and places when I am grieving, hurting, healing, and surviving. I am constantly amazed at what I have been taught in the valley!

Living God's Benediction

I believe there is such a thing as "living God's benediction". It is a step of faith, a prayer step, a step of determination, for life's journey.

When you find yourself wandering in the wilderness of Grief, if the choir has stopped singing in the cathedral of your soul, then pray God's benediction, a powerful prayer step toward your goal of healing your grieving heart. My grief version of God's benediction goes like this:

PART 1 - CHAPTER 8

> "O God of heaven and earth,
> In the twists and turns of grief
> bless me and keep me,
> make your face to shine upon me
> and be gracious unto me,
> lift up the sunshine of your
> Grace upon me
> and give me Your Peace."

Words I've Claimed

In Isaiah 25, we read of One who "will swallow up death for all time" (v8a) with the word of promise, "and the Lord God will wipe tears away from all faces" (v8b). In my grief, I have claimed these words of encouragement throughout my life in my own wilderness discoveries.

My Personal Wilderness Report

When my mother died in 1994, while I was interim pastor of our church, I experienced "a grief sandwich". I had a death and a funeral in Tallahassee right before leaving for my Mother's funeral in Tennessee. After our return from Mother's funeral, we had another death in our church in Tallahassee with three church member hospital emergency room patients at the same time.

In football, we have a penalty for "piling on" after the ball carrier is tackled and down. My grief during that time frame felt like life was "piling on" and I had no say or choice in the matter.

During that time of challenge, I rediscovered the meaning and comfort behind familiar New Testament words I had used almost carelessly, the words of Paul in 2 Corinthians: "Blessed be the God and Father of our Lord Jesus Christ, the Father of all mercies and God of all comfort; Who comforts us in all our affliction so that we may be able to comfort those who are in affliction with the comfort with which we ourselves are comforted by God." (2 Corinthians 1:3-4)

I had to "re-learn", "re-member", "re-mind" myself of the comfort of the Holy One: "For just as the sufferings of Christ are ours in abundance, so also our comfort is abundant through Christ." (2 Corinthians 1:5)

Rediscovering God's Comfort and Strength

I had to "re-discover" the palpable meaning of 2 Thessalonians 2:16-17: "Now may our Lord Jesus Christ Himself and God our Father, who has loved us and given us eternal comfort and good hope by grace, comfort and strengthen your hearts in every good work and word."

I was introduced, again, to those powerful words of Hebrews 4: "Let us therefore draw near with confidence to the throne of grace, that we may receive mercy and may find grace to help in time of need." (v16)

My faith was "re-activated", "re-newed", "re-affirmed", when I recalled the truth of Revelation 21, God tabernacles with us, He "lives" among us, He dwells with us. He is not a "resident alien" for even in that future time "God Himself shall be among them." (Rev 21:3) His Presence speaks to our grief: "and He shall wipe away every tear from their eyes; and there shall no longer be any death; there shall no longer be any mourning, or crying, or pain..." (Rev 21:4)

Grief, Hope, and Nailing Jell-O to the Wall

We do not grieve as those who have no hope, Paul reminds us in 1 Thessalonians 4:13. Yet "Hope" is a word that leaves many with a blank. Those who don't know hope. Don't have hope. Don't believe in hope.

My seminary professor, Dr. Wayne Oates, used to say, "Defining hope is like trying to nail Jell-O to the wall."

When Paul writes about suffering in Romans 8:24-25, he does so by writing about hope:

> "Hope that is seen is no hope at all. Who hopes for what he already has? But if we hope for what we do not yet have, we wait for it patiently." (Romans 8:24-25 NIV)

In the wilderness of "Why?" we often discover a hope that is not based on human wishful thinking but on God's Presence and Peace. Paul asserts in 1 Thessalonians 4:13, "We do not... grieve as others who have no hope." We do not grieve as if our only hope was our ability to nail Jell-O to the wall.

In the wilderness of grief, the writer to the Hebrews reminds us: "We have this hope as an anchor for the soul, firm and secure." In the midst of unrelenting grief, we may come to know the welcomed comfort of that assurance we call "hope".

The Redemptive Grief Discovery

The wilderness of "why?" is a good place to discover the gift of what Kirk H. Neely calls "redemptive grief". Neely, the senior pastor of Morningside Baptist Church in Spartanburg, South Carolina, provides an excellent observation in his book *When Grief Comes: Finding Strength for Today and Hope for Tomorrow*. Neely points to Luke's "compassionate interpretation" as to "why the disciples fell asleep in the Garden of Gethsemane."[31]

"When Jesus rose from prayer and returned to the disciples", Neely writes, "he found them asleep, exhausted from sorrow" (Luke 22:45).[32] Jesus found the disciples trapped in the wilderness of "Why?" wondering what fate awaited them. When would life be normal again?

Neely, who holds a doctor of ministry degree in pastoral counseling and psychology of religion, has been a pastor for four decades. He is the kind of pastor with whom people will talk and bare their souls. One of Neely's male church members, after the death of a daughter, told Neely "It takes me half an hour to put on my socks". A woman whose husband died asked Neely: "He was in every part of my life. What am I going to do without him?" Neely gave her…

A Priceless Answer

Neely's answer was 24 carat gold: "This is your opportunity to teach your children and grandchildren how a Christian faces such deep sorrow and continues to live life to the fullest."[33]

How?

"As difficult as it is to put one foot in front of the other", Neely concludes, "Christians in grief learn that 'they that wait upon the Lord shall renew their strength'… they shall walk, and not faint." (Isaiah 40:31 KJV)

Did you catch the "How?" "Wait upon the Lord". We should listen to God, the Holy One. Waiting upon the Lord, the Holy One of the Universe, is possible for the person of faith.

"Waiting" Equals "Screaming in Sorrow

Granted, this matter of "waiting upon the Lord" is a very hard and very difficult thing to do. You may feel, as did two of my prepublication readers, that if they were reading this section after their loved one died they would have thrown TGL across the room, one said, in a "fit of rage", the other said "screaming in sorrow".

I remember a time when I might have done the same thing!

There have been grief times when all I could do was try to hold on and "wait", "waiting" for God with my heart "screaming in sorrow"! Sometimes an encourager's comment cannot be appreciated until later.

Why do I now feel differently?

Without question one person who helped me was Henry Sloane Coffin, President Emeritus of Union Theological Seminary in New York, who wrote the Exposition of Isaiah 40 in *The Interpreter's Bible*, published by Abingdon Press. At the tender age of 25, I read Dr. Coffin's treatment of Isaiah 40:31, and it changed my understanding, maybe even my life. He helped me see what it means to wait…on the Lord.

Call it a "waiting upon the Lord" faith

"Those who turn expectantly toward God," wrote Coffin, "discover that occurrences are not 'bare events,' but advents of the everlasting God." Coffin said when Israel was at her national best she was "pre-eminently 'the waiting community.'" Coffin went on to write, "The early church was possessed by the same mentality, which unhappily has ceased to be the mind of contemporary Christians."[34]

Dr. Coffin's explanation response hit me between the eyes. His words shook me! He helped me see. "We," he said, "are not looking hopefully for God's arrivals on the scene in gracious power in historic happenings. Yet it is to this waiting mentality," Coffin points out, "that increases of strength are promised."[35]

Coffin convinced me I ought to try waiting upon the Lord. Waiting on the Lord, I learned in Hebrew class, is not like waiting for a stop light to change or waiting for an illness to subside. It's more like a choice I make to rely, to depend on, and look to the Most High God for strength and clarity in my life, in my daily challenges, even in my grief. Call it a "waiting upon the Lord" faith. I have learned "waiting upon the Lord" helps me find the way through my grief.

I received an additional "faith boost" from David F. Payne, who wrote in the Interpreter's Bible Commentary in 1979, his own interpretation of Isaiah 40:30: "Those who hope in the Lord shall find a strength for action beyond the ordinary human expectation."38 Hope and a strength for action, waiting does not get any better than that!

I've tried it for several decades now. I'm not saying I am a stronger or better person than someone else. I am only reporting what I have discovered. I find in all the ups and downs, in all the griefs and sorrows of my life, when I make a genuine personal effort to "wait upon the Lord", I am constantly being renewed and restored. For which I am eternally grateful. "Waiting on the Lord" works for me, and I pray it will work for you also.

The Chapter "Take-Away"

We do not live through the death of a loved one "alone", isolated, as the Country song says, "Oh lonesome me".

The One who "comforts all who mourn" is ever present, ever blessing, always comforting each of us in our personal grief circumstance. This is not a "line" for pastors, priests and Rabbis to assure professional security. This is a faith walk that any person as average as I am can find with confidence and follow with certainty.

The Divine Comfort we experience becomes real to each of us in our personal grief. The reality of One we know as the Holy One is an Ultimate Reality, not a pretend or a "make-believe" reality. In our grief, in the deep pain of every wilderness journey, we discover again One who comes near to comfort us in our tearful time of grief.

Death and grief help us see ourselves and our lives more clearly. Death and grief help us see today and tomorrow from a blessed perspective – God is with us. And the Most High God specializes in wilderness adventures!

I am praying for you and for your personal wilderness discoveries. I have a system for doing this. I keep a reminder on my desk to pray every morning of every day for the one reading TGL that day. So this is your day!

Your grief partner, and prayerful wilderness friend,

Fran Buhler

THE GRIEF LETTER

A Grief PS: How do death and grief help us "see"?

1. In your personal "wilderness", have you discovered God's Comfort and Strength?

2. Stop right now. Spend some time "waiting upon the Lord". Get rid of your personal notions of how long this "waiting" business should take. It's based on God's time clock, not ours. Be prepared to spend more time than you think it ought to take. Discover the absolute adventure of becoming part of "the waiting community."

3. Try living God's benediction for one day. Then one week. Try living God's benediction for a month; for a year. How about for a life time?

CHAPTER 9

HAVE YOU TRIED THE "ANGER BUCKET"?

Dear Reader, my Partner in Grief,

When my lifelong friend, Jimmy Hankins, died, I was upset. I was angry. Really angry! **Grief has the clout to make us angry.** Going through Jimmy's death, helped me relate to the following gentleman in his grief.

My friend and I were driving to an important meeting. He had just returned to work following his wife's funeral. Driving to our destination, he steered into the "By Pass" lane to access the beltway around the city to our meeting location.

Why This Matters

"That's what I did," he said, pointing to the interstate "By Pass" sign. He had missed work two days following the death of his wife in a terrible auto accident. The driver of the other vehicle was "at fault". As he continued, I listened. "I tried to 'by-pass' my anger, but it didn't work. I get angrier by the day… there's no place to take my anger so it just piles up higher and deeper."

The Anger By-Pass

In clinical pastoral care training and in grief ministry experience, I have seen the human tendency to "by-pass" anger. We accept anxiety, depression, tears, and trauma. We even allow denial. But anger, hostility, and rage are outside the range of acceptance. In fact, individuals often feel they are beyond the grief process when anger and rage blindside them.

Often, anger starts at the top. As my friend phrased it, "I'm sure I give the impression I'm angry at the universe. But to tell the truth, I'm angry at God!"

"What would you like to tell God?" I asked.

"It's unfair," he blurted. "She was such a sweet person, minding her business – and boom – she's gone!" I wondered: "Could I forgive someone for running a red light and killing my wife?"

The Anger Experience

Anytime death visits our lives, the response stage most of us try to "by-pass" is the anger stage. When we become over-loaded with grief, anger emerges. It is our anger – not someone else's. Rage and anger may emerge in our hostility and ambivalence. As Doris Jones asserts, we may experience:

- "anger at one who is gone,"
- "anger at doctors or hospitals,"
- "anger at an ex-spouse,"
- "anger at an employer for requiring a long distance move,"
- "anger at parents for not taking better care of themselves,"
- "rage for the poor choices made by our children,"
- "anger at government or insurance regulations,"
- "anger with the church, the pastor, the synagogue, the rabbi, the mosque, the priest,"
- "anger with God."[36]

Anger At God

Our anger with God may be an unmentionable emotion. We don't want to go there publicly, or in our family. Where death and grief are concerned, grief-thick anger with God goes with the territory. Unexpected anger and rage – whether directed at God or a family member – or at the situation itself – may spill out all over the place. Anger-based grief may be directed toward God or religious communities, expressed by not giving tithes or supporting financial offerings. Hostility and anger may be accompanied by withdrawal and passive-aggressive examples of emotional rage.

Controlled Anger is Legitimate

Where death and loss are concerned, yes, anger is legitimate. But the anger should be under control. If the anger is related to the cause of death, separation, and loss – and if the anger is under control--which means I am able to manage my anger without bringing harm to others or damage to property, then it's understandable.

Some of retired pastor Max Lucado's best preaching counsel addresses the anger challenge: "Are you angry with God? Tell him. Disgusted with God? Let him know. Weary of telling people you feel fine when you don't? Tell the truth."[37] Lucado's counsel is "face your grief with tears, time, and with truth."

Facing Grief with Truth

Excellent words on processing grief come from the tender thoughts of Doris Moreland Jones, director of the Middletown United Methodist Counseling Center in Middletown, Kentucky. These words are from her book titled: *And Not One Bird Stopped Singing: Coping with Transition and Loss in Aging* published by Upper Room Books. Jones discovered she could be "very grateful and very depressed at the same time." Jones' take on processing grief:

> "Grief and gratitude are not mutually exclusive. Grief is so capricious. It comes at unexpected moments and washes over us like a black blanket that blocks out the sunshine and smiles. It can be triggered by the melody of a song or the sight of a favorite jacket. Grief leaves us panting for breath. It is fresh and compelling. Grief saps vitality, leaving fatigue in its place."[38]

Jones, who describes her experience with spousal death as "amputation without anesthesia", expresses the experience as follows: "The death of a much-loved spouse causes the shrinking of the adult self. The loneliness is pervasive, consuming."[39]

Grief Associations

Grief associations are universal among all of us. A deep hurt, an emptiness, even days of anger have been reflected in comments I have witnessed. While we may eventually move beyond a particular association, grief has the power to permeate certain memories with a raw pain we may wish to avoid in those early months following the death of loved ones.

For Martha and her mother, shopping was always a joyous adventure, spiced with laughter and fun times together. Following her Mother's death, however, shopping pleasure often gave way to grief associations with the shopping experience.

George's family loved Bar-B-Q, often a grilled gift from his uncle. Following the uncle's accidental death, the grief association nullified his Bar-B-Q appetite for years.

Those early morning "pre sun-up" bass fishing hours on the lake with my father, as a kid and a young adult, gave way to other pursuits because of the painful association with his presence, his vault of stories, our shared laughter, and our ability to catch more fish than we ever needed. On the way home, we often detoured to give our "catch" to needy families. I still remember the smiles on their faces when we gave them our fish, cleaned, sliced, and ready to fry. But I don't care to fish like I used to. The few times I tried early morning fishing, I experienced a grief association of anger, anger because something and someone special in my life had been removed. It took me several years to work thru my anger-fed grief.

Fear and Loneliness Move In

One lady told me she never, ever wanted to be called a widow. Doris Mooreland Jones calls it the "salt without the pepper – the cup without the saucer". She then nails the feeling many surviving spouses have tried to describe: "The being less than whole. You feel so numb, yet you hurt so much."[40]

Listen to Jones as she shares truth from experience long ignored or denied.

> "Fear moves in along with loneliness. Grief touches us in our unconscious. Even we of the household of faith feel guilt and despair. We have physical fears, emotional fears, and spiritual fears. We go back to the old theology that we learned as children, which is as ill-fitting now as a dress worn to the senior prom. Sleeping alone is a toothache that covers your entire body that cannot forget when you were a part of another."[41]

An Anger Review

One of the most comprehensive treatments of grief anger may be found in *The Mourning Handbook* by Helen Fitzgerald. Anger emotions are not automatically a part of every person's grief. Yet if you find yourself in anger moods and realize you are experiencing anger episodes, consider...

Fitzgerald's Ten Anger Facts!
- "Anger is not part of every grief reaction."
- "Rage and anger are very strong emotions" and can be "frightening to you" and "to your family and friends."
- "Anger is an isolating emotion." Why? "Family and friends often don't know what to do with you or how to help you."
- "When a loved one dies, leaving you lonely and afraid of what your future will bring, you have every reason to be angry... it's okay to be angry. What's not okay is taking your anger out unfairly on

yourself or others."
- "Anger won't just go away." If it is ignored, it will "fester, growing larger and larger until it erupts."
- "Anger that is not discharged can create both emotional and physical stress leading to anxiety and depression. "
- "Anger that is not acknowledged and that is misdirected can create all sorts of problems in your life."
- "Anger can take over your life, making you miserable and the people around you miserable."
- "You may be short on patience, critical of others, complain about everything, or take your anger out on yourself and others."
- "Whenever you feel your anger reaches this level and it's out of control, I suggest that you seek professional help to gain a better understanding of what is causing your anger and how to manage it."[42]

Seven Common Anger Targets

Emergent anger as we mourn the death of one close and dear to us may target certain people or circumstances. You may experience…

- Anger at God
- Anger at the person who died and left you with loneliness and lots of legal stuff.
- Anger at yourself for something you said or didn't say to the one who is gone, or angry because you are still alive and he or she is gone.
- Anger at medical doctors, hospital staff, emergency personnel, even family.
- Anger at relatives and friends for lack of response, lack of understanding, lack of support.
- Anger at "the world" because everything goes on as though nothing happened!
- Anger at the changes forced upon you and your family, including the financial challenges you did not expect.

Anger Control

Controlling our anger is like controlling a volcano's lava flow. It just keeps coming. Where death and grief are concerned, the lava flow of anger erupts from the volcano of our grief. And you're mistaken if you think you can shut it off and stop it. Grief anger has been around longer than Mount Vesuvius. We need an exceptional strategy to combat our anger.

Martha Whitman Hickman captured the right perspective on anger in the context of grief. Not only is Hickman smart and well-schooled, her Phi Beta Kappa assessment of anger and grief are spot on. "My anger is legitimate," she writes, "and it will burn away sooner if I acknowledge and express it."

"Anger is part of our grief", Hickman explains. "Maybe we're angry at the loved one – for leaving us. Maybe we're angry with ourselves. Or angry at God." "As with other aspects of grief," Hickman points out, "we need to recognize anger and express it. We may need to be careful with relatives and friends. But we don't need to worry about God – we can let it fly."[43]

A frequent anger cause is the friendly warning we are bound to hear – likely from a friend, relative or work supervisor: "Shouldn't you be getting over this by now?" When someone in your life circle signals "Time's up!" let them know politely yet firmly that you appreciate their concern. Explain that every grief has its own schedule, its own unique timetable. Prepare yourself for the fact that the general population is impatient with most anyone's extended grief. And figure out ways to grieve in your own time – not when you are on your employer's time.

So what **is** an "Anger Bucket"?

Well, first of all, much of what we consider grief is actually anger. For example:

- When a loved one dies in an accident that may have been the other party's fault.
- When a loved one dies after an extended period of hospitalization and treatment.
- When a loved one dies with hard-to-understand pain and circumstances.
- When a child dies – for any reason. When death strikes via a natural disaster.
- When a spouse dies and leaves me all alone.

The causes of anger are potentially unending. Yet I'm not here to take your time with endless scenarios that may generate an anger response or fits of extended anger. I'm here to suggest a valid and effective approach to moving beyond anger responses.

Try Using the "Anger Bucket"

I've used the "Anger Bucket" personally myself and I have witnessed its effective use by individuals and families with whom I have walked and with whom I have grieved. I highly recommend it.

So what do you do with the "Anger Bucket"?

You fill it up. Put an imaginary "Anger Bucket" in your life in several convenient locations: By the trash cans in your kitchen and where you work, in your garage. Near where you sit in worship. Take all the anger from your life, past and present---no matter its cause, no matter its source, no matter how much pain it caused – and leave it in the most conveniently designated "Anger Bucket". When you leave home, when you leave work, when you leave your preferred place of worship, imagine a big bucket – an anger bucket – and deposit all your anger in the bucket and leave it there, moving on to embrace God's future for your life.

Anger is a typical by-product of many life circumstances like long illnesses, cancer, terrible accidents, horrific natural disasters, as well as most any of the circumstances associated with or leading up to the death of someone close to us. As humans, we have the capacity for both anger and grief, a potentially explosive mixture.

A Verse for the Valley: "Do not associate with one given to anger." Proverbs 22:24. Why? Because you will "snare yourself", scripture says, "and learn his ways."

Think about anger. Angry is a bad place to be. We can't use anger. Who is it going to help? It has had it's position in our lives long enough. Be done with it. As my colleague, Dr. Bill Shiell has said, "we can't retreat behind the walls of bitterness or hide out in the asylum of anger." From deep in your soul, give your anger to God (all of it), and for the sake of your life, leave your anger in your "Anger Bucket", and move forward, move God-ward, in your life.

That's what I did when my friend Jimmy Hankins died. We had been friends since the third grade. All the way through high school and beyond---until his death. He briefly owned a successful men's clothing store. He lived life to the fullest in spite of a long term illness that kept him bed-ridden for years. He was chipper even in his relative brief span of life. I visited Jim

THE GRIEF LETTER

every time we were in Lebanon, Tennessee, our childhood home. I still miss him. After every visit, as I backed out of the Hankins' drive-way, I left my anger in the streets behind me.

The Chapter "Take-Away"

Ask yourself: Will anger improve my life, my present or my future?

Will anger solve any of our frustrations, address our deep disappointment or speak to our soul-deep pain? Will a "fit of anger" fit me for anything?

Anger can become a dead end street. What we need is a path beyond our pain, through our grief, to the good future God has for us. The best thing to do with our anger is to simply let it go. Put it in the Anger Bucket, and leave it there. Acknowledge your anger exists, and make a renewed effort to manage your anger-infused grief.

Using the "Anger Bucket" is one of the very best solutions to "anger-twisted" grief we can ever use. Drop your anger in the "Anger Bucket" and move forward. Live today, relish this day, and look forward to tomorrow without allowing your anger to control you.

Your grief partner and "anger-bucket" user,

Fran Buhler

A Grief PS: Look beneath the surface of your personality and see it you spot some anger! Look behind your smile, under your "workout" time, outside your comfort zone.

1. Start using your "anger bucket" today, and every day. Make a mental note of the places in your life where you will place imaginary "anger buckets". As a helpful reminder, you may want to make an "anger bucket" location list. They really work!

2. Keep a list of your "anger" feelings. Reread the list from time to time. Challenge yourself to discard your anger feelings, working on them one at a time.

3. Keep a list for a week, then a month, of when you used one of your "anger buckets". Note the short and long term results. What have you learned? Monitor a three month and six month time frame and see what you learn about your anger.

CHAPTER 10

"WILL I EVER LAUGH AGAIN?"

Dear Reader and Partner in Grief,

What's the toughest grief you have experienced? I remember mine. Nothing else comes close!

The graveside service for my Mother came in the midst of a raging Tennessee thunderstorm. Family members squeezed under a grave-protecting funeral tent, enclosed on three sides. I resented the rain, cascading with a thick fog like a Smokey Mountain waterfall, surrounding us in a cell of inescapable grief. **It doesn't get much worse than a "cell of inescapable grief"!**

Why This Matters

At some point in our lives, we each find ourselves in the fog of grief. I overheard a grandmother asking herself and, for that matter, anyone within hearing distance of her granddaughter's casket, "Will I ever laugh again?"

When was the last time someone died in your family or your circle of friends? Grieving the death of someone close is a life-challenge. Perhaps that's where you are today.

The chapter question raises "the unspoken question" I asked in my heart at my Mother's graveside yet never asked out loud – "Will I ever laugh again?" To answer that question, walk with me as we work our way through several related observations and questions.

Grief Exposed

An eight year old says simply, "It hurts".

A 12 year old describes it in more detail: "It's like someone breaks your heart and you hurt all over".

A teenage girl in high school says: "It's not like any pain I've ever experienced before, and you feel it every day".

THE GRIEF LETTER

A grandmother recalls: "Of all the deaths I've lived through, this one hurts the most".

A husband excuses himself: "I still can't talk about it".

A single mom bathes her comment in tears: "To this day, it is the deepest ache I've ever known".

"She was the love of my life! Need I say more?" a grieving husband asks.

"It's been 20 years, and it still causes me to tear up at the oddest times. But I have to say – and I hope this won't be misunderstood. As a result of all these years of grief, I am a much better person now than I was then."

"It's ok to cry!"

Where death and grief are concerned, no matter who you are or how you were raised, it's okay to cry. It's also okay not to cry.

Where grief follows the death of someone close and central in our lives, the thing to expect is the unexpected. We can't actually plan and prep for it in advance. We meet the challenge to deal with death when it actually happens.

Personally, my grief pain experience is pretty simple. When I think I have my pain and grief under control, they hit me without advance notice, giving absolutely no warning. No matter where I am: at work, at home, visiting someone in the hospital, in worship, in a meeting, working in the yard, on a trip. Grief hits me head-on. I decided long ago I would never be ashamed of my grief, never apologize for my grief, never hide my grief, never deny my grief. I try my best to grieve honestly. I don't flaunt it or display it for show, but if my grief surges to the surface I never try to hide it or deny it, even if I'm in front of an audience.

So… when people ask you not to cry, you do not have to heed their wish. Grief is like politics – you can be open about it, even grieve in public, or you can be reserved with a preference for privacy. It's your grief, your call. You're in good company. Tears may be our necessary and welcome guide for our unexpected grief journey. The question before us is:

"Will we ever laugh again?"

Perhaps not, at first. Grief is hard and heavy (and even hellish at times).

Initially, we find it very hard to appreciate anything – anything at all – about our grief. Why?

Grief is initially too painful, dark and soul-shaking, too invasive. Grief does not entertain any thought of appreciation at all. Plus the reality of grief, in Max Lucado's words, is "the chill of sorrow". "It's cold." Lucado says, "in the valley of the shadow of death."[44]

However, if we grieve a healthy grief, we will at some point laugh again. But, don't be surprised if our laughter is mixed with tears. Tears and laughter are an important part of our grief. We will laugh again when we feel like laughing. We grieve – if we grieve well – as whole persons. We don't grieve only in our heart or soul or head. We grieve in every aspect of life – including our laughter. If we grieve naturally, normally, and openly, our grief, even our tears, will contain laughter at some point. We may find ourselves both grieving and laughing at the same time. We will probably grieve and laugh more openly, maybe even more often.

You can't make yourself laugh just to produce laughter. Your laughter comes from your life. Your heart and soul and personality, who you are, all of you, including your faith---especially your faith---yields laughter. Don't try to make yourself laugh when you grieve. You aren't wired that way.

Be yourself. Grieve, share, and in the midst of everything that's going on you will find yourself breaking into laughter. Let it come naturally. Don't try to start or stop it. Process your grief the way you would process any experience.

How we grieve begins as a strong human need. But grief becomes healthy and enriches life when we welcome grief, accept our grief, and choose to live our lives as persons who grieve our losses. Instead of pretending nothing has really changed and falsely believing we are above such human weaknesses as grief, we should see grief as a strength and move forward in the strength of our grief.

"You mean grief is not a weakness?"

No, never. God created us with the mental / physical / spiritual / emotional capacity to grieve. Grief is built into our design. Because grief is actually a healthy strength, when we grieve in positive, healthy ways, we encourage others in their grief and we become better able to connect with others in their grief. We even grieve better ourselves than we would in isolation.

THE GRIEF LETTER

"I'm grieving so hard I hurt all over, and it's not a weakness? What have I missed?" Sharon asked.

We never grieve alone. Even if no one checks on us in our grief, we never grieve alone. When we grieve, God is always present with us in our grief. God walks with us in our grief. "Even though I walk through the valley of the shadow of death, I fear no harm; for Thou art with me..." (Psalm 23:4a and b NAS) If we look to Him, God renews and restores us in our time of grief.

"So where do I begin?"

Begin where you are, with the way you feel. Grieve as hard and as long as you need to grieve. Take all the time you need. You can't rush grief any more than you can rush being alive.

As you live every moment you grieve through those same moments. At some point, when your grief has been healthy, God-breathed, and soul-deep, you will sense you are living life forward again. You are alive to each moment, in each day. For you, life is worth living again. Believe it or not, you find yourself laughing again.

After church one Sunday I heard a member say, following the death of her husband several months prior, "I've had to adjust to it, but you know I sometimes find myself laughing in spite of my grief!" The first time she wondered "How can this happen?"

Then she explained. It happened when her grandchildren were visiting, ages 4, 7 and 12. "My discovery is simple and I will share it with the world", she exclaimed: "Get yourself around children, be involved in their lives, and you will find yourself laughing in spite of your grief!"

But many live in relative isolation, with minimum human contact, and therefore do not have the normal stimulation to laugh that comes naturally from human interaction and family dynamics. If you're in that number, consider this chapter of "The Grief Letter" especially for you.

"Does Grief Leave Room for Laughter?"

How each of us responds to the death of another is a personal choice, and a reflection of our confident faith. By faith, grief has room for laughter.

How we grieve is also a function of the grief exposure we've had, how family members have modeled grief in front of us, and the death circumstances to which we've been exposed.

I may say "I will grieve the way I want to grieve." And that is true to some extent. But I cannot avoid or change the fact my grief will naturally imitate some of the family grief models I have grown up with or community grief styles that have influenced me in my grief until I become more selective, even intentional, in how I grieve.

While visiting someone whose wife died of cancer, the gentleman said he had been asked if he thought the death-of-a-spouse challenge could take away a person's ability to laugh? "And your response", I asked?

"Sure", he said, "you see it all the time. But that does not mean we are doomed to dwell in negativity. As for myself," he added, "I remind myself that even though death has taken my wife from me, there is a better way to think about this matter."

"And how is that?" I asked.

"First of all," he said, "she has not been 'taken' from me." Then he explained. "True, my wife died. She is no longer here with me. But she was not taken from me. She died for health and medical reasons. At her death, she transitioned to a different kind of existence, an experience beyond this life. I believe she is in God's Presence. I miss her terribly, but I know where she is, and sometimes when I'm thinking about the Grace of God and the reality of His resurrection power, I enjoy a private chuckle. The deep assurance I feel in those times of laughter is just amazing!"

"Even when you're living in grief," he explained, "you should still be able to smile and laugh at the silliness that is always part of life each day. As for me," he added, "death will one day come for me as well. But until death comes calling," he said with a big grin, "I plan to find something in every day to smile and laugh about."

His view reflects the perspective of a person of faith who has experienced great personal loss and is well aware of approaching death in his own life but still has the capacity to embrace life, live forward, and laugh.

The Faith Factor and Our Laughter

So the discussion comes back to our faith perspective. In the context of our faith, in the hope of resurrection, in the promise and power of the Holy

God to give new life beyond death in this life, we who believe, who trust His grace and Providential care, have every reason to punctuate our earthly grief with laughter.

Jackie Partlow was a high school classmate who became a mortician and funeral home owner. Jackie had the ability to "help" people laugh in tough times, even in a funeral home visitation time. I had the occasion to work with Jackie for several celebration of life funeral services of former class mates. For years, Jackie, who had been our high school class "Laugh Maker", was a funeral home owner-director in our hometown. By telling a laughable story or sharing something intrinsically humorous, Jackie possessed the professional grace and the personal sensitivity to ease a griever's pain, to use the power of a hearty chuckle to comfort those who mourn.

When done appropriately, grief always has room for laughter.

But it wasn't Jackie Partlow's sense of humor that made his unique persona possible and powerful. It was Jackie's personal faith in a God who shares our laughter as surely as our tears, a faith which enabled Jackie as a funeral home owner and director to "comfort those who mourn" in his own unique style.

"We interrupt this program!"

Here, we have a major grief pain point for me personally. After completing this chapter, I received word Jackie Partlow died. Because of a funeral in Tallahassee, Nancy and I were unable to make the Tennessee trip for the funeral of this classmate and friend.

As I changed the "has" to "had" in the Jackie Partlow paragraph above, I celebrated Jackie's life amid my own tears of grief and loss – while also laughing at Jackie's ability to use honest humor as a powerful means of human connection and comfort.

Grief is swallowed up in hope. The certain promise and the sure provision of eternal life are the springboards of joy and laughter. Our main goal is to grieve in healthy and transformational ways, not how quickly we can laugh again; however, grief-faith always has room for laughter. Which raises the grief question of how to handle holidays?

PART 1 - CHAPTER 10

Holiday/Holy Day Grief

Major US holidays pose special grief challenges, times when we grieve because of the "empty place" at the table, and laugh because of our love and appreciation for the one who is gone from our presence. I call it "reminder" grief, a grief created by the absence of one who has always been present on such occasions.

High, holy days in our respective faith traditions represent another grief hurdle we must negotiate, special calendar days with significant personal and often family meaning. Such occasions, because of past observance "together", become heavy grief "triggers", punctuating with pain the absence of the one we love and miss so deeply.

Include family days with special meaning as well: Birthdays, anniversaries, and other days with relational significance. Because grief is relational. Find something to laugh about, even if you have to create the laughter.

Spouse Grief: "As the season approaches, I spend days crying, unable to get in gear. It always seems to slip up on me, unexpectedly. And yet I laugh in my tears."

Couple Grief: "This will be our first Christmas without either of our parents. It will be a day of remembering good times and laughing about our shared life."

Parent Grief: "We spend the day doing all of her favorite things---activities, hikes, foods, reading and travel to favorite places, laughing---and relishing our big laughs!"

Mother-Daughter Grief: "We both miss him so much... I'm sure we'll both cry and laugh a lot."

Daughter-Mother Grief: "My father's death is something I'm still dealing with. Now, I need to give Mother a home with me. She can no longer care for herself. Dad actually cared for both of them. They laughed a lot. I hope we can too."

At-just-the-right-time-grief: "It's amazing! Your letter came at just the right time in our grief, when we really needed it. Because of your help, eventually we could laugh again."

Jesus' Personal Grief Journey Led to Laughter

Even Jesus experienced personal grief and laughter! The Gospel of Matthew reports Jesus' emotional-mental state. "My soul is deeply grieved, to the point of death..." (Matthew 26:38 NAS) Gethsemane, at the foot of the Mount of Olives, was Jesus' well-known personal grief headquarters. He went there to pray. He went there to grieve. He went there to weep. Over the years some have questioned the interpretive tradition that makes clear Jesus' personal, facing-my-own-death grief. Yet from an incarnational standpoint, what an affirmation of his humanity!

Dr. George A. Buttrick was Minister of Madison Avenue Presbyterian Church in New York City when he wrote the *Interpreter's Bible Commentary*, volume 7, on Matthew. Buttrick gives moving insight into Jesus' "Gethsemane grief." He captures and conveys Jesus' personal grief on several levels, referring to Jesus' "agony of prayer", his "loneliness of anguish", and his "soul agony."[45]

Buttrick draws the strong observation: "we cannot enter into his depth of sorrow," and calls it a "cup of rejection". In that "dread moment", he writes, "all his words and works seemed eclipsed in failure, and soon even his closest friends would desert him. It was a cup of lonely grief..." Buttrick concluded: "There is no human parallel: God 'made him to be sin for us, who knew no sin'" (2 Corinthians 5:21).[46] Dr. Buttrick leaves no doubt about the reality of Jesus' grief. Yet...

The New Testament Implication is "Jesus laughed again"!

And this is the significant point of my narrative. The time came, I believe, when Jesus laughed again. Jesus laughed with his disciples after his resurrection. Do you really think Jesus could prepare that post-resurrection seaside fish fry for his disciples in John 21:12, and the group not engage one another and celebrate his resurrection without the wildest laughter imaginable?

There is no record of such an exchange in the following verses of John 21. Yet, inevitably, it seems to me, there must have been a noticeable embarrassment among the disciples for their "disappearing act" at the time of Jesus' last hours at trial and His long, slow passage to death on the cross.

After all, as John tells us in chapter 19, "Joseph of Arimathea, being a disciple of Jesus" but not one of the twelve received Pilate's permission to remove the body of Jesus for proper burial. None of the twelve were available or so inclined.

Yet now stands Jesus on the seashore, beside a charcoal fire (verse 9) he built himself, welcoming the disciples without any evidence of bitterness or desire to even the score. From Jesus, only a welcoming hospitality to remind the disciples and all of humanity "…and lo, I am with you always, even to the end of the world." (Matthew 28:20b)

As with Jesus' disciples, there are no parallels for the pure pain of guilt. There are no time tables to indicate when we will laugh again. But if we grieve as people of faith, in hopeful and healthy ways, we will laugh again and we may also enable others to laugh again.

New Understanding When it's Hard to Laugh

As we grieve and grow in our grief, we discover new understanding even when it may be hard to laugh: Grief has no expiration date and God's comfort never wears out. Grief is a matter of living through life's toughest transitions…with God's Help. When we grieve in God's Providential Care rather than grieving in bitterness, grief is better. Life is better.

Read your Bible with a grieving heart, search for words of comfort. Allow God's Word to "help" and "heal". The key dynamic is "allow" it to happen.

We can't think our way through our grief. We have to feel our way out of our grief. We can't talk our way out of our grief. We pray our way through our grief. Our prayer need not be any more than "God help me!"

God is always available. While it certainly helps, we don't have to have a church or religious background to draw strength and comfort from God. We only have to turn to Him. Then we will want to become part of a faith community.

1. We must remember the promise, and claim the Presence: "God is near to the brokenhearted and delivers those who are crushed in spirit" (Psalm 34:18).

2. We must give ourselves permission to grieve. As the hole in our soul begins to heal, we gradually gain awareness and begin to appreciate the provisional grace of God.

Grief is hard and heavy. Circumstances compound our grief. The death of a loved one is a hole with jagged edges. Grief speaks to the hole in our heart, the slice of life and laughter wrenched from our lives.

Grief Relief: "When laughter and grief get together!"

Laughter is a bona fide, certified, as my aunt used to say, "sanctified", form of grief relief. Grace and healing plus life-purpose and laughter are God's answers to grief.

What does this "grace" talk mean?

Evidence of God's provisional grace means even in our times of sorrow and grief, there is reason to laugh again. In order to live through grief-laden days, we need the tension-relief and the sadness-relief of laughter. Laughter-relief is a gift from God.

Even grief has its moments of laughter. You know you are grieving when:

- You receive seven macaroni-and-cheese casseroles.
- Your work colleagues avoid lunch with you.
- You are tired, drained---no matter how much sleep you had.
- Friends don't invite you to their house to watch the big game.
- Neighbors see you at the super market and dash quickly to another isle.
- Your refrigerator has three chocolate cakes and none have been opened!

Laughter will definitely come again as a natural part of your life. When laughter shows up, welcome it. Don't ever feel guilty about it popping up in your conversations. You may still be in your personal time of grief and deep sorrow. But laughter, like a walk in the park or watching a movie, can be an emotional release. And don't you know your loved one or special friend would want you be experiencing moments of laughter and smiles in the middle of your grief!

Grief and Hope

In this world in which grief visits each of us, there is such a fuzzy feeling about hope. I encounter many people for whom hope is an "optimistic desire" that something will work out, but it's still "iffy" – not a sure thing. Yet hope is central here, especially here, in the time of death.

Hope in the Bible is an "assurance", a hope based on the promise of God –

not a hope dependent upon our optimism or our human ability to deliver. Hope in the Bible grows out of the provisional grace of God, having a distinctively divine dimension. We find such references in Jeremiah 29:11: "I know the plans I have for you… to give you a future and a hope." When we entrust our future and our hope to the Providence of God, we may live with confidence – we may hope in God's Promise: "We have this hope as an anchor for our lives, safe and secure." (Hebrews 6:19).

Even when we cannot understand or answer the "whys" of what's happening in our lives, the Hope the Holy One provides is all the certainty we ever need. The Hope of God becomes the Hope of our Heart! The Hope that anchors our lives depends not upon our strength and ability, but upon the Promise of God.

Key Verses for the Valley: As 1 Thessalonians 4 reminds us, verse 13: "For we do not grieve as those who have no hope." Hope is not something we generate under our own power. Hope is always God's gift! Verse 14: "For if we believe that Jesus died and rose again, even so God will bring with Him those who have fallen asleep in Jesus." Then Verse 18: "Therefore, comfort one another with these words." No fuzzy feeling here – this is a hope you can count on! And if that is not a reason to laugh, I don't know what is!

More Verses for the Valley: "Even in laughter the heart may be in pain, and the end of joy may be grief." (Proverbs 14:13). "A joyful heart is good medicine." (Proverbs 17:22). "And these things we write, so that our joy may be made complete." (1 John 1:4).

Our laughter never means the pain is gone. We are able to muster laughs in spite of our pain because we believe in the hope we have in the Most High God. In my personal grief experience, I have found healing in my laughter because laughter gives tears a different taste!

The Chapter "Take-Away"

"Will I ever laugh again?" is a straight up, honest question. I've tried to give you a straight up, honest response.

At our family graveside that day with the rain storm raging around us – like a cell of inescapable grief – I wasn't sure I would ever laugh again. Yet there is a path through our grief that brings us---when we may least expect it---to a time and a place where we are able to laugh again. In my experience, that day is worth the wait, whether it arrives after several months or lingers out

THE GRIEF LETTER

of reach for a time.

Until that day…

May God bless and keep you,
May God remain present with you,
And continue to give you strength, help, and hope…
Until you are able to laugh again.

Your grief partner, and laughing friend,

Fran Buhler

A Grief PS: More than anything, laughter and what we laugh about may be part of our grief, indeed, a very important part!

1. If you choose to trust God fully, completely, the day will come when you laugh again. Yes, it will happen. You can't order it or schedule it. You wait for it in anticipation.

2. In God's creation, grief and laughter belong together. Name two times you've laughed since the death of your loved one or friend. Do you recall why you laughed? Were you by yourself or with someone when you laughed?

3. Remember, "we do not grieve as those who have no hope." (1 Thessalonians 4:13) Jot down that verse or enter it in your Smart Phone. Carry it with you for frequent reference. Remember the verse when you laugh, and when you don't feel like laughing.

CHAPTER 11

GRIEVING ALONE IN THE "PAIN CLUB"

Dear Reader and Partner in Grief,

Even though we may be surrounded by other people, **grief is often a lonely place**. I've been there. I suspect you have too.

"We've outlived all of our family, and most of our friends," said Vivian, describing her experience following her husband's death. He was 89, she, 82. Vivian's daughter died three years before her husband. "To be honest," Vivian confided, "I do much of my grieving at church. No one knows, of course, and I don't always cry when I grieve. So I don't disturb anyone's worship. Most of the younger people have no idea who I am. Chuck and I loved our church and we had so many friends there." As she traced her grief, a tear eased down her cheek. "So rather than avoid church or stay away completely, I go there because I feel Chuck near me. I experience God's Presence. No matter how rough my week has been, I feel good when I go."

No one in the gathered congregation ever knows. No one even suspects. Vivian is grieving, alone, in the Presence of the Holy One!

Why This Matters

When a spouse dies, the survivor---no longer "a couple"---grieves alone, even if surrounded by family, even in church.

"Grieving alone" sounds like a verbal description for certain death situations. The most obvious ones, for example:

- Grieving alone when the spouse dies and the elderly survivor is no longer surrounded by family.
- Grieving alone happens with auto accidents or natural disasters when only one family member survives.
- Sometimes people choose to live alone. When death visits their family, they may go to the "visitation" at the funeral home, but they grieve alone.
- Others are alone, but not by choice. At least not their personal choice. Many are alone due to circumstance. Such as divorce, the

previous death of a spouse, or one who has recently relocated and doesn't know anyone. Those of us around them may be totally unaware of their particular circumstance and their profound "alone-ness".

Open our eyes and our ears and we discover circumstantial examples of people grieving alone in their particular life style, in "the Pain Club".

Military Grief

In public venues – sports events, worship services, special occasions, and national holidays – we often express appreciation to military survivors who have served our country. We also express appreciation to family members of military personnel. Such public gestures are appropriate. The recipients, and those they represent, need it. As a nation, we need it, too. These examples are appropriate ways for "we, the people" to remind ourselves of the high cost of freedom.

Yet think about what those occasions are like for a military widow, or widower, a childless military mother or father, or a fatherless military child when – due to the death of a military service member – family members grieve alone. "Dive beneath the surface of the war footage," writes psychotherapist Judy Heath in her book *No Time For Tears*, "and you will hear the anguished cries of mothers and fathers whose young men and women no longer rummage through snack cabinets or track mud onto their carpets, whose lifeless bodies will not bring along the grandchildren for whom they longed. This," she writes, "is true grief."[47]

Rev. Candace McKibben, Hospice Administrator and Chaplain for Big Bend Hospice in Tallahassee, Florida, calls this "one more harsh reminder of all that they have lost." Rev. McKibben, writing in The Tallahassee Democrat, our local newspaper, points to the inevitable "tension between the sheer joy for returning soldiers and the unspeakable sorrow for those who do not return."[48]

In case after case, when death visits a military family, the surviving spouse, parent, or child grieves alone – even when they grieve with family.

The Hard Grief of "Ambiguous Loss"

"Hard Grief" is often where and when we least expect it. Last night I came home after two funerals in two days, dog-tired, emotionally drained, flopped on the couch in our Fun Room and picked up the

October/November 2013 issue of AARP Magazine.[49] As I thumbed through, my eyes fell on page 12, a crisp side-bar review of "Lost and Found". See Allan Fallow's review below and note how it connects with *The Grief Letter*.

" 'Over the past century', writes Wil S. Hylton in *Vanished: The Sixty-Year Search for the Missing Men of World War II*, " '83,000 (US) service members have been listed as missing, of whom 73,000 disappeared in World War II, 56,000 in the Pacific theater alone.' 'Vanished' movingly recreates the hunt for 11 MIAs, shot down in a B-24 over the South Pacific in 1944."[50]

"Rumors of survivors caused families decades of 'ambiguous loss' – the grief of not knowing the fate of the disappeared. 'After diving to the plane's wreckage', says Hylton, 'I began to experience the same need for answers that's tormented the families all these years.'"[51] He found more than a few.

The description above registered with me because as a kid I had three uncles in World War II; one in the Army and one in the Air Force in Europe, one in the Navy in the Pacific.

My Air Force uncle had a good friend in the Air Force who was an MIA, whose plane was never found, whose remains were never recovered. My uncle never talked about it, wouldn't discuss it, in spite of all my childhood questions. Hylton's phrase, "ambiguous loss", calls to mind my uncle's hidden grief for one who was a "brother" in the midst of war, a "hard grief" my uncle bore in years of isolation and longing for some word to "clear-up" such an "ambiguous loss".

Difficult Grief

Indiana Hospice Chaplain, William H. Griffith observes, "There is no more difficult grief than that of a parent when a child dies." Combine that death-of-a-child experience with the "alone-ness" of a single Mom, or a single Dad, and you face the challenge of grieving alone.

"It's my 'solitary confinement'", Megan said, as she described her grief following the death of her 16-year-old daughter, killed in an accident. "We had so many wonderful conversations," she grieved, "and now no one answers my questions or hears how I'm feeling." When a single Mom grieves the death of an only child, she grieves alone, even if surrounded by friends.

THE GRIEF LETTER

Eye-Witness to Grieving Alone

I witnessed such an example. A mother with children, in an attempt to comfort a grieving divorced mom whose child had just died, made the mistake of saying to the bereaved: "I know exactly how you feel."

"Then tell me how I feel," the grieving Mom who had just lost her baby responded with a note of irritation in her voice.

"Well, it's obvious you grieve all the things mothers would do with their children, like proms and graduation, shopping for a wedding dress, and that kind of stuff."

"You're not even close," the single mom shot back. "None of that is on my mind. You want to know what I'm grieving?" she asked, "I'm grieving I'll never be able to change my baby's diaper, give her a bath, push her in a stroller in the park… or tuck her in bed at night… and I'll never have her father to do those things with us." When we comfort those who grieve alone, sometimes it's best to give our "presence" and our "here-ness," and forget about our assumptions and our pronouncements.

Difficult Grief 2.0

Women tend to outlive men, in marriage and in our society as a whole. Margaret Flanagan Eicher captures this example of Difficult Grief 2.0 in her poem "Survived by His Wife". Eicher published her poems in various magazines and anthologies. "Survived…" appeared in *When I am an Old Woman I Shall Wear Purple*, edited by Sandra Martz, published by Papier-Mache press. She published one of her earlier poems, written in 1944, when she was a member of the Women's Army Corps stationed at Fort Clayton in the Panama Canal Zone. She is deceased. Her words live on.

"Eyes swollen she lay in their bed – head covered, legs drawn up, cold though her forehead was damp – who had warmed herself in his warm flesh." "Now his absence was a constant companion: His hairbrushes, his keys, his clothes still smelling of him in his closet, covered like museum artifacts."[52]

"She shuddered, remembering the shoes he wore were still beneath the bed exactly as he left them, as if covered by a glass case. All of the things he had handled, used, inhabited, and finally left were covered or lying about like the frames of stolen paintings left behind."[53]

Living alone, surviving alone, doing grief alone, are distinct challenges. Yet living alone does not mean we are existentially alone, spiritually alone, emotionally alone.

"Homemade" Conversational Therapy

Example One: Years ago I knew a man who experienced the death of his wife when he was 35. He loved to fish the bass lakes of Tennessee. He devised the perfect way to grieve effectively in a manner that worked well for him. He would go to the lake fishing, pretending his deceased wife was in the boat with him. While enjoying his fishing trip along with the relaxation of being outdoors, he would have extended conversations with his wife, talking with her, spending "get away" moments with her.

"Fran, am I crazy?" he asked, "Should I be in an institution?"

"No, a thousand times No," I said.

Example Two: Three weeks following her husband's death, I followed up to check on the grieving wife. "Oh I hurt like you wouldn't believe," she said, "but our conversations have helped me through."

She explained she talks with her husband all the time. "I ask his advice, tell him what I'm doing, where I'm going. Run through my "to do" list for the day, and it helps ease the loneliness."

We need to do what works for us in our grief. This kind of "homemade" conversational therapy can become a big grief help in combating our loneliness.

In the Presence of the Holy One!

From the beginning God has offered to be with us in our alone-ness. The Genesis creation account includes God's assertion that it is not good for his creation to be alone (Genesis 2:18). And so the Most High God comes to us tenderly in our grief and stays as long as we wish, assuring by His Presence and Power, we shall never grieve alone.

Yet honesty and candor demand we examine other prevailing views about death, about grief, about God. We find these examples in our culture, in our neighborhoods, where we work, in our families, and in our houses of worship – regardless of the brand.

THE GRIEF LETTER

One aspect of grieving alone is the fact the solitary griever has no one to talk to, or listen to, no way to have needed conversations. This gives rise to bitterness from the experience of grieving alone. Often the bitterness is directed toward God, as we see in the following "grief zingers" about God, one-liners that represent the kind of thoughts real people express in "the pain club."

Grief Zingers About God

Note that each zinger below captures a typical "pain point", and for the sake of clarity---none of the zingers below represent my personal views. I mention them only because, even in times of grief, we must be vigilant in resisting false notions about God.

1. "I get so angry at the way God uses cancer to punish people."

2. "What have I done to cause God to take my child?"

3. "Why, why, why, why, WHY????"

4. "I can't believe God would allow such a tragedy to happen." (Said after a multi-car interstate highway accident with multiple deaths.)

5. "If God was really God, he wouldn't allow bad things to happen to good people."

I choose not to dwell on the twisted theology reflected in the "grief zinger" examples listed above. Most everything above flows from the fact God gave each of us the ability to choose and make decisions, plus the freedom to make mistakes and even the liberty to make bad choices. Who among us would wish to suspend the abilities, options and freedoms we have? Even when grief is difficult, like wrestling with an octopus, none of us would vote for a life without freedom of choice.

"Blessed are those who mourn"

Our mourning is love-based. We mourn so strongly because we loved so deeply. We can build on this new reality. We can actually move forward.

Keep in mind, this perspective on mourning comes from sacred scripture.

- From the Holy One of Israel to Isaiah in Isaiah 61:1-2: "The Spirit of the Lord God is upon me, because the Lord has anointed me to

- bring good news to the afflicted, he has sent me to bind up the brokenhearted... to comfort all who mourn..."
- Also in the New Testament: "Blessed are those who mourn, for they shall be comforted," words of Jesus' teaching in his Sermon on the Mount in Matthew 5:40.

In their book *The Right Words to Comfort You*, three ladies with personal insight into grief, Emily Thornton Calvo, Marie D. Jones, and Ellen F. Pill, give special words of comfort for this chapter and express my sentiment for this book: "God made friends so that in times like these, we have someone to talk to, to lean on, and mourn with." I sincerely hope *The Grief Letter* will be such a book – such a friend – for you.

Calvo, Jones, and Pill again: "May you find comfort and peace to carry you through each day. May you find faith and hope to keep you strong until this difficult time is over."[54]

"The Pain Club" is an expansive organization. Consider some who are eligible.

When Your Parent Dies

In her memoir *The Long Good-bye*, Meghan O'Rourke referred to her mother's death as "the jagged darkness of loss." As she grieved, she called her experience "the churning, dangerous waters of grief."

> "In the months that followed my mother's death, I managed to look like a normal person. I walked down the street; I answered my phone; I brushed my teeth, most of the time. But I was not ok. I was in grief. Nothing seemed important. Daily tasks were exhausting. Dishes piled in the sink, knives crusted with strawberry jam. At one point I did not wash my hair for ten days."[55]

In his book When Your Parent Dies, Ron Klug writes that "the death of a parent signals a break in one of the longest and deepest relationships we have had." We experience "an irreplaceable loss" that leaves us "empty", Klug says, and "like a wake-up call, confronts us with our own mortality."[56]

One church member explained her death-of-a-parent grief this way: "Someone at church told me I should be happy because my mother is in heaven." "Yes," she acknowledged, "I know my mother is in the presence of God. But that doesn't keep me from missing her terribly... because she's not here with me!"

"Because we take more responsibility for our parents than we do for friends or colleagues," Klug observes, "we often feel more regrets at their passing, a greater sense of unfinished business. And," says Klug, "these feelings strongly color our grief."[57]

The death-of-a-parent dynamic often generates a lonely grief. "When my father died," a friend confided, "my wife grieved as you would expect. But she grieved her father-in-law's death. She was not grieving her father's death like I was. And believe me there is a difference." Grieving the death of a parent, even though surrounded by family members who are grieving too, gives one the feeling of grieving alone. Solo grief is always a greater challenge.

Members of a Small, but Growing Club

A child whose parent chooses suicide becomes an instant member of a small but growing club. In my experience, I have found no reliable pattern for how children respond to and refer to the parent's act of self-destruction. Some children never refer to the parental death as "suicide". The child typically says: "My mother killed herself" or "My father killed himself". Others say "she passed away" with no inclusion of how she passed away. One son told me his father "just decided to 'check out'."

Jessica Lamb-Shapiro, author of *Promise Land: My Journey Through America's Self-Help Culture*, writes about the experience in the January 19, 2014 edition of the New York Times.

Ms. Lamb-Shapiro calls herself and her grief companions the "world's silent orphans". "After being under the impression for three decades that I'd never met anyone like me," Lamb-Shapiro met two others. Her mother killed herself just before her second birthday. In 34 years she had never met anyone else affected by a parent's suicide. Then in a single day her life intersected with two people whose parents had taken their own lives; two women, one whose mother killed herself, and one whose father killed himself.

So here were others whose fathers remarried, who also had "troubled relationships with stepmothers", had "difficulty forming attachments in relationships", and experienced the wish to shield people from the grisly idea of a mother violently abandoning her child."[58]

PART 1 - CHAPTER 11

Pregnancy and Infant Loss

While I was working on "The Grief Letter", I noted our nation's annual October 15 observance of National Pregnancy and Infant Loss Awareness Day, a day we grieve with those who have suffered the grief pain and the heartache of a death during pregnancy or the death of an infant.

It's a day to remember, as one infant loss website says:

> "babies who were born asleep,
> or whom we carried
> but never met,
> or those we have held
> but could not take home,
> or the ones who made it home,
> but didn't stay."[59]

Pregnancy and Infant Loss Awareness Month was created in 1988 with a proclamation by then President Ronald Reagan. The occasion was marked with verbal eloquence – whether from the President or a trusted speech writer:

> "When a child loses his parent,
> they are called an orphan.
> When a spouse loses her or his partner,
> they are called a widow or a widower.
> When parents lose their child,
> there isn't a word to describe them."[60]

Everyone in the Pain Club, and at one time or another that includes all of us, needs to be reminded of...

A Verse for the Valley: "...the day when the Lord gives you rest from your pain..." (Isaiah 14:3a).

The Chapter "Take-Away"

Yes, grief is often a lonely, painful place. Infant mortality at any level in any geographic region is always "frustratingly high", as our newspaper, the "Tallahassee Democrat", put it. Community observances across our country offer shared comfort and hope for those couples and mothers who may be able to conceive again. Such observances make us all aware that those who grieve infant deaths and unborn deaths should not grieve alone.

THE GRIEF LETTER

Our family was introduced to the grief pain of unborn infant death years ago. One of my three sisters and her husband suffered the pre-birth death of a child, a child hospital staff never allowed my sister to hold in her arms. My sister and I are each one of six siblings. I shared her grief in my tears. I could think of no words adequate to convey an appropriate response for such a heart-breaking, soul-shaking loss. In our collective grief, I fell back on words from Habakkuk 3:17-19a:

"Though the fig tree should not blossom, And there be no fruit on the vines, Though the yield of the olive should fail, And the fields produce no food, Though the flock should be cut off from the fold…Yet I will exult in the Lord, I will rejoice in the God of my salvation. The Lord God is… my strength…"

Pregnancy and Infant Loss Awareness Month is but one among many special commemorations on our annual calendars, prompting our individual grief, raising awareness, and comforting those of us who mourn alone in the Pain Club.

Your grief partner and "grieving alone" friend,

Fran Buhler

A Grief PS: Solitary grief is more widespread than you may be aware. Are people around you, at your work place, in your church or neighborhood, in a Pain Club? Are **you** in a Pain Club?

1. Identify your "Pain Club"---name it. How long have you been in it?

2. Remember you do not have to grieve alone. You may experience God's Presence right now during this very day, in this very moment, even in your Pain Club. God is very good at finding us in our own Pain Clubs.

3. Remind yourself repeatedly: As one who mourns, I am comforted. I am blessed.

To aid your memory, list at least three ways you are blessed. Can you add two more?

CHAPTER 12

"A GRIEF LIKE NO OTHER": GRANDPARENT GRIEF

Dear Reader and Partner in Grief,

Grief sometimes brings an element of the "unexpected" with it! **There are no flashing neon lights to signal grandparent grief;** so many times it goes unnoticed, unrecognized, unacknowledged!

I have known several grandparents who have suffered the death of a grandchild. If you turned to this chapter instead of skipping it, then I want you to find the help you seek.

Angela Thomas Pharr, in her book *Do You Know Who I Am?* writes about the "trembling inside" with such authenticity because she has been there. She describes herself as "standing at the edge of bad news". She writes of "that deep, abiding comfort your soul longs for", a comfort that "comes only from God", "from a soul quiet with Him" when you are in "a place to be still and know."[61]

Why This Matters

In my experience, as in Angela Pharr's, we must learn to ask God for the help we never thought we would need.

Listen to a grandmother talk about the death of her grandson: "I've experienced all kinds of grief," she said. "At my age, you name it and I've been through it: death of a parent, death of grandparents, death of my husband, death of good friends, death of a child. But the death of a grandchild – it's a death like no other!"

A Grief "like No Other"

Across the US, grandparent grief is devastating and lonely. More than 160,000 US grandparents experience the death of a grandchild each year. The grief devastation is more widespread than we think--- one in every 193,000.

THE GRIEF LETTER

The December 2013 edition of "AARP The Magazine" included interviews with grandparents of Sandy Hook Elementary School students murdered in the Newtown, Connecticut, massacre on December 14, 2012. Jan Goodwin called it "a grief like no other."[62]

"The grief is beyond description", one grandparent said after learning his grandson was among the 49 dead following the June 12, 2016, Orlando nightclub massacre in central Florida.[63]

"Forgotten Mourners"

A friend of mine refers to bereaved grandparents as "forgotten mourners". "People think it is not 'your' child that died," he observes, "so they don't equate the pain". Yet when a grandchild dies, especially a younger grandchild, the circumstances are often unusual, accidental or even tragic.

Grandparents are often expected to grieve by a different standard. As a grandparent member of our church said, "Grandparents are not given the same grief privileges when a grandchild dies. The notion seems to be: it's not your child, so it shouldn't hurt as much" she said.

For a grandchild to precede a grandparent in death, never seems like the natural order of life. Under such circumstances, our grief calls for help we never thought we would need.

Grandparent Grief is "A Consuming Pain"

"Pain does not occur in the abstract," writes Dr. Paul Brand, who says "no sensation is more personal than pain." Grief pain is more than personal, it is a consuming pain. Regina Easley-Young describes it as: "the lingering ache that accompanies a time of grief" and grandparent grief is always "a consuming pain."

How do we get the help we never thought we would need?

The three best selling drugs in the US are a hypertension drug, a medication for ulcers, and a tranquilizer. These are what Paul Brand calls "pain-mufflers". Often we may look upon pain as the illness rather than the symptom." In our grief, we often turn to the "pain-mufflers". It is an unfortunate fact. Many, looking for help, are heavily medicated. Our "pain-mufflers" hold out the hope we can self-medicate ourselves to happiness and peace again. But even if we drown ourselves in medications, the "pain-mufflers" will not meet our deepest needs.

When it comes to finding help we never thought we would need, this is the time we should turn to the resources of faith. I recall a third grader's comment who said "It's so much more fun when you know what's inside the Bible." I think of the grandmother who after the death of a cherished granddaughter wondered if, like the sorrows of Zion in Lamentations 1:12, "is there any pain like my pain...?"

This particular grandmother embraced the hope of relief in divine mercy from Lamentations 3:21-26.

> "But this I call to mind, and therefore I have hope: The steadfast love of the Lord never ceases, his mercies never come to an end; they are new every morning; great is your faithfulness. "The Lord is my portion,' says my soul, 'therefore I will hope in him'. The Lord is good to those who wait for him, to the soul that seeks him. It is good that one should wait quietly for the salvation of the Lord."

"So...when I find myself in need", this grandmother said, "I seek help. I 'wait' upon the Lord. I pray for deliverance."

Does Grief have a Plus Side?

The help we never thought we would need challenges our one-dimensional view of grief, a view that is somewhat negative, a view that rejects the notion anything positive and good can ever result from our grief.

Yet grief has a plus side. In personal experience and from professional observation, in spite of the penetrating pain, grief has a positive aspect to it. The experience of grieving has the potential to lead us to new outlooks on life. Grief has the potential to deepen our faith and strengthen our motivation to make our lives count.

Our grief experience has the potential to grind us down to the bone. Yet our grief also has the capacity to enlarge our compassion, raise our awareness and enable us to become more perceptive and more able to help others in their grief, while making our own grief more purposeful and more meaningful.

The open expression of emotion is natural and human and also important in our grief.

Grieving can be very painful, no question. But we may use our grief experience to work toward our own eventual emotional healing.

THE GRIEF LETTER

The Community of "Pain Survivors"

Every grandparent who grieves, in awkward circumstances or blessed company, joins the community of "Pain Survivors" because grandparent grief is like no other.

In a thank you note after the funeral of her grandchild, the grandmother expressed what happens all too often: "Not a person on our street acknowledged the death of our grandson. It was an auto accident, for heaven's sake, and it was all over the newspaper. Our daughter and son in law were comforted by the response of neighbors on their street, by friends in worship and at work. And I'm so thankful for the outpouring of love and support they have received. But George and I are really hurting. We expected our grandparent's and our parent's deaths, so we grieved as you would expect us to grieve. But this came out of the clear blue---a total surprise. No---a total tragedy! We had nothing to feel good about."

A Verse for the Valley: "Lord, you have been our dwelling place in all generations. Before the mountains were brought forth, or ever You had formed the earth and the world, even from everlasting to everlasting You are God." (Psalm 90:1-2).

By lifting our attention to the high places of God's Help, we assure we will be supported and comforted on our grief journey. God, our Keeper, our Comforter, will wipe every tear from our eyes. While our culture may not always recognize or give full attention and extend appropriate support to grandparents in grief, we may be alert to grandparent grief in our communities and neighborhoods, in our places of work and worship.

The Chapter "Take-Away"

As grandparents, our grief may not always be recognized and acknowledged. Grandparent grief sometimes slips beneath the radar of neighbors and friends.

We grandparents must ask the Most High God for the help we never thought we would need. For grandparent grief involves a death and a grief like no other.

Your grief partner and grand parenting friend,

Fran Buhler

PART 1 - CHAPTER 12

A Grief PS: If you are not a grandparent, feel free to move on. But if you are a grandparent, consider this:

1. Remind yourself of the joys of being a grandparent. Do not allow a grandchild's death to sabotage your special memories. Choose two memories you will always cherish.

2. Give thanks for the years you had with this grandchild, no matter what that experience has been and regardless of the circumstances of the child's death.

3. And remember, as grandparents, our families always need our prayer.

THE GRIEF LETTER

CHAPTER 13

"GRIEF IS A SACRED TIME"

Dear Reader and Partner in Grief,

I am writing you in your time of grief because I know personally how jolting grief can be.

I started "the grief letter" in 1993 because of my exposure to numerous individuals and families wrestling with the octopus of grief. Not that these families were any less equipped or prepared to handle grief; but because of grief's universal human challenge. **Sometimes, it takes a long time before we learn grief is a sacred time!**

Individuals and families receive no preparation for their time of grief. Without any prior thought, many ignore grief and others deny grief, as if one could elbow grief out of the room, shoving it aside with total disregard for the subsequent costly outcome.

Why This Matters

Back in 1993 and 94, due to my sudden change in career employment, exiting the consulting, marketing and project management arena, to lead and serve a flagship church in a challenging interim, I began thinking and asking myself, "Is there a way to help people see, feel, and experience the spiritual discovery: Grief is a sacred time?"

In the story of life from a faith perspective, death is not a period but a comma.

"Death is only the beginning of the beginning, not the end" was the way Billy Graham expressed it. If that is true, then it should alter our understanding of death and grief for ourselves and for others.

Grief is not against life but an important part of life. Grief does not "afflict" the dead. Grief "affects" the living. Genuine grief in the context of faith accompanies the griever into a sacred time of life. As one named Paul wrote in a letter to people living in Rome, "neither death nor life shall be able to separate us from the love of God" (Romans 8, a portion of verses 38-39).

PART 1 - CHAPTER 13

"Grief Is A Visible Piece Of Our Mourning"

We experience grief as we live our lives. We grieve and react to grief each time death introduces itself and invades our lives. Grief is a throbbing of the soul, a hammer-blow to the body, opening an envelope of emotions to support our staggering sense of loss.

Grief alerts us and those around us that the death narrative of someone's life intersects with our life in a powerful and personal way.

When we grieve, we experience substantial pain and multiple reasons for our grief. Grief is a purpose-driven emotional set. While the cry of grief commands our attention, the basic elements of grief compel our emotions. Yet we each experience our own distinctive rhythms of grief.

Grieving is a testimony to the relational fabric of our lives. If we lived in total isolation, without any contact with others, we would not grieve as we do. Instead, we would battle a profound loneliness, a pronounced isolation, and hunger no doubt for the "given community" we now take for granted.

Grief Counsel from The Academy

In my exploration of grief as a sacred time I have made no focused attempt to research views expressed by college and university faculty on the grief topic. However, I have found no shortage of academic professionals who also hold the view "Grief is a sacred time".

In my own city, Sally Karioth is a Florida State University professor in the College of Nursing. Professor Karioth began her work in death counseling in an era when many in university and medical settings ignored and often evaded death-related discussions. She believed discussing death and dying can be beneficial to patients and helpful to families. We spoke about her grief experience during a workshop at our church.

Certified in traumatology, Karioth assists students in times of crisis. She provided counseling and aided emotional relief efforts at the Pentagon following the 9/11 terrorist attacks. When asked about her experience with grief-shock, she was emphatic about the impact on her professional outlook. I made a note of two matters she mentioned specifically, when she said:

- "I've learned that healing the spirit is as important as healing the body."

- "I've learned that if a child is old enough to love, she is old enough to grieve."

I am thankful campuses are blessed with the presence and by the compassion of grief professionals like Sally Karioth.

Creating a Sanctuary for Grieving

When I read "Honoring Grief: Creating a Space to Let Yourself Heal", by Alexandra Kennedy, published in 2014, I became interested in her professional views because of a particular slant in her approach. A psychotherapist in private practice and a University of California professor in the Santa Cruz/East Bay area, her views about creating "a sanctuary" for grieving grabbed my attention.

Kennedy developed the powerful concept of "the sanctuary" while grieving the loss of her own father. "This strategy," she explains, "involves creating a specific place in our homes dedicated to healing---and then spending a limited time there daily. The sanctuary is a sacred space," she explains, "it becomes a crucible of healing when chaotic feelings are activated in grief."[64]

Later, Kennedy reports, "those who use the sanctuary find that they have much more focus and energy for their work, schoolwork, friends, and families."

Kennedy's work suggests we need to recover in our religious faith and practice the original "sanctuary" role-and-function in our grief, faith and worship. What if instead of thinking about the word "sanctuary" as a building or a certain space, we related the word "sanctuary" to a safe space, a protected place, where we experience the Comfort, Peace and Presence of the Holy One? I agree with Kennedy's findings and assertion about the role of a sanctuary space in our grief recovery. A "sanctuary" should be a "faith place" and a "safe space" to grieve, pray and experience God's Presence.

"Where is your 'sanctuary'?"

"I hope it's ok, me being here this time of day," Alice said, with a slight blush of embarrassment, as I entered our church sanctuary one week day afternoon.

"Sure," I replied, "the sanctuary is here to be used. Not just on Sunday," I added, introducing myself. I had never seen the lady before.

"I checked in at the church office to make sure nothing else was scheduled."

"You're ok," I told Alice. "Would you like some quiet time without interruption?" I asked. "I can put a sign on the entry doors for privacy."

"Oh, thank you, but I would really like to talk."

At the time I was still new on staff and could not recall ever seeing Alice in worship or anywhere else in church. When she told me her name, I did not recognize it.

I sat down anyway and she poured out her heart. Every word was about the death of her son, her only child, who lived only three days, a death that had happened 21 years ago. She had been in church, nine months pregnant, on Sunday. Her son was born on Monday. He died the following Thursday. I knew absolutely nothing about the lady or the death of her son. We talked an hour and a half. Actually, she talked, I listened.

She was not a member of our church. Her husband had left her shortly after she became pregnant. She now lived in another state and this was her first and only trip back to the sanctuary where she had worshipped the Sunday before her son was born on Monday and died on Thursday.

"This is my first and only trip back," she said. "I wanted to come back because I felt God's Holy Presence here, right here." Those were her words. Then she said, "Since that Sunday, including the day my son died, and every day since, I have felt the Presence of God. My life experience with God started right here, and everywhere I've been, I've lived in His sanctuary ever since" (I took that to mean "in His Presence").

"Grief is a sacred time."

"To lose a parent is to lose your past; to lose a spouse or close friend is to lose your past and your present; and to lose a child is to lose your past, present, and future." Those words from Daniel T. Hans, a pastor and author of *When A Child Dies*, make the case quickly.[65] In the words of Lynn Eib, author of *When God & Grief Meet*, "each death shakes a little different part of your world."[66]

THE GRIEF LETTER

New York Times Best-Selling Author, Melody Beattie, in her book *The Grief Club* states it best, better than all my seminary professors, better than all the theologians and Bible scholars I've read over the last half century, "Grief is a sacred time in our lives, and an important one."[67]

For Beattie, the grief process is a potentially "mysterious, transformational" experience.[68] Whether we grasp it or not, as Beattie asserts, grief is potentially a "transformational process."[69] She came to that view through her grief experience.

After her son died, Melody Beattie sat in her office surrounded by books about grief. These were books people had given her because they wanted to help Melody in her grief. Other books she had purchased herself. In her book, The Grief Club, Melody describes this personal grief journey she experienced.

"I'd open a book", she writes, "start to read it, then either put it on my library shelf or hurl it across the room." Beattie gives the most powerful, most penetrating, explanation I have ever read or heard. Witness her argument for yourself.

> "It's not that the books aren't good. Many are important and well written. The books didn't help me. Not one book led me to believe that this process I was in was a mysterious, transformational one. I couldn't find anyone to tell me each minute, whatever I experience is a valid, beautiful moment – however tragic it is. That's what I needed to hear: Grief is a sacred time in our lives and an important one."[70]

Sacred, Mysterious, and Transformational

So… fifteen years after her son's death, Beattie wrote her book on grief. Of the 13 books she had written at that point in her life, she expected her book on grief to be the most painful. She later said her book on grief brought her the most joy of all her books. Why? Because her grief was transformational.

Before you dismiss what you have just read as out of touch with the "deep-aching pain" of grief, consider this. If your challenge is one you can manage on your own and return your life to normal, I am happy for you. But if you are totally numb, drowning in unanswered questions, living in a darkness that drives out hope, hurting like you have never hurt before, now what?

That is precisely the grief circumstance in which Melody Beattie found herself.

In fact, I would say I am writing *The Grief Letter* out of a similar motivation to why she wrote *The Grief Club!* As she wrote in her introduction:

> "It's for people in pain, people who are numb, and people who aren't sure what they're feeling. It's for people who are broken; it's about trusting God and life to put us back together again."

Beattie did not stop there; neither will I.

> "It's about radical faith, enough faith to eventually turn to the same God... and ask for help finding and fighting our way back to life."[71]

Out of respect, I offer another Melody Beattie observation about her book that will, I hope, come to be true of the *The Grief Letter*. "The book is about getting through the time that starts when something happens that turns our world upside down, and we lose our old normal, until the new normal begins."[72]

In her 1979 book *Blessings*, with a British publisher, Mary Craig writes:

> "The value of suffering does not lie in the pain of it...but in what the sufferer makes of it... it is in sorrow that we discover the things which really matter; in sorrow that we discover ourselves."[73]

For it is in sorrow when we may discover the Presence of God.

A Verse for the Valley: "He (or she) who dwells in the shelter of the Most High will abide in the shadow of the Almighty. I will say to the Lord, 'My refuge and my fortress. My God, in whom I trust!'" (Psalm 91:1-2).

A Grief Quartet

Coping with our grief is no easy matter even with the Presence of the Most High. Listen to the following grief quartet in each griever's own words, suggesting the breadth and depth – the soul-deep scope – of pain and grief following a loved one's death.

Griever # 1: "My heart is breaking and the pain, at times, is unbearable."

Griever # 2: "I feel guilty about all the times I complained about her and wonder if I could have done a better job of taking care of her. I am exhausted."

Griever # 3: "I am just devastated. I need help more than at any time in my life."

Griever # 4: "This whole thing started with a "medical procedure". Who would have ever thought that 'a procedure' could be fatal? I hurt so much I don't know what to do."

Grief is tough any way it reaches us.

Unresolved Grief May Go Unnoticed: Get Help

Because of the sometimes hidden nature of grief---we do not always grieve in public or with a friend, in the presence of family or with a work colleague and maybe not in groups---it is possible to experience a stint of grief without making any progress, without moving through our grief process and back into a more normal mode of life without the grief indicators of crying, withdrawing from situations or mourning in the midst of regular duties, responsibilities or activities.

If and when this happens, we may need to seek professional help with a local certified grief counselor, a qualified pastor or a psychologist with certified grief counseling experience.

Conflicted grief, having strong and contradictory feelings in your grief, will benefit from counseling assistance. If you become stuck in your grieving, unable to move forward, you may be dealing with some form of "complicated grief", as do more than a million people a year in the US. Time spent with a qualified counselor can be sacred, enabling you to discover what really matters!

Don't let people rush you when you are grieving, especially for the first months, even a year. If over time, after five or six months, you feel you are not making any progress in your grief, maybe it is time to seek help. Be honest with yourself. If you need to, do it.

The Grief "Sneak Attack" is a "Big Deal"

Her "daddy" died on December 4, and she hasn't been home since. She lives only a three-hour drive away, and she hopes to gain the courage to eventually drive home. It's been four months.

She says she doesn't "stare blankly at the wall" as much as she used to. She can now focus better on her college class assignments. Still, she writes, "every once in a while, when I think I'm doing alright, grief sneaks up and reminds me that I'm not where I think I am."[74] The octopus specializes in sneak attacks!

Amy Jacobs wrote about her father's death in "Collegiate Magazine" in the Winter 2010/11 issue. Here's Amy's description: "For a season, you may not be able to absorb much of anything. I felt as if I swallowed the sea. I had so many emotions to work through---lots of feelings clanging around in my heart and mind---and I couldn't put anything on top of it. I had no emotional room to process. I couldn't watch movies or TV.I couldn't focus to read, and I didn't have the energy to think. Instead, I stared at the wall. In fact, I felt good about staring at the wall."[75]

A freelance writer, Jacobs demonstrates how one can go to the Bible for encouragement. Writing for a collegiate audience, she points to the promises of God's Word to make three assertions she has found true in her personal experience.

- Grief brings wisdom – Ecclesiastes 7:4.
- God is near – Psalm 46:1; 147:3.
- Comfort can be found – Matthew 5:4; 2 Corinthians 1:3-4.

Jacobs also checks in on the grief positive issue. "Grief will show you what you're made of, and it will show you what God's made of – stuff that doesn't change, leave, or die."[76]

Which raises the question… "Can grief be transformational?"

She aligns with the voices who see grief, and have experienced grief, as a transformational experience. "Grief has the potential," she writes, "to transform your life for the better."[77]

Amy Jacobs Evaluates Grief

> "I'm beginning to see the gifts that grief has given me. I wear my heart on my sleeve, and I'm now more transparent. I've come to like myself more when I'm broken than when I'm put together---turns out I'm truer and kinder this way."[78]

Let's hear Jacobs out:

> "I've learned to live with the contradictions. I'm both terribly sorry and grateful about the same experience. Awful has become awfully

good. Living my faith in the midst of layers of grief and a season of heartbreak has been the most challenging experience of my life with God—and I can say that grief is good and is a gift—continually driving me to God who brings peace and binds up my broken heart."[79]

Jacobs comes to a place where I have witnessed many in grief arrive, when she concludes: "That makes grief and all his friends easier to live with."[80]

A Chapter Pause

Pause for a moment and ask yourself: "What is my personal grief need?" When you picked up *The Grief Letter*, what were you hoping to find? Have you given your grief enough time?

The reason for the grief pause is because this is a good strategy to consider in our grieving. We do not have to follow someone else's grief direction or grief "trail"; we can choose the path best for us in our experience. Remember to exercise your choice of the chapter sequence as you read, according to your grief experience and your grief need.

The Chapter "Take-Away"

Yes, grief's sneak attacks are legendary, powerful, even feared. Yet in the testimony of real people, grief is a sacred time, can have positive benefits, and make a "plus" difference in our lives.

From a survivors' faith perspective, death is not a period, but a comma! Life goes on. Grief is a sacred time, leading us into God's good future.

Your grief partner and friend,

Fran Buhler

A Grief PS: To discover what really matters in your grief, take the following steps seriously:

1. Describe where and how you hurt the most in your grief. List how help has come to you.

2. Place God's grief bandages of grace around each grief. Discuss your grief with God, and also with a person you trust.

PART 1 - CHAPTER 13

3. Choose a "sanctuary" at your place of worship, in your home or apartment, in a space or place of your choosing. Go there to grieve. Journal your grief progress for reflection and review.

THE GRIEF LETTER

CHAPTER 14

"IS TRANSFORMATIONAL GRIEF POSSIBLE?"

Dear Reader and Partner in Grief,

You may not believe this, but three days after the service celebrating the life of a family member of one of our congregants, a note hits my church desk with some variation of the following expression: "Thank you so much for the care you have given us during this time of our overwhelming grief." Reference to "our time of overwhelming grief" has been the "expression of choice" in "thank you" notes I have received from grieving family members over the past two decades. Were they Christians? Yes. Was their grief still overwhelming? Yes.

Obviously, I do not know what your personal grief experience has been. But I do know this: **For many, grief is simply "overwhelming"!** In Luke 22:45-46, Jesus finds his disciples "exhausted from sorrow," filled with anticipatory grief for Jesus, their colleague and leader. The disciples were experiencing "overwhelming grief" because of their fear of what was ahead. From our own grief experience, we know the feeling!

Why This Matters

This is the challenge, therefore, when we turn the page to Chapter 14 and confront the question: "Is Transformational Grief Possible?" If grief is overwhelming, how in the world can that same grief be transformational?

In faith and trust, and fairness, I believe transformational grief is possible. A key ingredient, of course, is time. I believe this view clearly emerges from both the Old and New Testaments. This understanding has been voiced in faith traditions other than my own. This point of view where death and grief are concerned is evident in professional and academic circles serving our communities, including specialists in psychology, psychotherapy, social work agencies, Hospice organizations, and professional counseling services available where ever we live. Let's explore the matter.

Transformational Positives

"Death introduced me to an existence I knew absolutely nothing about", Roger observed, several years after his wife's death. An electrical engineer,

PART 1 - CHAPTER 14

Roger spoke with the classic precision of an engineer's mind.

"I have never felt so all alone," Roger reported. "Life was dark and ugly and several times I thought about scenarios – I'm talking suicide options – for ending it all!"

From Roger's low point, when he almost tanked in his grief, I recall the day when Roger shared some of the positive breakthroughs in his life. He checked them off like a litany of transformational positives, as if they should be displayed to support his feeling:

> He still battles loneliness, but his nights and days are not as dark and long as they used to be. He experiences new purpose, more energy, even joy.   ✓ Check

> He still misses her companionship, but he constantly celebrates his good fortune at what she brought to his life. ✓ Check

> He still knows moments of grief and sorrow, but he also enjoys days of gratitude for how she blessed his life as well as joy in new life experiences.   ✓ Check

> He still would like to take her to dinner and snuggle at bedtime, but he also gives thanks every day for the gift of her life. He believes he now has the opportunity---if he chooses---to use those gifts to bless this world.   ✓ Check

> He still talked to her about all sorts of things, and he had to confess, his grief "prayer talks" with God have made him a better, stronger person.   ✓ Check

When Grief Has A Transformational Influence

When Roger added it up, his grief had a transformational quality about it. He was not the same person he had been the night she died. He still missed her. He still loved her. He still had down moments, even "down days". Roger felt aspects of his life, aspects of himself, had been transformed in the totality of his grief. "To be honest", he said, "I even feel good about the transformation."

Several weeks before his own death, Roger said: "Through my grief I have become a different person. I'm even a better person. Not because of anything I have done, but because of the transformational impact my grief has had upon my life. And I don't mind saying", he added, "I'm a blessed person because of it."

In my personal experience with my grief following the death of a loved one, I would say transformational grief is the result of God's transformative grace. Transformative grief seems to be mostly Divine Grace with a "smidgeon" of human perseverance. Grief does not become transformative because we have special ability or strength others may not have. Yes, faith is important; but the transformative aspects of grief – like everything else in this life – are gifts from the Holy One. The transformational grief experience is ours because of the grace of God and His design for life and death and grief, not because of our spirituality, our religious preference, or our theological views

The words we use to explain our grief, to describe our grief feelings, are usually metaphorical. We talk with images and symbols.

A grieving gentleman: "Grief hit me like a punch to the stomach."

A grieving lady: "My tears are like Niagara Falls---they just keep coming."

Grief is like a flower. Wait a minute! Stop. Let's think about this one. Is grief like an octopus, or like a flower? Both, I say. The octopus and the flower are symbols of both the negatives and the positives of grief!

"Grief Is A Flower"

As the French poet, author and founder of the first endowed school of nursing, Madame De Gasparin, wrote:

> "Grief is a flower
> as delicate and prompt to fade
> as happiness.
> Still,
> it does not
> wholly die.
> Like the magic rose,
> dried and unrecognizable,
> a warm air
> breathed on it
> will suffice
> to renew
> its bloom."[81]

The warm air of God's Grace breathed upon our grief brings a transformative quality. Grief, even in its pain and sorrow, can in the power and grace of God become transformational. Grief can bring renewal of the spirit. As depressing and disappointing as grief can be, when warmed by the Breath of Life from the Giver of Life, grief enables us to blossom again.

Grief has two sides...

Think of faith as having a belief side and a behavior side, two sides of the same committed life. Here we meet another dimension of Romans 12:2 when applied to grief. "Do not be conformed to this world", Romans 12:2 urges us, "but be transformed by the renewal of your mind, that you may prove what is the will of God."

Grief is a "living sacrifice", per the language of Romans 12:1. When we find ourselves submerged in grief and sorrow, the believing side of our grief makes possible the behaving side of our grief as we live transformed lives in the face of our grief! The result of this transformation is the ability to discern in actual experience, "to prove", what is the will of God.

Grieving, like finding and doing the will of God, is potentially transformational.

"So... Is Transformational Grief Possible?"

The transformational aspect of grief is not, and has never been, experienced universally. Transformational grief experience is available to all, but it does not happen automatically. For a grief experience to become transformational, it must lead to or result in some significant change in the griever's perspective, outlook, everyday life and ultimately in one's quality of life long term. The question often raised is: "How in the world can grief be good?" It's a "deep water" question, so here's my best response.

Grief cushions the blow of death, but does not remove the cause of our deep pain. Grief releases the built-up emotions that threaten to undo us from deep within. Grief reveals what burdens us, whether anger, guilt, love, questions, or sorrow. Grief has the potential to move us into stronger faith and deeper spiritual experience. Grief, even in tragedy, watches carefully as God transforms grief into good.

On the highway of life, the grief lane may be life's most traveled way. The road of grief and sorrow often pushes joy aside as acute pain invades. As the psalmist confessed, "my life is spent with sorrow", and each of us experiences our share of grief-pain. Yet sorrow does not gain the last word, unless we allow it.

"How do we transcend grief?"

Dr. Catherine M. Sanders has an excellent answer to that question. With a PhD in psychology and her private practice experience, Dr. Sanders became known for her Tampa, Florida study of 125 bereaved individuals who had lost a spouse, a child, or a parent. Dr. Sanders followed each person through "his or her first two years of bereavement...met with each of them several times" and used that experience for an earlier book, *Grief: The Mourning After*.

In addition to writing journal articles and lecturing extensively on the subject, Dr. Sanders received the 1990 award for Outstanding Contribution in the Field of Death-Related Counseling from the Association for Death Education and Counseling. She also authored *Surviving Grief...And Learning to Live Again*. Dr. Sanders answer:

> "How do we transcend grief? As we view it in contemporary America, grief is seen as such a despicable ordeal that it is difficult to imagine that we can even survive grief. While I was going through my own bereavements, I had trouble conceiving of ever being without pain. I am not sure I even wanted to be without misery; it seemed appropriate that I should suffer. If my loved ones couldn't enjoy living, why should I? Yet, over time, grief gradually changed me. I've come to believe that if we can face the many lessons that bereavement offers us, we can finally triumph over sorrow. We have choices over how we will survive our significant losses. We can choose to maintain a bitterly cynical viewpoint, remaining in the conservation / withdrawal phase of grief, or we can confront the lessons of grief, painful as they are, and treat them instead as opportunities for our growth."[82]

When we do the latter, she writes,

> "We have opted for triumphant survival. Grief can then lift us up to new plateaus of living and loving. We are capable of deeper, richer relationships, immeasurable compassion, and an extraordinary ability to open our arms to life and adventure."[83]

"When this happens," Sanders asserts, "we transcend our grief and its pain."[84]

PART 1 - CHAPTER 14

"How can I turn my grief into a positive force?"

Whoever it is for whom you grieve, grieve with all your heart and soul. Don't hold back. Keep on grieving until you find something to which you can give your life, something you can "give back" to life. In other words, grieve until your grief runs out and serves no further purpose. Then grieve to new possibilities. Grieve until you become a grief helper.

Now your grieving has added purpose. You may still grieve for yourself, and that's ok. But now your grief has guided you into a time of life in which you now become a helping "medicine" available for the grief-sick needs of others. Having grieved your own heart out, you may now become a sensitive and effective grief helper when another heart is breaking.

"Grieving… can be a bridge."

Although we may feel helpless in our sorrow and grief, Arthur Golden suggests grief is "like a window that will simply open of its own accord. The room grows cold, and we can do nothing but shiver. But, it opens a little less each time, and a little less; and one day we wonder what has become of it."[85]

When it comes to the challenge of living through and living beyond our grief, Walter Anderson captures the battle in personal terms, in the first person singular: "I can choose to sit in perpetual sadness, immobilized by the gravity of my loss", Anderson says, "or I can choose to rise from the pain and treasure the most precious gift I have – life itself."[86]

According to Gerald Jampolsky, "Grieving can be a bridge to our experiencing a spiritual transformation."[87] As a child and adult psychiatrist, a graduate of Stanford Medical School, an author and an inspirational speaker, Jampolsky joins his professional voice with the voices of mental health, grief, and medical professionals plus clergy of all faith traditions who view grief as potentially transformative.

In 1959, Charles L. Allen, in his book *When You Lose A Loved One* expressed this transformative truth metaphorically: "Death is a doorway…to a larger life," for the one entering the passage of death, and for those who believe the "I am the resurrection and the life" words of Jesus.[88]

In 1994, and again in 2004, Verdell Davis published her grief classic *Let Me Grieve But Not Forever*. Before her book, Davis was the headmistress of a private school and served on the boards of several organizations. In 1987, when her husband and three friends were killed in an airplane crash, she faced "staggering pain...and wondered if there could ever be joy in her life again."[89]

Mrs. Davis writes about the emptiness and the questions that plagued her journey through sorrow. When I first read her story, I noted how her experience turned positive because of the "hope that anchored her soul when there was no desire to go on living". For Davis, her walk "through the valley of the shadow" was a bridge into "the light of hope" in which she discovered again "God's very special grace."

Judy Heath, psychotherapist (LISW-CP) and author of *No Time For Tears: Coping With Grief In A Busy World* knows her topic. Her four and a half month old son died of sudden infant death syndrome. As a wise man once told her, "Grief changes us, but how we change is up to us," leaving the future open to transformative possibilities. In her own experience, the "death of a loved one is life-altering and it can be transforming," asserts Heath.[90]

The Lessons of Grief

Every experience life puts in our path can be used for personal and spiritual growth. Dr. Catherine Sanders' has addressed the matter extensively in her *Surviving Grief....* She has produced an extensive series of "grief teaches us" observations which I merely highlight from Chapter 12 of her book:

"Grief teaches us..."
"to stop and examine what we truly want from life."
"the importance of living in the present...the value of every precious moment."
"the joy of spontaneity...the serendipity that is all around us."
"there is much to know about ourselves and our world."
"facing change is one of the hardest lessons of grief."
"we must trust our higher power to lead us on the right path"
"we have only now to let other persons know we love them."
"we need to keep reaching out to others."
"relationships can never be taken for granted."
"as we practice's grief's lessons, we slowly begin to transcend our grief."
"we change."
"we come to see grief as a death-and-resurrection experience."[91]

Elizabeth Kubler-Ross, a name associated with grief, specifically, the stages of grief, suggests grief can become a gift of growth as a possible outcome.⁹² Dr. Catherine Sanders in her book *Surviving Grief...* "believes there is a need to recognize and "identify a sixth phase of grief: spiritual growth." She believes "we haven't taken theory far enough until we incorporate spiritual fulfillment as the final phase of bereavement." The transformative evidence is out there – with clinical, psychological, theological, pastoral, and personal evidence.⁹³

"Is there comfort in sorrow?" Sorrows do not bring comfort automatically. Yet comfort always results when we live by faith and follow the "man of sorrows", who was "acquainted with grief". "Blessed are those who mourn, for they shall be comforted," Jesus said (Matthew 5:4).

What gave Jesus comfort?

A good clue may be found in one of Jesus' famous "last-sayings" on the cross. "Father, into Thy hands I commit my spirit." Even in the midst of a political, unjust, and harshly public death sentence, Jesus experiences the Father's comfort in his sorrow.

With an "into-Thy-hands-I-commit-my-spirit" attitude, each of us may also experience God's comfort in our time of sorrow.

"Is there discipline in sorrow?"

Yes, there is; the discipline of faith. Think of it as the discipline to believe God comforts all who mourn. Grief is an opportunity to grow and to expand our experience of God's Grace. Sorrow qualifies us for positive grief benefits. Human sorrow is born of a soul-deep pain, yet there is healing in its anguish. While it is always a bitter drink, an eventual strength takes root and blossoms from its bitterness. The shrouded sun is unveiled, the Presence of God warms the soul, and hope springs eternal from the depth of grief and despair.

Sorrow even has a mission, potentially. Like a flowering rose, allowed to shrivel in the dark until every fading leaf has dropped to the ground, yet when given appropriate light and nourishment generates new foliage and an abundance of new rose blooms. Sorrow has the God-breathed power to pull us back to life again.

"Is there healing in sorrow?"

Yes, there is healing in sorrow. Sorrow becomes a discipline of sorts. Yet, I must confess I did not come to know the discipline of sorrow until I had experienced several episodes of grief and the healing of my sorrow. Sorrow, when empowered by faith, facilitates a long-term, week-by-week, month-by-month, year-by-year healing.

Grief is not a curse or a punishment. Grieving will not kill us – "not loving" will. Grief is love's inevitable price. As the country music lyric put it: "I could have missed the pain but I'd a had to miss the dance." The stronger the love, the deeper the pain, the longer the hurt.

"Grief is a Gift from God"

Grief is a gift from God. Grief enables us to recover from the losses that shatter our lives. The God we may trust in the darkness of grief is the God we may count on in the confusion of grief.

Should not the God who redeems us from all our sin also have the purpose and the power to redeem us from the overwhelming sorrow of Grief?

Should not the God who is a lamp to our feet and a light to our path also light our Grief Journey?

A Verse for the Valley: "Be still, and know that I am God." Psalm 46:10a.

The God whose nature it is to forgive through the power of Grace Divine is the God who comforts all who mourn through the power of Grace Distributed.

The God who meets us in our fears at the cross of Jesus' suffering, also meets us in our tears in the soul-deep pain of grief.

Why not trust God with our Grief?

The Chapter "Take-Away"

Our grief experience may send us into an emotional storm, shaking us to the core. Yet our grief journey can also bring about personal transformation in important and meaningful ways.

Yes, grief can be overwhelming. Yet in the story of life from a faith perspective, death is a comma, not a period! And God's grace can be overwhelming too.

When we grieve spiritually, bone-deep, soul-deep, our grief is authentically ours and spiritually viable. We don't grieve according to the latest trend. "Copy-cat grief" is not our style. We grieve out of the depths of who we are as humans on planet earth. We grieve in the healing grace and mercy of the Great God of all Space and Time!

Grief, in all its mystery, is a potentially "transformational process". As I have stated: "For our grief to become transformational, it must lead to or result in some significant change in the griever's perspective, outlook, day to day life and, ultimately, in one's quality of life long term." As a griever I will blossom and bloom again---if I want to---if I choose to.

Your grief partner and transformed friend,

Fran Buhler

A Grief PS: Give attention to the "parched flower" of your grief.

1. Are you aware of your transformative possibilities? List one or two.

2. Allow the warm air of God's grace to begin your transformation. Experience God's grace personally, for yourself. Try out the transformational possibilities of your grief.

3. Relish the nurturing joy of God's blessing as you open to life, and blossom again. You can, you know. If you have the ability to grieve, you have the capacity to trust.

CHAPTER 15

GETTING OVER GRIEF: "IS CLOSURE THE BEST OBJECTIVE?"

Dear Reader, my Partner in Grief,

Getting over grief isn't like getting over the flu! We want to get over the flu "pronto"! Yet with grief, our goal isn't to get over our grief but to process our grief – so our grief means something to us and does something for us.

What can grief do for me, you ask? We have two choices. We may embrace positive grief or we may fiddle around with negative grief.

Positive and Negative Grief

Positive grief recognizes: "I was blessed having my loved one." There is nothing easy about positive grief. Yet positive grief lives forward by faith in the God who holds the future.

Positive grief recognizes both life and grief result from a divine-human process, helping us to restoration over a period of time. In a world where death is unavoidable, grief comes crashing in. Yet if we embrace it, grief becomes a form of God's gracious help. Working through the grief that hit us "head on" helps us move forward. We can engage life again. The best kind of closure comes because of the resurrection assurance we may enjoy by faith and trust.

Negative grief is mostly, well, negative; sees no positives at all and does its dead-level best (no pun intended) to find the worst in life, in death and beyond.

Negative grief has not a "thankful" bone in its body! Negative grief refuses to recognize how over time, God is able to restore us, if we allow it, if we welcome it.

Why This Matters

Grief is far more important than "closure".

"Closure" represents the cultural view that grief is something we stop, cease, put behind us, and "get over". And if you don't reach "closure" in a hurry, according to this view, there is clearly something wrong with you.

"Grief is something we get through."

An early voice against the "get over grief" crowd was Sharon Marshall, author of several titles including "Take My Hand: Guiding Your Child Through Grief". One of Marshall's sons died when he was four and a half months old. Her published view way back in 2001 is the view I have embraced since I was twenty-something in the 1960s. "Grief isn't something we get over. Grief is something we get through."[94]

"Grief is ongoing and individual."

In her book *In Lieu of Flowers: A Conversation for the Living*, Nancy Cobb writes: "Closure has become a catchword, an attempt to explain or contain people's search for meaning and their need to bear witness as they grieve..." "Anyone who has ever grieved," she adds, "knows there will be no closure...there will be only an opening, a void where someone was, and now isn't". "Closure suggests completion," writes Cobb, but "grief is ongoing and individual."[95]

Cobb gently nudges us toward reality when she writes: "Grieving is as natural as breathing; for if we have lived and loved, surely we will grieve." Shouldn't the "conversation" include the false assertion closure comes for those who believe in the promise and the hope of a future existence in the Presence of the Holy One?[96]

"...that great unending story fashioned by God's grace."

Is closure even the right objective? Isn't closure a false objective? Closure is a colossal misrepresentation. Even worse, closure is an insensitive insistence on a way of living after death that essentially copes with the loss by looking beyond it and pretending that everything is OK. What an unhealthy, inhuman way to live!

Thomas G. Long, Emory University's Bandy Professor of Preaching at the Candler School of Theology, expressed the appropriate Christian view of "closure" in the 2013 classic, *The Good Funeral*:

> "In the Christian faith we do not seek closure so much as we pray that all of our lost loves will be gathered into that great unending

story fashioned by God's grace."97

Dealing With a Culture of "Closure"

We don't "get over" loving someone, living with someone, doing life with someone. We don't say, "OK, time for closure!" Shut those feelings up and file them away.

If life is worth anything at all, it's about life memories, those special remembrances that make life a song to remember, a tune to whistle, all the days of our lives.

If the love was good, if the life together was good, we don't stamp it "closed". We savor it. Treasure it. We don't get over it. We work our way "through it" and "celebrate" it, always. "When we are experiencing personal grief," writes the Rev. Dr. John E. Baggett in his book, Finding the Good in Grief, "the most important thing for us to remember is that with God's help and the support of others, we can get through it."98

Even though grief may be the hardest work we ever do (because the octopus never gives up), doing anything to shove grief aside is unwise and unhealthy. As we learn to live with grief, we find a good life, even a happy and productive life, are possible again as we live by grief faith. Grief, after all, is a human thing and a "God thing". Why peddle the notion we ought to reach closure and "get over" something that is a God thing? The best closure is a sense of peace that comes from resurrection faith.

Is Closure "Finding the Remains"?

We see the extreme category of "difficult grief" when the circumstance of death or the cause of death results in the inability to recover the person's body because of how the person died or the conditions under which death may have occurred. For example, a death that occurs in military battle and identification of the remains becomes impossible, a death in a bombing incident, or because the body is "lost at sea"---any death in which the body is never recovered presents the so called closure challenge.

The faith perspective is radically different. For those who have no physical remains or "body" to provide closure, there is the closure of faith in the Most High God.

From the perspective of Christian faith, we know where the person is regardless of the cause of death or the circumstances of death. When we live by faith, death becomes a door, a passage, a transition from this life to the life beyond this life. The Most High God, the giver of life, the Presence we may enjoy throughout our lives, becomes the keeper of the place to which we go when life on earth ends and the everlasting experience beyond this life begins.

The First Law of Grieving

The First Law of Grieving is the simplest: "Grief has no formula," as Ellen Ashdown wrote in her 2008 memoir *Living By The Dead*.[99] Hang with me for a moment...

Dr. Ashdown became known in Tallahassee for writing about her life living beside Roselawn Cemetery, one of the City's best known and most used burial sites.

A Ph.D. in English, Florida Fiction Fellow, Phi Beta Kappa, and a writer for major textbook publishers, Dr. Ashdown captured the processes of death and grief in her own life and family, with Roselawn Cemetery always only a few steps away.

When we grieve, we live by the dead metaphorically, as does Dr. Ashdown literally. "In grief," writes Ashdown, "an absence is a presence." I have heard Ellen Ashdown's experience authenticated by numerous spouses who survived a loved one's death. Dr. Ashdown described in five words the experience of sleeping alone after a beloved spouse's death: "His energy vibrated beside me." She "breathed him in his unwashed jeans for months," she remembers. "Even his handwriting pained me", she concluded.[100]

In such a grief as this, in fact in all kinds of grief, closure does not help. The desire for closure becomes a false objective. Help comes from the Holy One who brings peace to our hearts, regardless of the timing or the specific circumstances of death.

What "I would have missed"

We are accustomed to getting over the flu in 3 or 4 days or a week, maybe ten days to two weeks in the worst of cases. But short-term grief, quickie grief, a grief span with brevity as the base measure, is not available in the catalogue of human grief. Yet this unsettling truth about grief's very nature and it's overwhelming presence does not leave us without hope or help.

Betty was honest: "I've never really reached closure in my grief", she acknowledged, "and I'm glad. I can't believe how much I would have missed if I had reached closure 20 years ago. I don't dwell in my grief, but overall it sure has enriched my life. I've discovered so much about love and life's true meaning and the joy of each day… and without some healthy grief along the way I would have missed it all!"

Bingo!

Grief Work is Ever So Daily: Four Facts about Grief

Bob Deits is known for his "Growing through Loss" conferences and conducting grief support groups. He writes from years of pastoral-counseling experience. Part of his legacy is the case he makes for "Four Key Facts about Grief". Deits has taught us that to build a foundation for grief recovery we must learn to work with our grief in specific ways. Consider the following four facts about grief:[101]

1. "The way out of grief is through it."

"This is the single most important fact for you to learn about grief", Deits writes. His observation is on point today even as it was in 1988, 1992, and 2000 for the three editions of his book, *Life After Loss*. "If you want to recover from your grief and grow through your loss, you must learn that there are no shortcuts to a good and full life after a major loss. You have to live through grief to resolve it."[102]

Deits' argument goes to the fact grief is so demanding we look for ways "to get out of going through it". Who wants to face grief? The heartache? The loneliness? Is it any wonder our common tendency is to try to avoid grief, get over grief, or wait it out?

2. "The very worst kind of grief is yours."

Take a hypothetical series of grief examples, every bad grief example you can imagine, then ask yourself which is the most painful? The worst grief example is always the grief that is yours. Makes no difference how you express it: "The worst grief is my grief."[103]

"My grief is the worst grief." "The worst kind of grief is always my grief."

3. "Grief is hard work."[104]

Grief is not an illness, or a weakness. Honest to goodness grief is very hard work. Grief comes at a time when we don't feel like doing anything. We want to go on cruise control and sleep through it. We want to "opt out", medicate out or consume ourselves with activity until we reach exhaustion and can't think or feel.

Yet when we grieve, there is much to do, grief that can't be passed on to someone else. There is no way around the fact grief is hard work.

4. "Effective grief work is not done alone."

Our cultural view is that grief is a solo affair---something we do in the solitary inner sanctum of the soul. Good grief does not exist, according to this opinion. Yet if and when our grief is shared relationally, either through strong friendships, shared experiences, or a healthy grief support group, the quality of our grief work improves.

"The more social your grief work is", writes Deits, "the better you will do with it. The more you talk about your grief work publicly, write about it in letters and share in the grief of others, the more effectively you will adapt to your loss. I don't mean to imply it's easy", writers Deits, "it is only necessary."[105]

God is in the "grief repair" business

Grief is brokenness at "the heart and soul" level, and God is in the grief repair business! Mending broken hearts is one of His specialties. If you have been to the dark place called "grief", and called upon the Most High God, then you know from personal experience.

"To walk through grief is a heroic journey," writes Therese Tappouni. "No other challenge in life approaches it."[106] Nobel Prize winner and two-time Pulitzer Prize winner William Faulkner said, "Between grief and nothing, I will take grief."

As we walk the path of grief, even with tear-saturated eyes and heavy hearts, we grieve for the purpose of healing our aching souls. Choose "nothing", and our grief sours like a bad bottle of milk left out of the refrigerator for three days. Grief counselor, Therese Tappouni, concludes her book on *The Gifts of Grief: Finding Light in the Darkness of Loss* with a final blessing: "May each year take you further from grief and deeper into gratitude for the gifts that will last a lifetime."[107]

THE GRIEF LETTER

The Bible Speaks to Grief and Grace

Grief and grace come together in a theology of grief that begins with the very nature of God as revealed in the Bible. "The Lord is gracious and compassionate" the psalmist announces (Psalm 111:4) and Paul reflects the same experience generations later when he writes in his second letter to the Corinthians, "My grace is sufficient for you..." (2 Corinthians 12:9) referring to the nature and action of God toward his hurting ones.

Each of us experience "the bitterness of death" (1 Samuel 15:32) and "the valley of the shadow of death" (Psalm 23:4). We know "the sting of death" (Hosea 13:14; 1 Corinthians 15:55-56) and "the suffering of death" (Hebrews 3:9). Yet death, in the biblical scheme, does not have the final word. The Revelation, to John, Chapter 21, announces a new heaven and earth, a holy city in which the tabernacle of God is among His people, "and they shall be His people, and God Himself shall be among them... and there shall no longer be any death; there shall no longer be any mourning, or crying, or pain..."

Grief brings "a sense of exploration"

In 1998, Thomas J. Davis wrote about his personal grief experience following the death of his wife. Davis' wife died following a 19-month struggle with a difficult disease. Davis' candor and reflection are helpful – whether we have walked a similar path or may one day find ourselves on a similar journey.

"Many good books", writes Davis, "detail the illness and death of a loved one and reflect on the relation of faith to the devastating grief one experiences when watching a loved one die." Davis goes on to observe: "It has been my experience, however, that the nature of grief changes somewhat over time." Davis is a Presbyterian minister who teaches the history of Christianity at Indiana University – Purdue University at Indianapolis.[108]

In his book *God In My Grief,* Dr. Davis observed "the grief of the first year that followed (his wife's death), "carried a 'newness'. Though the grief was real and painful, it was something I had not experienced before." He describes a period of adjustment during which "... I tried on the role of the grieving person." It took some time to adjust to that role," Davis explains. "It was like listening to a song I didn't know", says Davis.[109]

Then Davis describes a sense of exploration, plumbing the depths, gauging the boundaries that, for him, softened the harshness of death's song." Davis writes: "Or, maybe the newness didn't soften the harshness; perhaps I was simply too much in shock to hear anything that first year." Dr. Davis' subtitle is the stuff of an enriched life under the blessing of grace...

"The Music of Grace When Life Lives On."

Dr. Davis asserts "there is a sense of permanency that sets in after the first year that calls a different tune for grief", "the more permanent side of grief", he calls it, "and the ways Christian faith relate to that grief."[110]

Davis' experience with grief following the long term illness and death of his wife makes the case the sound of our grief is important because "grief is so incredibly isolating." It is hard to communicate our loss in ways that resonate with others. It is simply hard to share our feelings with others. Davis' book is "a song sung in the key of grief". He has a special analysis and observation for the "you-need-to-reach-closure" crowd.[111]

"Others need to know how grief lingers and debilitates, not just right after the death of a loved one but for a long time afterward. In my experience, and I'm sure in other's as well, there's a tendency to get rushed; people want you to move on. I hope this book says, 'Don't rush me. Walk with me instead.'"[112]

Following the death of one close and dear to us, we face the universal question: How do I let go? How do I move forward? We can easily become stranded in regret, resentment, anger, or even self-pity. We may become stuck in a negative mode.

Grief Attitude Makes a Difference: A Grandmother's Song

When I was a kid, my paternal grandmother used to sing a song:

> "God will take care of you
> Thro' ev'ry day
> o'er all the way;
> He will take care of you,
> God will take care of you."[113]

The most important grief stage is when we arrive at that time and place in our healing when we can say and sing those words and mean them. Ultimately, faith offers the upward way through our grief.

One of the realities of this life is that, for many, grief gets complicated. Grief and the grieving process may slow our grief progress, may even stop us in our tracks. If so, consider the Ezekiel verdict which follows.

The Ezekiel Verdict

Jesus borrowed "the good shepherd" motif right out of Ezekiel 34. While the chapter clearly relates to God's displeasure with Israel's priestly "leadership failure" to be good shepherds at the time, it is appropriate to read Ezekiel 34 in relation to the Ezekiel model of how a good shepherd should function and what a good shepherd should do.

Read Ezekiel 34:12, for example, in the context of grief and note how God's intended "shepherd care" should be lived out in a grief context. Read the text "as if" the care for his sheep is an example of God's "grief work":

"As a shepherd cares for his herd in the day when he is among his scattered sheep, so I will care for My sheep and will deliver them from all the places to which they were scattered on a cloudy and gloomy day."

What if that "scattered on a cloudy and gloomy day" includes the scattering of grief and sorrow when a loved one dies?

In the New Testament, 1 Peter 5:2, 3, 4, and 7 connect with the Ezekiel theme.

In 1 Peter 5, the elders, the leaders of the church, are admonished to "shepherd the flock of God among you" (NAS), to cast all your care/anxiety/concern (v7) "upon Him", upon the "Chief Shepherd" (v4) "because He cares for you" (v7).

Like the song says: "God will take care of you." Even in our time of grief and sorrow, thru every day, over all the way, God will take care of you."

Grief and the Metaphor of Baptism

Life is shaped in the example of Christ's own life and death. Where grief is concerned I find the metaphor of baptism useful and comforting, even prophetic, because baptism includes a dual symbolism – both a burial and a raising up! As Paul writes in the New Testament book of Romans, we have been baptized (i.e. buried) into Jesus' death and baptized (i.e. raised up) into Jesus' life. Listen to Paul's explanation to the "church" in Rome, via the words of Romans 6:3-5:

PART 1 - CHAPTER 15

"Do you not know that all of us who have been baptized into Christ Jesus were baptized into his death? Therefore we have been buried with him by baptism into death, so that, just as Christ was raised from the dead by the glory of the Father, so we too might walk in newness of life. For if we have been united with him in a death like his, we will certainly be united with him in a resurrection like his."

The Chapter "Take-Away"

Getting over grief isn't like getting over the flu. But help is available! In a world in which grief is so widespread, so consuming, and for many – so depressing, this word from God's Word offers comfort and hope and even makes me smile! Laughter bubbles up within me. Because...

In the grief attitude of faith, not even death has the final word! God's resurrection power has the final word. Talk about closure? Now that is closure!

Your grief partner and friend,

Fran Buhler

A Grief PS: God is in the grief repair business. You may discuss your personal or family need with the Most High God. Describe for yourself your grief attitude. Then...

1. Take a few moments and talk to the Most High God now. Be honest.

2. Choose a verse in the Bible that speaks to you in your grief. Claim it. Practice it.

3. God is also in the resurrection business! Exclusively, I might add!!!

PART 2

GRIEF ADVENTURE IS A LIFE CHOICE

Part 2: Grief Adventure is a Life Choice

"Grief, an adventure? You've got to be kidding me!" "And who in the world would want to make grief a 'life choice'?"

The questioner was someone who had been through a difficult and painful family death.

The exchange occurred when a member of our church asked if I was still writing "the grief book". The discussion convinced me, more than ever, this Part 2 with Chapter 16 had to be included. I knew the association of "adventure" with "grief" would be a roadblock to many. Yet I also knew the whole idea of grief adventure had an authentic biblical basis, so why not make the case?

Why This Matters

Early in my life, like everyone I knew, I thought of grief as a heavy emotion lasting almost forever. Yet the more I experienced grief, dealing with the matter personally, the more I noticed the adventure aspects of my own grief. My grandparent's deaths sparked in me and in our family an active interest, an adventure, into our family history. The deaths of high school and college friends caused me to look harder at life, to ask what life is all about and to treasure family and friendship, not knowing how long either would last.

The more I observed individuals who had grieved for however long they needed to grieve, the more I became aware of people who made the choice to live the grief adventure in much the same fashion as one might prepare to visit the Rocky Mountains or climb Mt. Everest!

TGL offers a GPS for grief and sorrow, gently guiding the reader on a grief adventure born of faith, leading to grief behavior change long term. That's why we call grief a "journey". Give yourself grief-time and faith-time. Everything takes time, plus God's grace.

What This Means

Again and again, from people of faith, comes this notion that following the death of a loved one life is "a soulful journey of grief"---an adventurous journey. I kept coming back to my seminary discovery in which "adventure" becomes a verb. In the Book of Judges, Chapter 9, we find Jotham's parable, given on the top of mount Gerizim, south of Shechem, addressed to those assembled. Jotham reminds the gathered assembly of his father's action in their behalf. In the KJV, "...my father fought for you, and adventured his life far, and delivered you out of the hands of Midian." In the RSV, the father "risked his life, and rescued you from the hand of Midian."

In a similar fashion, Jesus fought for each of us. He "adventured" his life and delivered us out of the hands of death. Yes, we each must die. But in the life of faith, we transition to a greater experience. Through the power and in the presence of the Holy One, we adventure life at a higher, more meaningful, level.

The Bible word for "life" is "way"; translated literally as a "journey", a "path", or "road". Per Psalm 1:6: "the way of the righteous". Isaiah 30:21: "This is the way, walk in it." Or Jesus himself in John 14:6: "I am the way, and the truth and the life." In Acts 9, Luke writes about the early Christ followers as those "belonging to the Way," that is, the "way of faith" in Christ Jesus, which is the way of faith in God.

A Hymn and a Verse for the Valley

"Great God of every blessing, of faithful, loving care;
You are the fount of goodness, the daily bread we share.
How can we hope to thank you? Our praise is but a start;
sincerely and completely, I offer you my heart."[114]

"For the Lord comforts His people, and will have compassion on His afflicted Ones." (Isaiah 49:13c).

Yes, like life and faith, grief is an adventure, a life choice, a way to grieve with purpose and live with promise. What serves us well in life and faith carries us through our times "in the valley".

Are you ready for your five-chapter grief adventure?

Part 2 Chapter Previews

Chapter 16 encourages us in "The Soulful Journey of Grief" as we make the life choice to begin "feeling our **way** out of grief", a decisive grief adventure that could take a while.

Chapter 17 helps us move beyond the "waddle-waddle" stage as our grief adventure over time leads to personal growth.

PART 2

Chapter 18, if we embrace the grief adventure challenge, will help us discover joy again.

Chapter 19 examines the personal benefit of grief-faith, a comfort that comes only from God, because faith matters.

And Chapter 20 wraps up Part 2 with "The Adventure of Faith: The Promise of a 'Presence'".

Your friend in the adventure of grief,

Fran Buhler

A Grief PS:

1. You now, because of your strong personal and emotional needs, focus on your immediate grief needs. Choose your two biggest grief/faith needs to work on first.

2. Focus where you hurt. Give yourself time to grieve. Don't allow your "schedule" to pre-empt your personal grief needs. If you are hurting and need help, get professional help.

3. Among the mountains of life and faith, the highest peak you will climb is your ultimate faith adventure, involving "The Promise of a Presence". If you have not experienced the presence of the Holy One, you have missed life's most meaningful experience---and most rewarding adventure!

CHAPTER 16

THE SOULFUL JOURNEY OF GRIEF: "FEELING YOUR WAY OUT OF GRIEF"

Dear Reader and Partner in Grief,

Maybe the following example captures your grief experience. "I thought my grief was long gone," the caller confided over the phone, "but I hit a rough patch last night and literally cried myself to sleep."

The octopus has an open disregard for letting go! **Grief is defiant. The soulful journey of grief takes time.**

"Recovery is a matter of the heart rather than the head," writes Paul F. Keller in his slim 18-page booklet, How to Grieve. "You are not going to think your way through your grief," says Keller, "as much as you are going to feel your way out of it." Keller's powerful little guide connects with grieving individuals and families to open hearts and help them heal.[115]

What This Means

"Some survivors try to think their way through grief," writes Carol Staudacher in "A Time To Grieve". "That doesn't work," Staudacher writes bluntly, and then explains. "Grief is a releasing process, a discovery process, a healing process. We cannot release or discover or heal by the use of our minds alone," Staucacher asserts. "The brain must follow the heart at a respectful distance," she writes.[116]

Why, we ask?

Because, as Staudacher insists: "it is our hearts that ache when a loved one dies. It is our emotions that are most drastically affected." "Certainly the mind suffers," she says, "the mind recalls, the mind may plot and plan and wish, but it is the heart that will blaze the trail through" what she calls "the thicket of grief."[117]

Paul Keller's "chapter opening" quote above may be the single most descriptive paragraph in my grief experience about "working with your feelings." What follows is designed for anyone "feeling" and "thinking" your way out of grief.

Many in our population regard grief as a sign of weakness. From this point of view, grieving is something you simply do not do in public. In public settings, many of us are not comfortable with the "feeling" side of grief. We tend to put a false "brief-grief" face on the whole grief phenomenon, as if we should grieve on cue---and then get on with life.

Why This Matters

The death and grief collisions in our lives are always unavoidable, sometimes unexpected, and many times more complicated than we anticipated. There is no way we can organize ourselves to avoid death or grief. "I believe the hardest part of healing after you've lost someone," said singer Chonda Pierce in a radio interview, "is to recover the 'you' that went away with them."[118]

We cannot remodel the reality of death to avoid grief. Too many of us believe we can actually evade the grief experience and get away by not showing up! Yet the truth is we grieve whether or not we show it publicly. We need to attend our grief, be present in our grief, choosing to live forward, making grief adventure our life choice.

The Grief Flu-Model

Grief is normal and acceptable in our culture as long as we follow "the flu model" – three days and back to work. In my experience, eighty percent of the time, grievers observe a three-to-five day "flu model".

The 'flu model" has become the universal grief standard. Its acceptance is pervasive. Its practice, demanded. And we need to rid ourselves of it. We need to do the "feeling" and the "thinking" necessary to contend with this false notion of what grief is. We should take the time grief requires. Maybe that means rethinking our post-funeral tradition of "three days and back to work." Maybe it means rethinking what we know about grief.

The Grief "turn-around"

Grief demands time, and attention. Yet it can be worth the cost.

Our soulful journey of grief in which we gradually "feel our way out of grief" has the potential to produce a "turn-around" in our lives. "A turn-around" means literally a "repentance" (to use the Bible word), an "about face" (to use a military term) in which we turn and go in a different direction. Grief when combined with faith has the potential to help us move from the pit of grief despair to the upward road of personal appreciation for the Mercy we have experienced and the Grace we have received. So here's the question...

"How do we practice responsible grief?"

We recognize that as grieving individuals we are still responsible to our families and to our employers.

My wife and I have a friend who sits on a national policy board in the field of public education. Not long ago, her husband died. She deals with the "grief at work" challenge every day. She addresses her major responsibilities and her profound grief by seeking to acknowledge her grief and manage her responsibilities. She takes regular "grief breaks" during the day. She times meetings, travel, and other demands so that her schedule includes "built in grief times".

Our friend also follows a "grief honesty" practice. She never denies her grief. She feels that would be unfaithful to her wonderful marriage. She neither claims nor pretends her grief is not a problem. She does not flee from grief's transparency. If in an important meeting or conversation she is unexpectedly overwhelmed by her grief as it surges to the surface, she simply acknowledges the source and the reality of her grief and goes on with the conversation or the meeting discussion at hand.

She also times her days off strategically in recognition of her grief needs, but she maintains a responsible work schedule and respects performance expectations that go with her job and her level of responsibility.

A 30-year Perspective

"Don't take my grief away from me," writes Doug Manning, using the single, simple, spiritual statement he has trademarked. Since 1982, former pastor Doug Manning has committed himself to grief ministry. For thirty years, Doug has devoted his time to writing, counseling, and leading seminars in the areas of grief and elder care. In numerous ways, this is exactly what our culture and even our best friends try to do – take our grief away from us.[119]

In Manning's book by the same title, *Don't Take My Grief Away From Me: How to Walk Through Grief and Learn to Live Again*, he lays out the rationale for "the grief letter's" success, why the letter struck a universal chord in the human heart.

"You give yourself permission to grieve by recognizing the need for grieving," Manning asserts. Then he drives home the assertion: "Grieving is the natural way of working through the loss of a love. Grieving is not weakness or absence of faith. Grieving is as natural as crying when you are hurt, sleeping when you are tired, or sneezing when your nose itches." Manning says grief "is nature's way of healing a broken heart."

"Grief is not an enemy – it is a friend," in Manning's view. "It is the natural process of walking through hurt and growing because of the walk." "Let it happen," Manning says, "Stand up tall to friends and to yourself and say, 'Don't take my grief away from me. I deserve it and I am going to have it.'"[120]

Permission to Grieve

Isn't that precisely what the original "grief letter" did? In a society that demands closure, and even schedules closure for us if we let it, "the grief letter" gave people permission to grieve, a ticket to grieve, in the face of cultural pressure to reach closure.

Women and men in every mode of dress and style of attire have approached me – from jeans to pinstripe suits, from dressy dresses to slacks and shorts – each with tear-filled eyes, stopping me to retrieve from a purse or a pocket, the crumpled grief letter, wrinkled and worn from days and weeks of folding and unfolding to say: "Thank you for my letter, I needed permission to grieve."

I never planned or conceived or designed the grief letter in such fashion. Like many ministry initiatives, the thought and follow-through were quick and hurried in order to get on to the next thing. Grief has a way of calling us to a "higher agenda."

"The Bible asks our Question"

"How long must I bear pain in my soul, and have sorrow all day long?" (Psalm 13:2) poses the question every griever asks, as once again, the Bible asks our very human question. "My eye is wasted away from grief, my soul and my body also. For my life is spent with sorrow, and my years with sighing..." according to Psalm 31:9b-10a, a familiar experience for grievers.

Even though those are words from the Bible, if those words were all I had, I would not have what I need in my grief. I give thanks for Isaiah's words, "He will swallow up death for all time..." (Isaiah 25:8). I give thanks for

THE GRIEF LETTER

Jesus' promise, "Blessed are they that mourn for they shall be comforted" (Matthew 5:4). These words of Isaiah and of Jesus include you. These words also include me. We remember the Holy One of Isaiah 53:3 as "a man of sorrows, acquainted with grief", words all Christians associate with the life and death of Christ.

In this 21st century, what King Agag of the Amalekites in 1 Samuel 15:32 called "the bitterness of death" is pervasive, prompting a variety of attitudes and behaviors.

1. The way we grieve always reflects our view of God. God-less grief, it must be said, abounds in the US and in our world today.

2. We cannot expect someone else to make sense of our loss, our grief pain, our soul-deep suffering, for us. We must do our own "grieving and believing" and respect the "grieving and believing" of others even if it differs radically from ours.

3. We who grieve will always have to suffer those who have all the answers, are quick to tell us what has happened and why, because they have everything figured out.

4. We live in a culture inhabited by persons who have a deep need to openly express their inner hostility toward God or any belief in God. Unfortunately, many people of faith tend to shy away from such individuals. We need to listen...begin a relationship of acceptance of the person in spite of their hostility, and see where it goes.

5. The high frequency of "difficult death" and "hard grief" have made popular an old proverb: "If God lived on earth, people would break His windows." In today's often hostile environment, some would like to break His nose!

Grief is a time to venture forward in our lives, not retreat or withdraw. Faith and love and prayer are our best tools, our most powerful responses and the areas in which we are most likely to experience breakthroughs and new possibilities!

Bitterness is only a hiding place, not a solution. We can hide out in our anger and we can blame someone or something else, but we cannot bring our loved one back to this life again. "How long, O Lord?" has been the cry of the ages. Over time, the faithful have come to live and to believe the Most High God will see us through our grief to new life again.

To answer the question, "how long?" we must dare to speak the language of faith because we have embraced the life of faith. We must dare to be people who love because, as the Song of Solomon reminds us, "love is as strong as death" (The Song of Solomon 8:6c). Faith and love are the best tools we have for life's grief journeys.

God's Word Knows Our Grieving Hearts

Sometimes, strange as it may seem, even reading the Bible backwards helps the grieving heart. I was grieving the deaths of two close friends while thumbing through scripture, hardly giving much attention to the texts, until three passages jumped off the pages of God's Word---as if they were aimed for my hurting heart. I could never explain why or how the trio of texts grabbed my attention, but I was surely helped by each verse in succession, and by all three verses in tandem. Sometimes, I believe, scripture texts "find us" when and where we are hurting before we have the clarity to "find them". This may be the best part of a "soulful journey"! May I share my discoveries in sequence?

Psalm 63:1: "…My soul thirsts for Thee…" (NAS)

Psalm 62:1: "My soul waits in silence for God only; from Him is my salvation. He only is my rock and my salvation. My stronghold: I shall not be greatly shaken." (NAS)

Psalm 23:3: "He restores my soul…" (NAS)

The Life and Grief Choice

In the Christian faith tradition, when I seek comfort for myself and when I am comforting those who mourn, I turn to the resurrection promise laid out in multiple New Testament texts. One especially good example is the story of the death of Jesus' friend, Lazarus.

Read the Lazarus episode for yourself in John 11 and follow my observations. Note Jesus' own personal grief because, as verse 5 attests, "…Jesus loved Martha, and her sister, and Lazarus." Note Jesus' response after his arrival, in verse 33: "He (referring to Jesus) was deeply moved in spirit…" When they took him to see Lazarus' body, "Jesus wept", verse 35. Jesus shed tears, as Jesus' grief was real and evident. Jesus experienced the human side of grief.

Faith embraces the exchange between Martha and Jesus from verse 20 thru verse 40. Please read these verses for yourself.

Why We Stake Our Faith Here

We stake our faith on Jesus' assertion in verse 25, his response to Martha's exasperation:

> "I am the resurrection and the life; he who believes in me shall live even if he dies, and everyone who lives and believes in me shall never die. Do you believe this?" Jesus asked. (John 11:25-26 NAS)

Belief in the power of God, the Holy One, to make His promise of resurrection an unmistakable reality for those who dare to believe and trust in Him, is the "leap of faith" at work here. *The Grief Letter* is not about a grief sadness for which there is no remedy. It involves a life choice, for which there is redemption! Yes, grief is real. The pain is soul-deep and powerful. When we experience the shock of grief in our lives, we need "the Bread of Life"--- not cake and cookies.

The answer via divine grace is the fact of Christ's resurrection, as Paul describes in 1 Corinthians 15. Check verses 12-19; consider verses 20-49; and dwell on verses 50-58. Be aware the dual questions of verse 55 are a direct quote of Hosea 13:14. Grief is inevitably "me-centered" and that is understandable. But as we grieve, our grief must become God-centered as we make our life choice by the way we answer Jesus' simple question: "Do you believe this?" When we believe Jesus is the resurrection and the life we make a God-centered confession. We "choose" the Bread of Life---over cake and cookies.

A Verse for the Valley: "Fear not, for I am with you; be not dismayed, for I am your God. I will strengthen you, yes, I will help you, I will uphold you with My righteous right hand." (Isaiah 41:10).

Grief is hard, no matter the angle of the grief experience, no matter the relationship prompting the grief. Our grief always relates to our "belief", to our faith or lack of faith, and to the One in whom we trust. The soulful journey of grief---in the strength of faith---leads ultimately to the recognition: Grief is an adventure and a life choice.

"...put your hand into the hand of God."

The opportunity to attend and graduate from Carson Newman College in Jefferson City, Tennessee, now Carson Newman University, just north of

Knoxville, was an early blessing in my life. To the professors under whom I studied and the coaches under whom I played, and for the athletic scholarship that paid for my education, I am deeply grateful.

In the Carson Newman University Library one day, pursuing a sociology class assignment, I came across a poem published in 1908 by British sociologist Minnie Louise Haskins, known as "The Gate of the Year."

"I stood at the gate of life and said, 'Give me a light that I may go safely into the unknown,' and a voice replied, "Go out into the darkness and put your hand into the hand of God. That will be to you better than a light, and safer than a known way.""[121]

Quite often, especially in my own "soulful grief journeys", I have returned in my mind to Haskins' words when facing a major decision, considering the next life adventure, or grieving the death of one dear to me. Her words have inspired me again and again, especially after the deaths of so many members of our family.

What Grief Reveals

Our grief showcases our view of God. When we find ourselves soul-deep in grief, ripping us into tears, taking us down into our own solitary silo of sorrow, leaving us in pain and sadness, we discover what we really believe about death and about God.

In our grief, God knows our sorrow. The Holy One understands our gnawing grief, comforts our broken hearts; and, in time, heals our sorrow-torn, sorrow-worn, spirits.

What we behold in the New Testament gospels of Matthew, Mark, Luke and John is the story of God's resurrection power in the face of death. Jesus' raising of Lazarus from the dead, a revelation of God's presence and power in Jesus, leads directly to the trumped up trial and crucifixion of Jesus, before his ultimate resurrection on the first day of the week.

So I write about grief and the celebration of life and faith within the Providence of God. "Grief never ends… But it changes. It's a passage, not a place to stay. Grief is not a sign of weakness, nor a lack of faith… It is the price of love." – Author Unknown

THE GRIEF LETTER

The Chapter "Take-Away"

While grief is defiant and, like a stubborn octopus, has an open disregard for letting go, tears are the divine lubrication for our grief adventure. Grief becomes a matter of both the heart and the head. We must "feel" our way through our grief long before we are able to "think" our way out of our grief. Our best feeling and thinking come together as we live by "faith" through our grief, as we "trust" by faith beyond our grief.

For one who has experienced "the soulful journey of grief", "walking the winding, sometimes confusing, hallways of grief" repeatedly over the years, the sacred tears of grief are intended by the Holy One as a solace for the soul. I am thankful the grief adventure is an available life choice. I am grateful for the opportunity to share life, faith and tears via "the grief letter."

Your sometimes tearful partner in the adventure of grief,

Fran Buhler

A Grief PS: For your grief adventure…

1. Have you trusted God as a life choice? Faith is an adventure. Describe for yourself your adventure of faith.

2. How would you describe your grief adventure? Tell yourself right now…

3. The "how long" question of Psalm 13:2 can only be answered by faith---not by a calendar. In the privacy of your own heart, ask yourself: What is my faith answer?

CHAPTER 17

GRIEF ADVENTURE LEADS TO PERSONAL GROWTH: BEYOND THE "WADDLE-WADDLE" STAGE

Dear Grief Adventure Partner,

We've done 16 chapters together; I want to share a true story with you, one of the best grief-related experiences I have had. "The biggest mistake I made in my grieving," a man told me a good six years after his wife's death, "was to get stuck in the 'waddle-waddle' stage of grief." He described the "waddle-waddle" stage as those years after her death when he did not believe there was any life for him beyond her death. So instead of living his life, he slipped into a daily "waddle", in his words, "just going from one waddle to the next and wasting every day God was giving me!" **The "waddle-waddle stage" has an octopus trade mark!**

Why This Matters

When we grieve---if we are open to it---the grief adventure takes us to a renewed level of living and a higher level of faith leading to personal growth.

May the pressure we feel in our culture to get over our grief be overtaken by our progress at working through our grief, even growing through our grief adventure. Yes, it is possible to experience personal growth through our grief, moving beyond the 'waddle-waddle' stage.

"Broken For Good"

At 3 am, three days into her freshman year of college, Rebecca Jones' father died. At the age of eighteen, she found herself challenged like never before!

Everything she believed, "the hope she had always carried in her Christian faith", was put into the fire of "deep grief". A full decade after her father's death, Rebecca put her grief journey on paper and published it. The amazing thing about Rebecca's ten year grief experience is that she came to the place and time when she could write: 'I am not happy Dad died, not one bit. But having been there, with it having happened, I can look you straight in the eye and say: 'I am thankful.'"[122]

Rebecca eventually wrote about "how you can, in time, learn to be thankful for that for which you are not actually happy!" You see, Rebecca Rene Jones refused to allow herself, though slipping and sliding in her grief, to become a "waddle-waddle stage" captive. She titled her book, *Broken for Good: How Grief Awoke My Greatest Hopes*. Her subtitle speaks to the truth of this Chapter 17.[123]

Witness to Grief Contrasts

During my 21 years officiating funerals and memorial services, I have examined "the Grief shelf" in brand name and independent family-owned bookstores in 20 states across the US. I have also checked "books in print" every few years to identify titles I may have missed "at the bookstore." I have made considerable effort to assure my "due diligence." I do not claim my search and review have been academically acceptable or exhaustive, merely that in the course of constant ministry schedule crunches I have sought to monitor what has been available for the grieving person as well as the grief helper.

This "search and read" exercise has informed *The Grief Letter* and, I hope, has been helpful to your reading. From my reading and research, and from my pastoral experience, I have noted the vast variety of grief circumstances and experience. If I have done a good job reflecting the "grief landscape", then the following examples have added strength because over the last 21 years each is typical of two grief "faith" contrasts I have witnessed.

First Example

First, I share a conversation with the manager of a brand-name bookstore in a southern urban center. She had been helpful when I arrived, steering me immediately to the store location shelving titles of interest. Later I stopped by to thank her. In the course of our conversation, I asked the universal question I often ask.

"Have you had a death in your family in recent years?"

"Not recently", she said, "but my grandmother died 12 years ago... (pause)...and that really threw me for a loop." (Without any hesitation, she immediately knew the exact number of years since her grandmother's death! Many of us have a mental calendar of the personal, family and friendship grief we have experienced.)

Tears appeared in her eyes, as she paused, "It was…my world started coming undone. Plus, my family's Irish---so you don't cry!" Again, she paused.

"It was…the roughest…time…in my life."

"I'm sorry to dredge up your pain," I said.

"Oh no," she jumped in, "I'm actually feeling relief---like a heavy weight has lifted. This is something I should have talked about long before now." As she continued, I listened.

"My parents were not "believers" so I didn't have any preparation for how to deal with death, especially their deaths. Never thought about it!" Then she added, "So when they died, it was like 'whamo', I was bouncing off the walls. I didn't know where to turn for help."

She was looking at the floor, then at me---to see if I was listening.

I was.

"This whole grief business… is the toughest thing… I've… ever… EVER… dealt with," she said, slowly, deliberately. Then out of the clear blue she pointed the conversation in a different direction.

"After the deaths of my parents", she said so softly I almost missed it, "I put forth extra effort to always honor and cherish the memories of my parents. But I made a conscious choice to live with an 'every day' sense of purpose and to use my grief to motivate my life development as I met the career challenges before me."

Did you hear it? She used her grief adventure to inspire and motivate her personal growth. She went against the grain of grief and moved forward with her life.

Second Example

My wife and I received a note in a 2014 Christmas card from the wife of a deceased cousin. The daughter of a retired pastor, she is a gifted and published fiction author of renown, a person for whom I have great admiration. In her note, she referred to her Father's death---a death about which Nancy and I knew nothing until the daughter's Christmas card arrived.

"It has been a year of challenge for me. My 89-year-old legally blind father moved in with me in April. He passed away at my home on Aug 1st. Watching him struggle at the end is a memory I shall take to my grave. There were many teachable moments in that experience. But, as he reminded me the night before he died, 'There is grace in dying.' It was a comfort to hear that reassurance from him at the end of his life. Now, having made it through, I realize there is grace in living, too. I am more sure of it than ever!"

In the dual accounts above, the grief contrasts jump off the page! The family backgrounds, personal career interests, and grief experiences are varied as one would expect. Regardless of the first lady's lack of family faith guidance, she wrestled the octopus of grief and then moved forward with her life and career. In spite of all the grief and difficulty the second lady lived through, she named the challenge. She claimed her hope. In her grief, she spoke to the promise of the Most High God.

Although my grief contrasts above are between a person and family without a "faith" heritage and a person and family with a significant "faith" history, I intend no criticism. I extend only good will and my strongest sympathy to the former whose grief was so difficult and to the latter who experienced the heightened grief that comes with personal day-to-day caregiving.

These two contrasting examples, while being miles apart in their individual faith practice and direct contrasts in their respective family faith traditions, have one singular similarity. Each demonstrates personal growth in their respective grief adventures.

Through the acts of faith and personal choice it is possible to live with Grace and Gratitude, to grieve all we need to grieve, and live forward by faith. Grief can be helpful and bring healing. The grief adventure may also lead to personal growth.

The Healing Sorrow of Grief

Sorrow can be very difficult because from Day One sorrow zaps our physical strength and steers us toward the "waddle-waddle stage". Sorrow often imposes a long loneliness. Yet the healing sorrow of grief helps us become better, stronger, more able to engage life and more likely to be grief-sensitive in someone else's time of sorrow.

Someone asked, "What's it like doing so many funerals?"

You learn, I replied, that even though there is pain behind every death, we do not all grieve alike. There is the potential for God's comfort and peace to cover every pain, not eliminate the pain but to cover it, making it bearable. You also learn the pain often goes beyond losing the loved one. Sometimes the grief experience leads to estrangement within families with conflicting views about faith and death, differing priorities or personal clashes.

If you pay attention, you see examples in which the grievers' grief-pain does not have the last word. You see sorrow-filled families pull together, grieve together, laugh together, and move forward together. Quite often, you see a family of "faith" as they embrace their sorrow, look to God in Christ Jesus for Comfort and Hope, and then you see them transition into a future God-given joy, a matter we shall examine in Chapter 18.

There are those who wish for a faith without the tears of grief. Such a faith would be possible only in a world or a life without love.

Verses for the Valley: "The Lord is good to those who wait for Him, to the soul who seeks Him. It is good that one should hope and wait quietly for the salvation of the Lord" (Lamentations 3:25-26).

What an adventure! Yet...

Waiting is not an American virtue. Many of us view patience as a weakness, preferring instead a "hurry up" and a "get moving" obsession with getting ahead, winning, beating the competition. Where grief is concerned, there is no alternative to waiting, even waiting patiently, for the Lord, because the octopus never gives up! In fact, the adventure of grief begins smack dab in the middle of the waiting.

How to Experience the Adventure of Grief

The challenge of moving forward with life – following the death of one close and dear to us – confronts every survivor. How do I move beyond "the waddle-waddle stage" of life? How do I live forward? How do I experience the adventure of grief and growth?

When death and grief invade our lives, the effective response is to put all of our energy and effort into moving forward because that is possible, purposeful, and positive. "One of the saddest things in life", says Cos Davis, a clinical pastoral therapist in Franklin, Tennessee, a suburban community in the south shadow of Nashville, "is to grow bitter rather than better, to die to life before you die, to finish poorly." When this happens, you die to life while still living.[124]

Writing in the March, 2011 issue of "Mature Living", Davis describes a typical example of the "need-to-move-forward challenge" from his professional practice. A year after her husband's death Mary was "stuck" in her grief. Her husband died suddenly. Every time she went to clean out his closet, she was "regretting the critical things she had said to him", writes Davis. Then Davis adds: "After a year she was unable to move his boots from the hearth where he had left them the night before he died."[125]

Cos Davis' summary represents a universal example of an inability to move forward: "Mary had suffered a great loss, but she was beginning to realize she was also losing out on life. Someone she loved deeply was gone, and she remained. She needed help to grieve and permission to get on with her life." Mary faced the classic challenge of living forward. Moving forward following the death of someone dear to us is much more difficult "to do" than it is "to discuss."[126]

Five Choices Move Us Forward

In decades of experience with numerous grief situations, individuals able to move forward in their personal growth, even under the profound load of heavy grief, seem to do so by making five choices. These five choices enable them to experience the adventure of grief. They choose to live forward in their lives by making choices we can make in our lives.

1. Embrace life as a gift from the Holy One.

This is the first of several choices. We recognize life is from a Source outside of our personal ability. We acknowledge life is bestowed by a Power beyond any human possibility to duplicate. Life comes from One who is wholly other, from the Most High God. This personal life choice, this faith choice, begins the adventure. Choose to embrace life as a gift from the Holy One. A good place to make this choice is on our knees.

2. Choose to accept your death-loss.

Choose not to deny the loss, but to accept the loss. Acknowledge the loss, accept the death, along with the giant void the death leaves in your life.

How do we accept someone's death? The way I do it is by celebrating their life and everything about their life that enriched and enlarged my life. I accepted the fact the death of my father and mother may have subtracted from my daily life but their deaths could never lessen their contribution to my life and never remove their influence and beneficial presence from my memory. I could always treasure the time I had with them and not even their deaths could take that away.

3. Give yourself time to grieve.

I see people in my work who say they are going to grieve their loss but then never give themselves "time" to grieve. Grieving comes naturally, yet grieving takes time. The challenge I see is not with grief resistance, but a lack of grief assistance! We often do not create the time it takes to grieve. And that is a choice.

Occasionally, I will concede, I see someone who seems to intentionally do the "busy-busy" drill as a means of avoiding grief---or as a way of coping with grief. Yet I see far more examples in which the griever is acting with good intentions and really wants to grieve, but is caught in a "schedule" that shoves grieve time aside and pushes on while life presses down. Sometimes grief is as simple as having time to grieve, giving to yourself "the gift of time" to grieve. In some circumstances, we have to make time to grieve---regardless of the consequences!

4. Be grateful for how blessed you are.

Identify what you are thankful for, and be intentional about it. You will find it is an act of faith and excellent therapy. Cos Davis has a memorable line: "bitterness results from denying your blessings."

"Including thanksgiving each day", Davis says, "will make a great difference in your attitude and your life." Remember, being thankful is a personal choice. Gratitude is a powerful energy with medicinal and healing qualities. Include the daily personal motivator: How can I be productive today?[127]

In her book *Simple Abundance: A Daybook of Comfort and Joy*, Sarah Ban Breathnach urges the use of what she calls "a gratitude journal". She explains the use of this simple tool with four steps:

> "... each night before I go to bed, I write down five things I can be grateful about that day."

> "Some days my list will be filled with amazing things, most days simple joys."

"Other days – rough ones – I might think I don't have five things to be grateful for."

"Real life isn't always going to be perfect or go our way."[128]

I believe she is on to something. For as she acknowledges: "Real life isn't always going to be perfect or go our way, but the recurring acknowledgement of what is working in our lives can help us not only survive but surmount our difficulties." We often focus so heavily on our loss and grief – what isn't going right – we can't see the joys that remain a part of our lives. I have found gratitude to be both a beneficial and a reliable tool in my coping arsenal, and I highly recommend its use.

5. Embrace life as a growth adventure

The death of your loved one does not define your life unless you allow it to do so. The death of my parents was a life defining circumstance for me, yet I did not allow their deaths to define my life. Their deaths left a hole in my life but their deaths did not take away from me the joy of living forward in my life or the joy of remembering their lives.

Life and grief have one thing in common: Each is a brave adventure leading us into personal growth. We venture into what Dr. Doug Dortch, Pastor of the Mtn. Brook Baptist Church in Birmingham, Alabama, calls, "the good future God has for us". We ought to be as committed to growing in our grief as we are to living our lives. Turning our grief into a growth adventure avoids the "waddle-waddle" temptation.

Five "Am I's?" for Every Griever

Use these five "Am I's?" as a "positioning exercise". The answers chart our progress. Are we stuck in our grief or are we beginning a grief adventure that leads to joy?

"Am I" growing bitter or better?
"Am I" dying to life while I'm still living?
"Am I" stuck in my grief or living forward in my life?
"Am I" allowing a great loss to rob me of a greater life?
"Am I" living more for what I have found rather than dwelling on what I have lost?

God has given each of us the gift of choice. We may choose as one person said, "to waddle in my grief." Or we may choose to let go and move forward, acknowledge our loss and give ourselves time to grieve. We may consider how blessed we are and embrace the adventure we have before us. But we must choose the adventure!

"Grief is as much about finding as it is about losing..."

"Grief is as much about finding as it is about losing," writes pastoral counselor Bob Deits. "It is not an illness," says Deits, "but a process of recovering your balance after life has dealt you a major blow." Working your way through the considerable challenges of grief and recovery will require a discipline – there is no other word – that can add a positive dimension to your life experience – and to your grief. You can emerge on the other side of your grief, as Deits says, "considerably stronger and more compassionate" than you were in your life prior to your growing experience with grief.[129]

Yes, grief is an adventure – "as much about finding as it is about losing." Talking with someone who has moved forward in their grief and lived through their grief is "like talking to an adventurer," as Deits expressed it. Those who have moved through their grief "talk more about what they have found than what they have lost."[130]

Prayer and the Adventure of Personal Growth

Honest to goodness prayer goes with grief's territory and is actually a stimulant to personal growth. Our grasp of a blueprint for personal growth often emerges from our prayer life. Our first glimpse of "what could be" often flashes before our soul's radar screen as a result of quiet prayer and reflection.

Consider your own grief prayer life. First of all, do you actually have an active prayer life? Or is it just something you nod about affirmatively and go your merry way in total reliance upon your own spiritual strength and intelligence? Make your prayer personal, positive, and intentional. Pray what you feel. Pray about what is best for you. Here's an example for starters:

> God, our Father,
> Help me be open to your purpose in my life.
> I believe my grief is an adventure with purpose.
> Help me grow in this adventure of grief.
> Help me make good decisions as I become
> responsible for my own grief progress.
> May I be unafraid to ask for help when I need it.

THE GRIEF LETTER

Help me resist the temptation to rush through
my grief to reach the false objective of closure.
Help me move forward with a sense of peace.
In your Holy Name I pray, Amen.

The Ultimate Grief Prayer

If prayer is a challenge for you, then pray the Ultimate Grief Prayer:

"God help me. Amen." (You don't even have to say "amen" for it to be effective.)

The Chapter "Take- Away"

Perhaps the biggest temptation in our grief experience is the thoroughly human tendency to "waddle" in our grief, to slip and slide this way and that, to grieve without any real purpose other than to feel sorry for ourselves. The "waddle" opposite is a clear, focused sense of purpose---in grief and in life!

Now…we move toward the more serious grief work of personal growth. What lies ahead may not always be pretty, but it can be meaningful. And it can lead to personal growth in the days ahead.

Grief isn't supposed to be a day in the park---it's grief, after all. And it's work, for sure. No one ever called it "grief play"! Yet this is the feature we must come to recognize and appreciate, the adventure of grief leads to personal growth if---and it's a big "IF"---after a grief appropriate period of time we by-pass the "waddle-waddle" option and choose the grief adventure!

Your grief adventure partner---former "waddler"---and "growing" friend,

Fran Buhler

A Grief PS: Ask yourself:

1. Am I grieving forward? And growing? Or waddling? Is the experience stretching me in the right places? In my acceptance of death and loss, in my personal growth, in my relations with others, am I grieving forward, and growing?

2. Describe (for yourself) your grief adventure into personal growth in a

paragraph or two, a page if necessary. Write it. Ponder it. Remember it. Come back to it in six months. Then make sure you move on.

3. Ask yourself: As I grow, what am I finding? What am I losing? Do I consider it a positive trade-off?

CHAPTER 18

THE SOUL SIDE OF GRIEF: THE ADVENTURE OF GRIEF FINDS JOY AGAIN!

Dear Grief Adventure Partner,

If you push me to the wall to learn what I believe about grief, it is captured in this chapter title and subtitle. The latter, by the way, is also our TGL subtitle. **The truth of this chapter title and subtitle overcomes even the strongest octopus!**

Bob Diets, one of the best grief guides of our time, in the third edition of his Personal Guide: Life After Loss, provides considerable evidence for our Chapter 18 subtitle: "The Adventure of Grief Finds Joy Again!" Examine the five bullet quotes below from Deit's book. As you read each bullet, describing "life after loss", what do you discover?

- "Their lives reflect the events of the past, but are focused on the future. Death and loss do not dominate their thoughts."
- "They have a sense of joy that is more solid than most people's because they know there is nothing life can deal that they can't handle."
- "They are compassionate people."
- "They have more patience than most folks."
- "They have a reverence for life and a deep appreciation for human relationships."[131]

When you consider the evidence, isn't it obvious? They know joy again!

Why This Matters

Knowing joy again isn't a matter of personal determination, family connections or lucky circumstance. Knowing joy again comes when we reorient our soul focus from a total obsession with what we have lost and give open consideration to the life that is opening to us and the future possibilities before us. Knowing joy again is a gift from the Most High God as the grieving heart opens to the sunshine of God's grace and welcomes God's gift of personal peace and joy.

Verses for the Valley: "Those who sow in tears shall reap with joy." (Psalm 126:5).

Isaiah speaks of the "ransomed of the Lord", the redeemed, those who have been delivered by God's grace, who "find gladness and joy, and sorrow and sighing will flee away." (Isaiah 35:10).

Jesus himself sounded the same note: "You will be sorrowful, but your sorrow will be turned to joy." (John 16:20b).

God's grace carries us in our grief until that time when, in His strength, we choose to live forward again with energy and purpose…"so that our joy may be made complete." (1 John 1:4).

The Adventure of Grief Leads to "Soul Focus"

"No life experience is more common than losing someone dear to you", writes Bob Deits. His guidelines for the adventure of grief-work, so simple and to the point, are powerful, practical, and dependable.

Dr. Diet's four guidelines "will help you get started and keep you going when you grow weary of the task." I've quoted Diet's guidelines below followed by my commentary in parenthesis. I believe Diet's four guidelines constitute what I call "soul focus", adding purpose, responsibility, intention and patience to the grief experience.

- "Believe that your grief has a purpose and a destination." (The adventure must start somewhere and move toward an objective. Grieve with purpose.)
- "Be responsible for your own grief process." (You have to "start your engine" to experience the grief adventure. You cannot sit back and wait for it. You are responsible for your progress.)
- "Don't be afraid to ask for help." (Benefit from the adventure of others. Be intentional about it.)
- "Don't rush it." (Adventure deserves time and requires patience. Relish it.)[132]

Why Call Grief "an adventure"?

Grief is an adventure because our grief is a first time experience. Every grief is different, though similar. When grief comes again, even though we've been through it before, it's different the next time.

So, whatever the death situation may be, we've never been here before. We're not sure what comes next. We're not sure where we're going. We have mixed impressions, maybe even mixed information, about what's ahead. We may think we know what life will be like in six months, a year, five years. But we don't. And if we are honest with ourselves, we know we don't.

The adventure of grief is a matter of personal faith and divine providence. Our grief involves life choices: "What do I believe about death…life…and the future?" "Can the adventure of grief lead to personal growth?" "Can the grief adventurer find joy again?"

Of course, this may be hard to believe or accept until we experience it ourselves. And that is why I wrote hundreds of individual "grief letters", year after year, for 21 years; and why I write *The Grief Letter*.

The Adventure of Healthy Grief

The question I often hear is this: "Is there a healthy way to deal with death in our lives?"

Yes, I say. The healthy way is to deal with it honestly, openly, the way it feels to you. Grief is very personal and every person's experience will not be the same. And healthy grief is always an adventure.

As we navigate our own grief adventure, we need to accept the reality of death. We must face the truth or remain stuck where we are. We must deal with our initial personal emotions about the death and navigate our way through the long spiral of grief emotions to follow.

For people of faith, we draw solace from the comfort of knowing our loved one has gone to be with God. Our soul focus is to trust the One who gives Life and the One who receives us in Death. We begin the process of adjusting to life without the one who has died. The adjustment will likely be slow and hard, perhaps bitter-sweet. There may be other lingering issues with which we must cope. Yet in time this grief path leads to joy.

Grief can be Good: A 50-year Perspective

It's been half a century since Granger E. Westberg published his 64-page booklet Good Grief. Yet his offerings are as strong and relevant now as then. Westberg held a joint professorship in medicine and religion at the University of Chicago and a professorship in preventative medicine at the

University of Illinois' College of Medicine. Dr. Westberg knew how to write brief and deep.

In the preface of his grief classic, Westberg asks, "What can be the result of good grieving?" Fifty years later, I cannot improve upon his observations:

1. "We come out of our grief experience at a slightly higher level of maturity than before."

2. "We come out of our grief as deeper persons, because we have been down in the depths of despair and know what it is like."

3. "We come out of it stronger, for we have had to learn how to use our spiritual muscles to climb the rugged mountain trails."

4. "We come out of it better able to help others. We have walked through the valley of the shadow of grief. We can understand."[133]

Finding Joy Again

Dr. John F. Baggett is a United Methodist pastor and mental health professional. In his book, *Finding the Good in Grief: Rediscover Joy After a Life-Changing Loss*, Dr. Baggett addresses from a Christian perspective the grief expectation of knowing joy again. Having served parishes in Kentucky, Tennessee, and Chicago, he has the ministry mileage to tackle such a challenge. Dr. Baggett is a graduate of Vanderbilt Divinity School, with a PhD from the University of North Carolina.[134]

Joy Will Return

Note Baggett's following words:

> "When we are in the midst of our journeys of grief, we may feel we will never know joy again. Yet many who have walked before us through the valley of sorrow testify to the reality that joy will return if we allow it to. If we have eyes to see, there are happy moments in each day and times of joy in each season of life."[135]

The Joy We Possess

Consider the truth of Baggett's view below:

> "But for people of faith, joy is much more than this. The apostle Paul

wrote of a boundless joy in the midst of his troubles. Joy is a feeling we possess in our hearts at all times, even when we are having the most difficult of days. It does not depend on the successful pursuit of pleasure or material things. It is not conditioned upon whether life is going the way we wish it would."[136]

A Durable Joy

Note the following Baggett quote is backed with the assurance of divine promise.

"The joy of our faith is a durable joy. It dwells within us at all times because God's love dwells within us. It is a taste of that perfect joy we will know in the life to come. Death never can defeat us. Suffering and sorrow will end. And nothing will separate us from the love of God."[137]

A Welcomed Reader Mix

I realize readers may come to this book from other faith traditions. My Christian focus may be a challenge for you. I sincerely hope you will not turn away. My primary motivation is to help you in your grief, not to pressure you or try to "convert" you. If you come to this chapter in grief, needing help, I suggest you look to the resources of your faith tradition. Seek out your pastor, priest, rabbi, or imam and discuss openly the grief challenges you are experiencing. I pray you will take the simple steps below.

"The Soul Side of Grief---Let God Lead You"

When death and grief befall us, the experience affects us differently. For some of us, it's only natural to become super active and busy, busy, while others may become lethargic or practically comatose." Early in our grief, it pays to heed our body for physical signals. If we feel like crying, we should cry. If we feel like sleeping, we should sleep.

For the longer-term, however, our souls signal needs and questions that physical rest and grief's tears cannot address. It's what I call the soul side of grief.

1. Let God lead you.

2. Allow your faith to help you. If you have not experienced faith, take your first step of faith, now. Pray the most powerful prayer you can pray: "God

help me!"

3. Make your relationship with God a permanent partnership.

4. Allow the Most High to comfort you as you mourn.

For your best grieving, you need a clear head, a thankful heart, a purposeful intention, and soul-deep determination. Warning: Over-consumption of medications, alcohol or drugs negates your grieving purpose, period. Opioids will never be the answer for our grief. You will never drug yourself to life. Reject the drug abuse option to overcome grief. Grieve and grow…with a clear head.

Expect the Ten-Day Blitz

The process of knowing joy again begins where all grief begins. The first days after the death, as news of the death spreads, it goes viral. The immediate blitz bombardment – all with good intentions – lasts three to five days. The avalanche of phone calls, texts, emails, Facebook posts, visits, food, flowers, runs a good ten days. Faces and circumstances change, but the grief schedule is often similar for everyone.

"Suddenly Alone!"

In her book *Suddenly Alone*, Dolores Dahl writes about the "grief opportunity" typically available if we "care enough" to think and act strategically – and thoughtfully. Listen as Dahl describes to her loved one the grief experience of being "suddenly alone".

"… there was so much activity following your death that I had no time to be lonely, no time to digest the fact you were gone. I was overwhelmed with the support and the love that filled my home during those first few days of disbelief and confusion. But, as is always the case, everyone returned to their own homes, their own lives, shortly following the memorial service… and I was alone."[138]

The Chapter "Take-Away"

Soul-deep sorrow needs the soul side of grief, the adventure of grief. There is no better path. What lies ahead may not always be pretty, but it can be meaningful. In a matter of time, with a more consistent soul focus, your grief will transition to a more joyful daily outlook.

THE GRIEF LETTER

"Suddenly alone" is a grief adventure opportunity! Approach it as an adventure. A venturesome spirit is a helpful approach to life and a joyful heart is good medicine.

Your grief adventure partner and soulful friend,

Fran Buhler

A Grief PS: Remember to use the Ultimate Grief Prayer from Chapter 17: "God help me!" plus the gentle advice of Chapter 18: "Let God lead you."

1. Give three reasons why you are thankful for the soul focus and the gift of the grief adventure you have experienced.

2. Name two joys you have experienced since praying the Ultimate Grief Prayer in Chapter 17, or following the advice of Chapter 18.

3. Based on your personal grief experience, what thoughtful advice would you give someone who is still grieving and in pain, and needs to discover and experience joy?

CHAPTER 19

THE PERSONAL BENEFIT OF GRIEF-FAITH; "A COMFORT…ONLY FROM GOD"

Dear Partner in Grief-Faith,

So much has been written about faith, is it possible to add anything that hasn't been expressed?

I think so, especially where grief is concerned. **Our faith is still faith even when we are grieving.** That's why I call it "grief-faith". When facing grief in our own lives, as well as helping others in their grief, we need to experience the personal benefit of faith, what we might call "faith-ability."

Why This Matters

We often think of faith as a glowing torch, a flame so strong nothing can snuff it out. As if the strength of our faith is the key---and it's up to us. Everything depends upon our strength!

Yet, in reality, we come to our own faith and discover it often is no more than a flickering flame, glimmering perhaps, but hardly glowing. It is hard to believe that even a flickering faith will carry us as long as it keeps on flickering. Why? Our faith is not in the flame nor in ourselves but in the Holy One who created the flame and carries us through each day. A flickering grief-faith receives life-giving oil from the Holy One to fuel the lamp of hope. Faith matters!

How Faith Works

It is an old story. But faith has been around much longer than the story!

Decades ago, the need for a suspension bridge across the Niagara River (as in Niagara Falls) presented a huge construction challenge. How do you get a heavy iron cable, weighing tons, to span the river, a cable strong enough to support the loaded trains crossing the river? How do you suppose the bridge builders addressed the problem?

First, they flew a kite---yes, a kite---with only a string attached, from one side of the river to the other side. The string had a cord attached. The cord had a rope attached. The rope had a stronger, heavy duty rope attached. The heavy duty rope had a small cable attached. The small cable was strong enough to sustain the final iron cable needed to support the bridge and all the future trains that would be crossing the river one train at a time.

This huge bridge needed for train transport of heavy cargo could never have been built but for that little kite-string!

Isn't that the way faith works? Doesn't faith start out as a "kite-string" faith long before it becomes an "iron cable" faith? Our "faith-ability" grows stronger as we work our way, excuse me, as we trust our way through each day of grieving.

Faith necessary to bridge life's small, seemingly insignificant challenges, increases strength as we use our faith over time, until faith the size of a mustard seed grows into a faith strong enough to bridge the grief chasms of our lives, bringing us eventually across death's divides. Sometimes our faith may be like an iron cable. And sometimes our faith may be no more than a kite-string. But the Holy One in whom we place our faith makes the difference. Faith in the Most High God is the key to faith-ability!

"Faith...and the rivers of our grief"

The personal benefit of faith is never more significant, never more critical, than when it spans the rivers of our grief. Our faith is the sure trust of the heart, going far beyond mere intellectual belief. In the darkness of grief, sometimes faith is all we have to hold on to. Faith in the Holy One, faith and trust in the One who defeated death, faith in Jesus, the one who said to his colleagues and disciples in Gethsemane, "My soul is deeply grieved, to the point of death..."(Matthew 26:38)

Frankly, I am drawn to a Savior who, in the Incarnation into human flesh, has experienced the depth of human death and grief. God the Father knows what death feels like because He has experienced the death of His Son in human flesh. Maybe we sell God short in the death and grief department. After all, He has been there!

The personal benefit of faith manifests itself in the long term healing process that accompanies our grief journey.

"Faith...and the Healing Process"

In *The Mourning Handbook*, Helen Fitzgerald speaks to the healing process that leads toward restoration.

- "While I can't tell you when you will recover from grief, I can assure you that people do recover.

- "And while some sadness will always be there, the tears and grief will become more manageable as you integrate them into your life and live with them.

- "I do know that the intense pain of early grief goes away after a while, leaving an ache that will also subside.

- "I know countless people who have had to endure shocking, devastating losses and yet have gone on to live happy and productive lives."[139]

Grief Help in "a whirling sea of grief."

Following the memorial service for her husband, the grieving wife described her life as "a whirling sea of grief." Then she added, "and would you believe all two of my friends wanted to talk about was the weather!"

Do our conversations typically circumvent matters of grief and faith. Even when someone dies and we speak to the family, we hardly ever talk about grief and faith! We talk about the weather. We talk about the past, the future, what we've been doing, where we're going, what's happening at the office, what's going on in our community.

We talk about everything before we get around to saying the lamest phrase human kind ever delivered: "Now, if there is any-thing-at-all-you-need, don't-hesitate-to-call". With that "one-size-fits-all" comment, too many of us feel we have done our duty. Because they never call, we are convinced we met their every need. But haven't we left the grieving person drowning in a whirling sea of grief?

Have we given a thoughtful, meaningful condolence? Not really. Have we extended a helping hand? Hardly.

Fortunately, it is neither my nature nor my habit to be so blunt, but after a life-time in churches and funeral homes, in "visitations" and at "gravesides", it is time to speak up. **Those who grieve deserve better.** We who wish to comfort, need to get our act together. When we comfort those who mourn, we should be Christ-like and helpful – genuinely helpful.

THE GRIEF LETTER

Grief help is about the one grieving, the one whose heart is broken, whose soul throbs with a never-ceasing ache; it is not about the "grief helper". In the living of our faith, in the practice of our faith, we have a responsibility to prepare ourselves, to coach ourselves, in effective ways to comfort those who mourn. Part 4 will offer such help.

One thing is certain. We do not help others in their grief when we continue to peddle the grief clichés of the past. If we care, we owe it to the God we say we follow and serve, to sensitize ourselves, to prepare ourselves, to help others on their grief journey.

Positive Suggestions

I credit my wife, Nancy, for my favorite "condolence of choice". Hundreds of times I have borrowed her classic condolence, a simple but strong, heartfelt expression: "We hurt with you ".

Many words will do their "comforting" work if we really mean them, such as: "I am very sorry". The griever can tell if we speak from the heart or if we're just spewing words.

Silence Speaks. When I enter into a situation where the grief is heightened by the circumstances of death, sometimes I feel words actually get in the way. A number of death examples come to mind: When a spouse, family member, or good friend has been killed or died in an accident; a child dies in child-birth; a loved one dies after surgery, or a long, multi-year decline leading up to death; a military representative came to the front door to deliver the news.

For the one grieving, a time of pronounced "alone-ness", such as funeral-home silence, at-home-by-yourself silence, or in-the-middle-of-a-crowd silence, can be heavy and overwhelming. Introduce a human presence into those silence examples, and it speaks a comforting language to all who grieve, saying: "I'm here. I care."

Presence Speaks. To one torn apart by grief, presence speaks---often louder---with more meaning---than words. If the intent of our heart is right, and we add a bit of intentional thoughtfulness, then our words and actions will probably be appropriate and comforting.

Our presence always makes our words more powerful. Grief follows death as night follows day. Grief also follows love and care. We do not grieve for one we do not love, one we do not know or one for whom we do not care.

Grief is a relational barometer, a measure of what another life meant to our lives. When grieving another life, recall what the person meant to you and let those memories guide your grief. An informed grief becomes a healing grief.

When Grief Adds Sorrow to Our Pain

We find ourselves thinking no one ever grieved like we grieve. Yet the bible narrative is loaded with examples of grief and sorrow we have never read or we read right through without a pain pause or a grief pause.

One we easily overlook is Nehemiah 1: "The words of Nehemiah the son of Hacaliah..." in verse one, sets up Nehemiah's personal discovery from one of his brothers. When Nehemiah hears about the suffering, survival status of Jerusalem, he "sat down and wept and mourned for days..."

In the New Testament, we find examples of unexpected, overlooked, grief. In Luke 24, after Jesus' resurrection, on the road to Emmaus, Jesus encounters two travelers who do not recognize him. When Jesus opens a conversation with them, Luke's narrative announces: "And they stood still, looking sad." The exchange that follows reveals they were grieving Jesus' death.

Isaiah wrote about "the day when the Lord gives you rest from your pain" (Isaiah 14:3). I believe that promise. In my experience, that day has actually come for me and for other "believers" I have known. I also believe the Isaiah promise connects with another promise in the Book of the Revelation, verse 21:4c, where we read: "...there shall no longer be any mourning, or crying, or pain." God's Grief Help is long term. We don't have to worry about running out of Grace.

God's Presence in Our Grief

Speaking from graveside experience with hundreds of hurting grievers, God's Presence in our grief, though beyond our comprehension, is not a mystery. We actually sense it. We receive Help from it. We endure and carry on day to day because of it.

God's Presence is powerful and always comforting. God's Presence is both Gift and Challenge---a gift of divine comfort in our time of need and a challenge to believe, to live by faith, at all times---even in the presence of death.

THE GRIEF LETTER

Grief clogs our emotions and releases our tears because...grief hurts. Grief hopes. Grief helps. And grief heals. When grief adds sorrow to our grief pain, grief faith adds God's Presence and Comfort to our lives.

A Strategy for "getting through"

I have discovered a strategy for getting through the ever-so-daily grief and pain. Here's why and how it works.

Where grief is concerned, we are impotent. We can't avoid grief, can't stop it, can't prevent it, can't tough it out. We can't "choose" not to grieve; can't "decide" we prefer not to grieve. For grief will override most choices or decisions we may attempt. But we can choose to embrace our grief. Accept our grief. Add grief to our lives. Deal with our grief and the grief of others as best we can. We are not helpless.

We may also choose to embrace through our faith the ultimate source of help. Again, it's our choice. We have the opportunity to make the same choice the psalmist made, the choice made by multitudes of the Jewish faithful who made their regular faith journey to Jerusalem to claim God's Promise as recorded in Psalm 121:1-8.

Psalm 121 is "a song of ascents", that series of psalms from Psalm 120-134, also called "Pilgrim Psalms", sung over the centuries as the Jewish faithful made their journeys of ascent to Jerusalem for the observance of annual religious feasts and festivals. Some interpreters believe "the hills" may have been the "high places" where the baals, the local fertility gods, were worshiped. In its history and in its truth, Psalm 121 is a soaring prayer of faith, a powerful reminder of the Presence of One we may claim in our grief.

"My Help Comes From the Lord"

"I will lift up my eyes to the hills—
   where does my help come from?
My help comes from the Lord,
   the Maker of heaven and earth.
"He will not let your foot slip—
   he who watches over you will not slumber;
indeed, he who watches over Israel
   will neither slumber nor sleep.
"The Lord watches over you—
   the Lord is your shade at your right hand;

The sun will not harm you by day,
>   nor the moon by night.
"The Lord will keep you from all harm—
>   He will watch over your life;
The Lord will watch over your coming and going
>   both now and forevermore." (Psalm 121 NIV)

"View the Present Through the Promise"

Using the words of Thomas H Troeger, view the present death of your loved one and your experience of that death through the promise of the Holy One, as follows:

> "View the present through the promise, Christ will come again.
> Trust despite the deepening darkness, Christ will come again.
> Lift the world above its grieving through your watching and believing
> in the hope past hope's conceiving: Christ will come again.
>
> "Probe the present with the promise, Christ will come again.
> Let your daily actions witness, Christ will come again.
> Let your loving and your giving and your justice and forgiving
> be a sign to all the living: Christ will come again.
>
> "Match the present to the promise, Christ will come again.
> Make this hope your guiding premise, Christ will come again.
> Pattern all your calculating and the world you are creating
> to the advent you are waiting: Christ will come again."[140]

The personal benefit of grief-faith does not flow from the strength of our faith but from the One in whom we place our faith.

Verses for the Valley: "Do not grieve as those who have no hope. For if we believe that Jesus died and rose again, even so God will bring with Him those who have fallen asleep in Jesus. Therefore, comfort one another with these words." (1 Thessalonians 4:13c, 14, and 18).

"A Comfort that Comes only from God…"

By stretching our faith and embracing our grief, accepting our grief along with the soul-deep pain and the ever-so-present numbness that marks our grief, we adopt the strategy of simple faith and strong trust. By lifting our attention to the high places of God's Help, we assure we will be prepared, supported and comforted on our grief journey, wherever it may lead.

THE GRIEF LETTER

With help from the Holy One, get through your moment of grief and pain. Get through this hour. With God's help, get through one day, then the next day. Get through a week, a month, a year. Get through "right now". Get through today. And we are on our way. God is our Keeper, our Comforter. As Revelation 21:4 proclaims: "He will wipe every tear from our eyes."

The Chapter "Take-Away"

Then one day, we look around, check our personal grief meter, and realize we have been the recipients of a Grace even stronger than our Grief. Like a distant star in the darkness of night, the thought registers in our soul---I am "getting through" my grief and pain.

My pain is not totally gone. But God is with me on this grief journey. And I am getting through it.

And you are!

Your grief-faith partner and friend in the Faith,

Fran Buhler

A Grief PS: Think about the personal benefit of grief-faith...

1. Remind yourself of the benefits of your faith in your life. Can you list some of them?

2. If you are not a faith follower of the Most High God, would you like to begin your faith journey?

3. Start your faith journey right now. Pray: "God help me. I trust in you." And mean it with all your heart.

CHAPTER 20

THE ADVENTURE OF FAITH: THE PROMISE OF A PRESENCE

Dear Partner in Faith and Grief,

As you grieve, I know you are hurting. **Could you think about your grief as an expression of your faith**, as another life-based example of how the Holy One actually follows through and "comforts" all who mourn?

Every person's life is like a Smart Phone photo gallery, telling a story of adventure. Or you could liken it to a scrapbook. The question is: Will our Smart Phone photo album or our life "scrapbook" tell our faith adventure?

- Our high moments of joy as well as our low times of protracted grief.
- The joys of love and family adventure, along with the radical pain of giving up special ones we love while offering tribute for the joy they brought to our lives,
- The stories of times past we don't want to forget, and the present and future faith adventures we don't want to miss.

Why This Matters

In the words of Rebecca Turner and Paul Simpson Duke, "When sorrow floods the troubled heart," how do we respond? What do we do when we no longer have music from the life of our loved one? A child's laughter, a parent's hug, the one gone from our lives? Where do we turn for hope and help? To whom do we look for deliverance?

Resurrection Faith

In the adventure of faith, we cultivate a steadfast spirit. We develop tenacity, a spiritually tough faith that "keeps on keeping on" throughout our lives. We live with a Resurrection Faith, as Stephen Starke says, "uneclipsed by doubt and dread". Such a faith lives the life of obedience to God by giving thanks for His deliverance and facing the future, encouraged and strengthened by His Grace.

THE GRIEF LETTER

In the words of "Scatter the Darkness", by Stephen P. Starke, we find an Eastertide encouragement in our grief for all our faith adventure days:

> "Scatter the darkness, break the gloom:
> sun, reveal an empty tomb
> shining with joy for all our tomorrows,
> hope and peace for all tomorrows,
> life uneclipsed by doubt and dread:
> Christ has risen from the dead!"[141]

Grief and Grace

The Grace of God pierces the shroud of grief around us---letting us know we do not grieve alone. "Grace shows up," Karen Hering says, "in the experiences of loss and grief." In my own grief, I have certainly experienced this truth. I remember Paul Tillich's sermon, "The Shaking of the Foundations," in which he asserted:

> "Grace strikes us when we are in great pain and restlessness.
> It strikes us when we walk through the dark valley..."[142]

Playwright Eugene O'Neill said all of us are broken and each one of us "lives by mending. The grace of God is glue," O'Neill said. In my experience, and the experience of grieving individuals I have known, I like to state it this way: God's grace is stronger than all our sin---and greater than all our grief! [143]

The Adventure of Faith and the Music of God's Comfort

When we grieve, we need a different music, the music of faith, the music of God's comfort. We need assurance and peace from the Most High God. God never guarantees to shield us from trouble and tribulation but He does promise to deliver us, to bring us through our dark days to days of sunshine again.

In 1989, Rebecca Turner and Paul Simpson Duke left us their joint forever blessing in "When Sorrow Floods the Troubled Heart", from the 2010 *Celebrating Grace* Hymnal:

> "When sorrow floods the troubled heart
> and clouds the mind with fears,
> affliction presses from the soul
> the bitter flow of tears.

God's weeping children raise the prayer:
'Almighty God, how long
till tears shall cease and silence break
and grief be turned to song?'"[144]

A splendid example of hope, prayer, patient endurance and the process of transformative grief!

In the gross darkness of our world, with the demons of darkness pulling at our very lives, we live a faith that is human and therefore flawed, a faith focused on a sovereign God. There will be times when we slip and fall and fall again, but if we hold fiercely to our faith, because of the Lord God in Christ we follow, we shall in Him overcome the world. In the course of what Meghan O'Rourke calls, "the long goodbye," her metaphor for death and the separation that follows, we have the comfort of Scripture: "In the world, you have tribulation", Jesus said, "but take heart for I have overcome the world." (John 16:33)[145]

Even in times of death and disaster, living in the iron grip of grief, we may hold on to this confident hope. In the life of faith, the Presence remains with us. In the deep darkness of life, in our pain, in our faith, even in our doubt, regardless of how joyful or difficult the journey, whether in dreams achieved or dashed in disappointment, the Most High God always holds a remembrance of each of us when we are at our best – even though he knows fully our very worst. Here---in our particular grief circumstance---the focus now changes.

A Radical Change in Focus

The story is no longer about your loved one, remembered in my "grief letter". The story now becomes the Most High God he or she sought to obey and the Holy Savior he or she – and we – trust with our lives.

In the midst of physical pain and medical challenge – or even accidental and tragic circumstances – we cannot fake our faith. The "words", the "letters" of our lives, during the good times and during trials and tribulation, speak of a deep and abiding faith that marks our journey – or to use Jesus' analogy – faith the size of a grain of mustard seed, in fact, just a speck of faith.

The Grief Letter always reflected the dual "touch" each of us needs – the "human" touch and the "Divine" Presence. Because of the Presence of the Most High, we enjoy the cup of redemption, a cup of salvation we sip and savor for all eternity.

In the adventure of faith, we cultivate a steadfast spirit. We develop tenacity, a spiritually tough faith that keeps on keeping on until the very end of our days. Yet in our moments of greatest spiritual strength, we are unable to go it alone. We need something beyond our own strength, our own determination, beyond our ability as humans on planet earth.

When my mother died, and when my father died, people said so many complementary and wonderful things about them. And I certainly appreciated each person's intent. Yet to be honest, though personally treasured and appreciated, none of those remarks "comforted" me. They made me feel proud of my parents, but they did not comfort me. In my soul-deep grief, I needed a comfort stronger than the experience, the expressions, or the tribute of other people.

The Promise of a Presence

I found what I needed in the second book of the Bible. I found a promise from the Holy One, a Presence promised in Exodus 33:14: "My Presence shall go with you", a Promise to Israel in the Exodus, echoed throughout the subsequent pages of the bible.

Could this include you, and me? Can we embrace this Promise and believe it includes us?

The same God, the same Divine Force, who guided Israel, stands ready to guide and comfort each of us through our soul-deep grief and beyond! I found the Promise and the Presence I needed in God's Exodus Promise, a Promise for all the exodus journeys and experiences of life.

I also found the Promise in Jesus' words in John 14:1-3: "Let not your heart be troubled; you believe in God, believe also in me.

"In my Father's house are many dwelling places; if it were not so, I would have told you, for I go to prepare a place for you.

"And if I go to prepare a place for you, I will come again, and receive you to myself; that where I am, there you may be also."

I also found the soul-comfort and deliverance I needed in Jesus' simple, straight forward words: "Blessed are those who mourn, for they shall be comforted."

Verses for the Valley: "For He shall give His angels charge over you, to keep you in all your ways." (Psalm 91:11). "I am the resurrection and the life. He who believes in me, though he may die, he shall live." (John 11:25).

The life and death of a loved one causes each of us, as people of faith, to grieve our loss, but not to stop there. We can move forward, looking to the One who daily bears our burden, who makes it possible to experience the adventure of faith in the sunshine of His Grace.

"The Coming Joy"

Jesus did not avoid the subject of death, even when the issue at hand was his own death. In John 16, the disciples puzzle over the meaning of Jesus' mysterious sayings in verses 1 – 33. Go get your Bible. Read the text slowly, allowing it to sink in, as you open yourself to another part of the mystery. God is with us even in times of death and loss. His Presence brings Joy!

Jesus speaks bluntly though prophetically to his disciples:

- "… you are filled with grief." (v6) "… you will weep and mourn…" (v20)
- "You will grieve (v20) "… but your grief will turn to joy." (v20)
- "Now is your time of grief…" (v22)

Note Jesus' analogy in verse 21 – his grief-pain comparison to a mother giving birth in which the pain of birth brings joy, a human example of a God-Truth!

Don't miss Jesus' confident assertion in verse 33: "I have told you these things, so that in me you may have peace…" This "peace" is what our Jewish friends call God's "Shalom", the peace of God! God has always been in the "peace-giving" business.

May we, from every faith tradition across this earth, agree on one aspect of our faith? The Presence does not play favorites. To those who believe, God, the Holy One, gives Peace, and God's Peace brings joy in the heavy patches of grief we all experience!

Yes, the life-long challenge of how we handle grief speaks to what Isaiah called "the day of grief and desperate sorrow" that invades each of our lives at one time or another.

Personally, I want the photo albums and scrapbooks of my life to reflect my faith adventure. I want them to profile the Holy One who collects our grief tears, the God who does not remember our sin (Jeremiah 31:34) but Who "keeps track of all our sorrows" (Psalm 56:8).

The challenge is to follow the ancient Voice described by Isaiah. "Your ears will hear a word behind you," according to Isaiah 30:21, "This is the way, walk in it." I find this Voice of Isaiah 30 connects with those words of Yeshua, the one called, Jesus, who said: "I am the way, the truth and the life" (John 14:6).

The Chapter "Take-Away"

Why allow the octopus nature of grief to hold sway in our lives?

According to Psalm 56:8, God put the psalmist's tears in a wineskin, which is like saying: "He collects all our tears in a bottle." This is a "word" we may believe and trust, a word on which we can rely: God is, and always has been, in the tear-collection business. God's main agenda--- right up there with creation, forgiveness and redemption---includes a world-wide, "full service", "24/7" Grief Department. From the Most High God, His grief-grace is available now and for all time.

"Let 'the Pope' Speak"

What I have in this chapter called "the Promise of a Presence" has been echoed by noted faith leaders, past and present. On June 17, 2015, Pope Francis spoke to families mourning the loss of a loved one, calling the experience "one of the more painful events every person has to deal with."

"May we, with Christ-like tenderness and compassion," the Pope urged, "know how to be close and offer consolation to families suffering the loss of a loved one. Above all," the Pope stressed, "may we always be witnesses to the love which was revealed through His cross and resurrection, a love stronger than death." Indeed, the greatest promise and assurance of all time.[146]

Another Pope's Request

At this point in *The Grief Letter*, I am reminded of the day I visited Frank Pope at his "home" in a Tallahassee, Florida, assisted living facility. We reviewed some mental notes he had filed away about his last "wishes for his funeral". We enjoyed some laughs, as we always did, and I knew in the providence of the Most High God I would have only a few visits left with

PART 2 - CHAPTER 20

Frank before his journey home.

What had drawn me to Frank and Savannah's Country Buffet, a local lunch "hang out" in Tallahassee---where an interesting assortment of people share lunch in the midst of busy days---were his crazy "one-liners" about politics, the latest news about the Florida State Seminoles' baseball and football teams, or funny stories from his youth playing minor league baseball.

But this day, Frank was focused, smiling as always, but focused. I think he knew his time was short, when he gave me the best funeral and grief advice I've ever received. "Fran, let 'em out before the pews get hard."

For *The Grief Letter*, it's time to do that now.

Your grief partner and forever friend,

Fran Buhler

A Grief PS: Grief is something to think and pray about. "The Promise of a Presence" is worth reading the Book of Exodus...and the entire Bible.

1. Describe your faith adventure in words that are meaningful for you.

2. What has faith taught you? Make a list to keep for future reference when facing tough challenges.

3. Do you really believe you can "faith" your way through your grief and life's challenges?

This is a good time to take a break from TGL. Give yourself at least a few days, a week or maybe a month. When you feel like it, move on to Part 3.

PART 3

THE TEN COMMANDMENTS OF GRIEF

Part 3: The Ten Commandments of Grief

There comes a time in our grief when we begin to mull over different questions and aspects of our grief. When that time comes tends to vary with each of us. The questions that weighed upon us in the early weeks and months (and maybe even years) of our grieving, when emotions were sometimes overwhelming, begin to give way to other equally challenging questions that persist in gnawing at us until we give them attention.

After we've been able to "get through today" for a whole lot of "todays", we've handled "the body blows" of grief, and even come to "own our grief". After we spend time in the "'why?' wilderness", and just as we become regular users of the "anger bucket" and regular members of the "Pain Club", and some of us turn to a grief help "we never thought we would need", then comes the time when we begin to sense a strange nuance in our grief.

Questions we had never even thought of previously begin to swirl up from that deep reservoir of grief we call the "soul", bubbling to the surface of our thoughts and emotions. Followed by other related thoughts, until the thought begins to take off, grabbing more of our attention span. Yet always more questions and yearnings: "Is grief a sacred time?" "Is transformational grief possible?" Then the granddaddy of them all: "Is closure the best objective?

What This Means

We are grieving---no question about it. But now, it occurs to us, after days and months of wrestling with that tireless octopus, we are slowly moving through our grief. In fact, it is beginning to feel---when we don't fight it---like a strange sort of experience, an adventure.

In Part 2, we began to see what that means as we examined the dimensions of the grief adventure: How it leads to personal growth, finds joy again, carries a personal benefit and actually may become an adventure of faith!

Why This Matters

This matters because---just think about it---doesn't it mean we are moving through "the grief of grief" and are now beginning to wrestle with and explore and maybe even choose the adventure of grief as our own personal, life choice?

And that matters so much because it means for us grief will not become a dead end street, no pun intended. Our grief is gradually becoming a door to new life choices and experiences. Our grief is taking us beyond our potentially stagnating grief into a purposeful grief. In the process, we find our now purposeful grief moves us toward and focuses us on new personal growth.

In the fullness of time, through the power of the Most High God, grief begets growth. Is not this precisely the time when we should give serious attention to "The Ten Commandments of Grief"? Does it not also make good sense that attending to and observing "The Ten Commandments of Grief" should prosper us as we grieve?

Verses for the Valley: In Psalm 116, the thanksgiving psalm, giving thanks for deliverance from death, the psalmist cries out: "The chords of death encompassed me, and the terrors of Sheol (the place of the dead) came upon me; I found distress and sorrow, then I called upon the name of the Lord (verse 3)…"What shall I render to the Lord for all his benefits toward me? I shall lift up the cup of salvation, and call upon the name of the Lord"(verse 12).

So what may we expect to cover in Part 3?

Part 3 Chapter Previews

Chapter 21 offers a welcome discovery when we experience a death among family or friends. The best thing we can do involves faithful observance of "The Ten Commandments of Grief"."

Chapter 22 offers "12 Steps from Grief to Healing" for your personal grief benefit and progress.

Chapter 23, "The Grief Text and the Social Media Epitaph," recognizes we have entered an era in which an epitaph tribute to one's life is likely not to be chiseled in stone and placed in a cemetery, but shared on a Facebook post!

Chapter 24 offers four strategic steps to deal with family grief. Five redemptive family actions welcome God's help with family grief. The chapter includes an unusual forgiveness story for **both** the forgiver and the forgiven.

PART 3

Chapter 25 has a blunt announcement about the personal agony of "The 'Woe-is-me' Disease".

The chapter addresses the cure, how to escape the self-centered orbit. It reminds us the answer is not reliance upon our personal strength and steers us toward Bible texts offering encouragement, hope and grief-strength.

Chapter 26 recognizes confusion abounds when it comes to grief and faith, and addresses the straight-up question: "Are Grief and Faith Enemies or Friends?"

Chapter 27 addresses ten significant questions and answers about grief and guilt, including the strategic question: "Is there such a thing as 'guilt removal'?"

Chapter 28 addresses the question that eventually concerns most of us in our grief and offers 27 grief clues as a barometer for our progress. With the chapter finale, "How do I know I'm getting better?" we can do our own assessment of our personal progress.

After our exhausting wrestling sessions with the octopus, Part 3 will help us with some of those grinding grief concerns that don't go away quickly!

Your grief partner and "seeking to be obedient" friend,

Fran Buhler

CHAPTER 21

THE TEN COMMANDMENTS OF GRIEF

Why This Matters

Were you ever told, "Don't touch that!" and you touched it anyway?

Then...**don't read the Ten Commandments of Grief. They will change your approach to grief!** As you read, look for two commandments to which you need to start giving more attention.

If you're my age, you grew up on the "Thou shalts", as the Ten Commandments are listed in the Old Testament Book of Exodus, Chapter 20. But if you're my grandchildren's age, "Thou shalt" seems a little strange. So...take your choice.

1. **Thou shalt grieve. / Allow yourself to grieve.**

Some will ask, "Why?" thinking, "No one can force me to grieve. I'm in charge of my life. I don't need to grieve." They have yet to meet the octopus!

In my experience, the octopus makes sure we grieve whether we want to or not. The question is: "Will my grief be healthy?" Facing the reality of death is a healthy thing to do.

God designed us to grieve. We humans are wired to grieve.

Grief is a safety valve that keeps us from exploding in private or imploding in public. No grief, no gain.

Trust God and grieve. You'll be glad you did. You will be healthier, too.

2. **Thou shalt grieve honestly. / Be honest about your grief.**

Fake grief is grieving the way you think you are expected to grieve or grieving the way you've seen others grieve, so you adopt their model. All of us experience the grief expectations in our American culture. "Take 3 or 4 days off and then get back to work."

Grieve what you feel, not what others expect. Grieve your heart out. Grieve until it hurts… then grieve past the hurt.

Honest grief will lead to healing along the way. If you live a "no grief" life, your life is a lie. Live an authentic life and you are going to grieve. Grief goes with our human territory.

Trust God, be open to your feelings of grief – and grieve honestly.

3. Thou shalt grieve for as long as you need to grieve. / Don't put a time limit on your grief.

We live in a culture where grief has a prescribed time length. Whether stated or held silently, the attitude is prevalent. Brief grief does not exist – not even in America.

Grief is a long-term emotional and mental process. For some, grief may be a life-long process. Grief's intensity may vary, but it can last a long, long time. Grief takes time. And when we resist, grief grabs whatever time it needs.

The grief clock, the grief calendar, the grief experience can't be managed like our daily calendar: "Oh, well, I'll allow 30 minutes for my grief at 7pm today, and 40 minutes next Tuesday at 6am." What, pray tell, is going on at 10am and 3pm?

Don't try to shove grief aside, push it away, bury it "inside", deny it, defy it, or not try it. God created grief. If you reject your grief, you're rejecting God's first aid.

Trust God and grieve for as long as you need to grieve.

4. Thou shalt grieve in your own way. / Grieve your way, not someone else's.

Grief is ever so personal. Give yourself permission to grieve.

Grief is not "one size fits all" or "one style expresses all." Different people – from different cultures and backgrounds – grieve in different ways.

Express the grief you feel, the way you feel it, whenever you feel it, however you feel it. Authentic grief is do-it-yourself grief. Don't imitate others.

Someone else cannot do your grieving for you. You can't grieve by proxy. You can't spell grief without an "I" – and it should be a capital "I".

Trust God and grieve your way.

5. Thou shalt respect the grief of others. / Always respect the grief of others.

Don't expect or insist that everyone grieve the way you grieve.

Respect the grief of others, regardless of how they may express their grief.

Grief is sacred territory. Always enter the halls of human grief with respect for those who find themselves in the dark hole of grief. Don't be guilty of the thoughtless invasion of another's grief. Ask God to help you respect the grief of others.

6. Thou shalt embrace the grief process. / As you grieve, embrace the grief process---don't hold back.

The grief experience is not a grief "point", but a grief process, a process we experience over time, not a series of steps we quickly take in 1, 2, 3, 4 fashion. Grief comes and goes. And we can't always control grief's coming or its going.

Grief has its triggers – a thought, an experience, something we see, hear, or read. Something someone says, a song, a scene, a task. Whatever it may be, it will trigger giant economy-size grief in a heartbeat.

Grief's currency is time – your time, your life time. Grief is a life-long process.

Some individuals fight grief. I say wrap your arms around your grief – embrace the grief process, and give thanks for your grief.

7. Thou shalt trust the grief process. / To get through today, you really need to trust the grief process.

"How can I trust a process?" is a frequently asked question. The answer is: We trust "the grief process" the same way we trust any other process. Take the "plant growth" process or the "cold weather process" for example. For grass or plants in our yard, we till the soil, plant, fertilize, and water – then trust the plant to grow. When we have a cold weather forecast, we protect sensitive plants by covering them or bringing them inside. In all aspects of our lives, we encounter times when we "trust the process." It's the same with our grief.

Yet the grief process does not happen overnight.

"What I hate about the grief process," she said, "is the pain." Her remarks came four years after her husband's death. She didn't sugarcoat the painful days she experienced along the way. But her story does not end amid the pain. Two years later, the same person said, "In a strange sort of way, it's the pain that heals."

We hurt because we loved, because we loved deeply. Eventually, love works its way into and through the grief process, into the pain, into the soul-deep grief, and the emotional wounds begin to heal. The pain begins ever so slowly to subside. Because, you see, the pain brings healing. The pain brings peace.

Grief can be scary, unsettling, confusing. But grief is not our enemy. Remind yourself: Grief is not my enemy. Grief is from God and emerges from my very human feelings. As I trust the grief process, I may walk a long, hard road, but I walk in the direction of recovery. Even though I may move through an up and down, zig-zag pattern of emotions and hurt, I live life on the upswing and I grow in a healing direction.

In her title Living through Mourning, Harriet Sarnoff Schiff captures the right slant on life's unavoidable mourning process:"

- "Without the process of mourning there can be no recovery."
- "Any surgical patient will attest to the fact that before he was healed and felt well he endured varying degrees of pain. No patient can avoid that process."
- "No bereaved person who has endured the death of a special person can avoid the process either."[147]

Trust God. Trust the grief process; allow the pain of grief to bring healing.

8. Thou shalt fully participate in your grief. / Let go, and participate fully in your grief.

Don't hold back. Don't hold out. Let go, and grieve – no matter what it looks like, no matter how it feels.

Whatever you may have expected, your grief will likely be different. Don't back away, participate fully and personally.

Grief has the capacity to shake us and shock us. But if we participate in our own grief, fully and emotionally, it doesn't leave us where we've been.

Over time, healthy grief, participatory grief, moves us forward in a positive direction. Trust your grief and become a full participant.

9. Thou shalt allow your grief to move you toward healing. / Give yourself permission to heal, to move toward healing.

Grief isn't a dead-end street. God didn't create grief to be a negative destination. But... we need to work with our grief, not against it.

The purpose of our grief goes beyond our grieving. With our participation, the grief process moves us toward healing, toward wholeness, toward recovery.

We may live a "doughnut life" with a grief hole in the middle, but we are able to function as a whole person again. Healthy grief actually helps us engage life again, as healthy, life-loving persons.

Trust God for your healing.

10. Thou shalt remember to return the favor. / Use your grief experience to become a grief helper.

Remember those who came along-side you in your grief. When you're ready and able, come along-side a friend, family member, a neighbor, or even a stranger – in their grief – and do for them what someone else did for you.

Pray for them. Trust God and accept the power and opportunity you have to help another person in their grief. Reach out, and touch. Reach out, and give. Reach out where you live. Reach out and help someone move a step closer to healing – the way someone helped you.

Through God's grace, crawl out from your deep, dark hole of grief. Crawl out – and help someone else crawl out, too. The sooner you trust God, the sooner you help someone else with their grief, the sooner you begin to heal yourself.

Don't be a Lone Ranger, riding your grief through life all by your lonesome.

You need people contact to live. Trust God and live.

If you ask: "Why do I need ten commandments?" Or: "How can I in my grief respond to 'commands' when I can't even focus my thoughts or even my days?"

Those are fair questions and very human reactions.

Try this: Back away from the "commandment" feeling, as if someone is "telling" you to do something. When you consider the commandments of grief as helpful suggestions from a friend, you experience a different feeling. As Janice, whose husband died in a horrible accident, said to me, "I found the Ten Commandments of Grief very helpful because I could hear God saying 'give yourself time'. She went on to say one person had suggested she give herself "permission" to grieve.

"Death is an Unalterable Fact"

James R. White is a veteran counselor and hospital chaplain. In his little book *Grieving, Our Path Back to Peace*, he gives meaningful counsel for the "need" to "give yourself time": "The first thing to realize about the grieving process is that you can't sit down and chart out how long it is going to take you to 'get through it'."[148]

The Third Commandment of Grief reminds us: "Thou shalt grieve for as long as you need to grieve." James White suggests, "The relationship that was yours with husband, wife, brother, sister, mother, father, son, daughter, grandparent, grandchild, or simply close friend will never be there again in this life. It is an unalterable fact. Your loss will change the scope of each day for the rest of your life."

We may "tear up" years from now on a special day in our memory that calls to mind how much we miss this special person. Is there anything wrong with that? Absolutely not. "One does not seek to escape grief," White writes, "but to embrace it, work through it, allow it to heal the hurt, so that we can move on with our lives in full light and recognition of what has happened and how God has changed our lives as a result."

The Chapter "Take-Away"

If while reading this chapter you sensed God's Presence and were helped and encouraged by the Ten Commandments of Grief, then trust God, trust yourself, and live forward. Make the discovery yourself. God will go with

THE GRIEF LETTER

you.

Your grief partner and friend,

Fran Buhler

A Grief PS:

1. Pick three of the "Ten Commandments of Grief" helpful to you personally.

2. Choose two "Commandments" you would like to start following. Name them, then consider how you would make them part of your personal "grief touch" when extending your condolence to someone.

3. Which Commandments are the most difficult for you? Why? Ask yourself: Is my difficulty with this Commandment compounding my grief?

CHAPTER 22

WHY TWELVE STEPS FROM GRIEF TO HEALING?

Grief needs a starting place.

Dealing with deep grief---under the best of circumstances---is always difficult. As a grieving young mother asked, "Where do you start?"

Deep grief imposes a heaviness on the soul. Creates a numbing sadness. Administers the sting of sorrow. Opens the door for confusion, unanswered questions, relentless pain. We sometimes experience frequent anger. We are stunned, often overwhelmed, by unexpected anger. In deep grief, life is shrouded in gray and experienced in tears. Where's the solace?

"It takes time," they tell us.

"Well, how much time?" we wonder.

And nobody knows. Still…

"Grief needs a starting point."

Like love, no matter what all is going on, grief needs a starting point. In a sense, that's what "the grief letter" was about, an acknowledged starting point. And that's what this book, TGL, is about. Where the love was is where the grief will be.

Could this chapter be your starting point?

Don't worry about the implication of starting at Chapter 22!

Some of us started at Chapter 1, others at Chapter 4, and a bunch of us at Chapters 10 or 11. That's ok. That is the personal nature and the personal differences of grief. Because grief is an important step---an indispensable step, really---for building a future life of joy.

"Steps you take by faith…"

Even though "12 steps" became known because of Alcoholics Anonymous, these 12 steps get you pointed in the right direction to deal with the death

THE GRIEF LETTER

of someone dear to you.

You are not on a time clock.

You don't have to report your progress to a grief monitor.

You should not have the mindset you are going to charge through these 12 steps and be done with your grief. In fact, as you read and process the remaining chapters of *The Grief Letter*, you will find yourself relating again and again to specific steps among the twelve in this chapter.

So instead of thinking of these as 12 "quickie" steps, approach them as thoughtful, sometimes unfolding steps, you take over time. Steps you take by faith, as your "wait" upon the God of the universe.

For Your Personal Benefit

Plus, there's a grief-sized bonus. These particular 12 steps from grief to healing translate into two frequently ignored imperatives proven in the grief experience of many with whom I have walked:

- Trust God's grace in your grief. It helps cover the unknowns.
- Trust God's power in your pain. It smooths out the rough spots.

Your Grief will Tell You What it Needs

As you move through the 12 steps, consider Martha Whitmore Hickman's words: "If I can let my resistance down, be calm in my soul, my grief will tell me what it needs from me at each step along the way." Hickman adds: "… the process will not be cheated. It will take as much time as it needs."[149]

So enter the 12 steps with the long view. Instead of thinking how can I get through this grief as soon as possible, ask yourself: "How can I get through my grief and process my grief appropriately, no matter how much time may be required?"

Try the steps. See what you think. More importantly, see how the 12 steps help you "feel" and "believe". Grief is all about feeling and believing. No matter how long it takes, may each step bless and keep you – and help you.

PART 3 - CHAPTER 22

12 Steps From Grief to Healing

1. Accept your pain.

The pain of grief means you are alive and human. I have known persons who tried to run away from their pain. Others tried to hide it. Some often deny it. Be gentle with yourself in your pain and others in their pain. Hurting is not a weakness.

Actually, the reverse is true. If you've experienced the death of a loved one or close friend and you don't feel any pain, then you do have a problem.

The pain of grief accompanying the death of someone close to you is a divine signal you are on schedule. As you accept your pain, trust God – pray.

2. Own your grief.

Your grief is exclusively yours. It is unhealthy to resist grief, deny your grief, pretend you don't feel it. And it never helps to ignore your grief or reject it.

The healthy response, the best response, is to take ownership of your grief even though the pain of personal loss hurts deeply.

When you own your grief, pain still pierces your body and soul and leaves you exhausted, totally spent for days at a time. Grief ownership does not make your grief any less painful or bring brevity to your sorrow.

But when you own your grief, don't try to run away from your grief. Stand up and face it, deal with it. Find ways to faith your way through it. Pray. Trust God. Own your grief.

3. See the love connection.

You grieve and hurt so deeply because you loved and cared for someone you lost. Be thankful you hurt because you loved. Be aware you grieve because you cared. See the love connection.

Consider the alternative. If you had not loved, if you had not cared, you wouldn't hurt so much. Who would prefer that alternative? Never love anyone, never care about anyone, and you can avoid grief altogether?

But...in the process you will experience something more hellish and far worse. You will know the pain and grief, the awful cost, the terrible consequence of never having experienced the joy of loving someone else.

Trust God. Claim the love connection. And pray.

4. Know the depth.

When you grieve, the pain measures the depth of your loss – and also your love. It's a life principle: Love deeply, grieve deeply.

The scale of your emotional pain gauges the enormity of your loss. Isn't the blessed experience of deep love and strong relationship worth celebrating?

Know the depth of what you're dealing with. Grieving deep loss is an emotion of the soul. Trust God in the depth. Pray.

5. Accept your loss.

The pain and grief you experience help you accept your deep loss in the death of your loved one. When you accept your loss, when you come to terms with the reality of life without the one you grieve, then you are able to move forward.

Your ongoing journey through grief and loss becomes an adventure in healing, and eventually in helping others. Pray. Trust God, as you accept your loss.

6. Chart your path.

You loved and cared, you therefore have the ingredients within you to chart your path for healing. Your pain and grief will help you. It is time to give appropriate love and care to yourself. The time will come when you will be able to offer love and care to help the healing of another. Try to stay focused: Chart your path toward healing. Pray.

But what if I grieve because of guilt, a deep-seated guilt that I did not love and care as I should have? What if I grieve a heart-breaking guilt that I was unfaithful or that I betrayed my spouse, family member, or friend who is now deceased?

If I did not love and care before, now I have the opportunity to confess my wrongfulness, to amend my attitude, and to ask forgiveness.

It is time to receive forgiveness. So you can heal, and chart your path to wholeness. Trust God and chart your path.

7. Don't instruct others in their grief.

Your pain and grief are **your** pain and grief – not the grief of someone else. Don't make yourself the self-appointed expert on the grief of another.

We each experience some commonalities in our grief, but we each grieve in our own individual way. Respect the grief of others. Come along side and be sensitive, gentle, helpful. Don't allow yourself to become a grief bully, one who always knows what's best for someone else's grief.

Every community, every church, every temple, every mosque has a grief sergeant who always knows it all and instructs others in their grief. Don't do it.

Trust God and you won't need to do it.

8. Avoid self-centered grief

Don't run from your pain and become a prisoner of your self-centered grief. Then you grieve yourself to death. Self-centered grief opposes God-centered grief. When we place ourselves in the center of the grief equation, we move from healthy to unhealthy grief. Healthy grief includes prayer.

God's design for human grief puts God in the center of our grief to heal the soul-deep devastation. When we place ourselves in the center of our grief, then we become roadblocks to our own healing. God-centered grief brings healing.

Trust God. Avoid self-centered grief. Keep God in the center of your grief.

9. Offer support to others.

At some point, even in your grief, you recover awareness of what's going on around you. Your experience of pain and grief actually trigger awareness and insight into the pain and grief experience of others.

Pray for them. You choose to listen better, and to express your care. The time comes when you offer grief support, as appropriate, to someone suffering the pain of a great loss. Out of the depth of your pain, you speak words of comfort and care. You offer help. You pray for them the way others have prayed for you. Trust God and offer help to someone whose heart is broken.

10. Don't expect ditto grief.

Within our individual lives, the grief of one loss is not automatically the same as another loss. We grieve different losses differently. Don't expect carbon copy or duplicate grief from one death to another. Don't pray ditto prayers. But pray.

Trust the Holy One with your present grief the way you trusted Him with your prior grief.

11. Allow yourself to heal via the "...upward process of healing."

Don't ever forget your pain and your grief have the divinely designed purpose and the empowered potential to bring you healing. Yet it does not happen automatically. You have to help it happen. Pray about it. You cannot begin healing and you will not ultimately experience healing unless you allow yourself to heal. Desire it. Want it, seek it.

Trust God, and allow yourself to heal. Allow yourself to hope again.

When we hurt so deeply, how do we find hope? James R. White, a hospital chaplain and veteran counselor, offers insight and help on our way to peace as we begin to hope again. White calls it the "upward process of healing."

> "People in grief wonder if they will ever feel okay again. Not only do you face overwhelming emotions of loss, you can feel discouraged or even ashamed when your grief doesn't disappear quickly or happen in neat orderly stages. For all people who have experienced loss, moments of joy and normalcy mix with moments of sadness and anger. Being moved again by painful emotions you thought you had tamed isn't a setback. It's part of an upward process of healing. And when you allow your grief to be accompanied by hope in God, grieving can be your path back to peace."[150]

12. Embrace the joy of healing.

The experience of pain and grief does not mean you will never know joy again. The outcome involves your choice. You may choose to grieve and accept your healing. Or you may run from your pain, become a prisoner of your self-centered grief, and reject the God-powered healing only healthy grief can bring to pass. Choose to trust God, giving thanks for his healing Grace. Trust the Holy One and embrace the joy of your healing. Don't feel doubt or guilt over your joy of making progress thru your pain. These are challenging steps. I will be praying for you.

A 12-Step Bonus: The Short Question

I've read the Psalms, Romans 8, Ephesians1, Job; I've read the whole Bible, and I agree with James R. White: "The toughest answers are the shortest ones." I also believe the toughest questions are the shortest ones. Like, "Why?"

Some people I have known used the 12 steps to answer the "short question".

Years ago, I was attempting to comfort one whose daughter had been ripped from her life by a horrible interstate auto accident. I did not know the lady very well, was not sure what kind of faith she had or how she was dealing with her sudden, unexpected sorrow! She met me at the door with grief so heavy she was literally heaving as she breathed. She pointed toward a chair, across from her chair. As we sat, I noticed an open Bible on the lamp stand beside her chair. Clearly underlined was the Verse for the Valley below:

A Verse for the Valley: "The eternal God is your refuge, and underneath are the everlasting arms..." (Deuteronomy 33:27).

As the lady talked, and I listened, she touched seven or eight of the 12 steps we have just reviewed. She had such strong faith, I learned, a faith in ONE WHO carried her through her days of sorrow, and all the times of grief to follow.

May her response encourage us and give us strength to face our own grief.

When Our Time Comes...to die...or to grieve...

I shall always remember the first time I read about the one who wrote the expressions below:

"Should it be ours to drain the cup of grieving even to the dregs of pain, at thy command, we will not falter, thankfully receiving all that is given by Thy loving hand." Think about it.

When it comes our time to die, we will have "drained the cup of grieving" in our lives on numerous occasions – both for ourselves and for others. As Emory University's Thomas G. Long has written, the quoted words opening this paragraph "gain even more strength when we know they were composed by Dietrich Bonhoeffer in a German concentration camp only months before his execution. Who said them is as important", Long asserts, "as what they say."[151] To me, Bonhoeffer's words become just as relevant and real when responding to a death as they are in the process of facing one's own death.

The Chapter "Take-Away"

"12 Steps from Grief to Healing" assure us of one important thing. The 12 steps give us a "do-able" starting point without any penalty, without any negativity. And a grief starting point is essential.

If we were unable to get moving forward in our grief way back in those early chapters, we need not panic. We need not worry. We need to use the 12 steps to help us get moving forward in our grief now. Grief is not about how soon we get started, but how well we grieve once we get started. Now it's time to grieve in high gear.

The Most High God will be with us every grief step of the way.

Your 12 Steps partner in grief,

Fran Buhler

A Grief PS: Over time, good grief is super important, because it leads to healing…

1. In your grief, note carefully as you begin the 12 steps what you are experiencing.

2. Select three steps you need to consider taking in the immediate future, for healing.

3. Whenever your steps become a challenge or increase in difficulty, remember those words from Deuteronomy; "God is your refuge", your certain help in your time of need.

CHAPTER 23

THE GRIEF TEXT AND THE SOCIAL MEDIA EPITAPH

Dear Reader and Partner in Grief,

We have entered an era in which an epitaph tribute to one's life is likely not to be chiseled in stone, but left on a Facebook post. Social media have become an integral part of our grief experience.

Why This Matters

Not long ago I received a text message, an hour before the graveside service began, from a family member in another state. The family member and the deceased had not been speaking for several years, due to a bitter disagreement. The text was to me – not to the family or a particular family member. Since the family had scheduled a "family-only" graveside service prior to the memorial service at the church, I had an opportunity.

In conjunction with my planned graveside remarks, I read the text and witnessed a scene of family healing, a burial and a "reach out" communication that brought a family back "together" for the first time in years.

Social media provide soul-deep message systems, technology that "touches" lives, a tribute to the special person who died, along with a personal reminder that says "I'm remembering you". Social media "touches" make possible a realization that instantly, many friends, even strangers, care. Along with you, they feel the plunge of grief too. Then comes the realization: "I am in the midst of many who care!"

"The Grief Text"

Texting is now the communication link with many families. Below I share an "incoming" text example revealed in my IPhone following the sudden auto accident death of the daughter of a good friend. The father was texting me as we began assembling thoughts for her eulogy.

THE GRIEF LETTER

The father's text:

> "John 16:33 was my mother's favorite.
> I'm working on something unique to
> describe her faith. The dark moments
> of our life will last only so long…
> our time with her was a gift from God!"

The father continues:

> "Christmas joy is not a given 4 those who mourn
> the loss of a parent, child, sibling, or good friend.
> Looking @ an empty place @ the table brings
> unimaginable pain, pain that is deep & not always
> fleeting. Such pain rooted in suffering will
> come, as it should, but so will joy… joy
> in Christ's presence with me even as
> I look @ an empty place @ the table…"

My return text:

> "Thought about you last night. Be glad you're a
> man w/ feelings, not a stump – like some men.
> Remember this, after a big hug she would swat you on
> the back & say go have a good Christmas!"

Paula Clayton, my personal assistant for 16 years, commented about the recent death of an extra special neighbor on her street. Paula was deeply touched by a Facebook post summing her neighbor's significance in social media epitaph style:

> "She gave without effort and
> loved without expectation."

Consider these examples of "the new normal".

Some may suggest the Internet is not the best channel for grief or for comforting "those who mourn". I say, why not? Does it not depend on the Internet "user" and what is expressed in a given communication? Let's welcome the trend, and help improve grief ministry via the internet.

The message "I'm so sorry", "I care", "we are remembering you" is personal and needed – whether in a card, email, text, tweet, Facebook post, phone call, or in person.

Human grief is bound to go viral – just as it is prone to go emotional – and Internet-based vehicles for delivering the right message in a timely, sensitive manner are like flowers ordered and dispatched for grieving recipients. The "sender" has control. The card attached may contain words that comfort, lift, and encourage---or words that sting with insensitivity.

Prior to a service celebrating life and resurrection, scheduled in our sanctuary recently, two grandchildren were taking "selfies" – pictures of oneself in a special setting for transmission and sharing with someone else not there – for the family "digital scrapbook". In this context, it was a thoughtful thing to do.

An older adult observer saw it differently, thought it disrespectful. When I shared my take on it and that I would appreciate a family member being that thoughtful of me, the critic repented immediately, asking, "Why didn't I see it positively instead of negatively?"

The Power of Remembrance

Boil grief down to its essence. Grief equals absence. Someone in our life is gone from our life. Our special person is missing. Absent. Not present. All of our sorrow and grief stem from the absence of one who is now no longer present. A proven way to keep our special someone present, even beyond death, is via our power of remembrance.

Remember the one gone, missing, absent from your life. **Recall** your special connection, and give thanks. **In remembering**, we call to mind the person's presence, personal impact, and powerful connection with our own life. **Our remembrance** provides a memory image of the person's life and fills the missing image from our lives. We have our **memory**. We also have our social media treasures.

Social Media Memory Bank Treasures

Jan told me she discovered her best treasure after her daughter's death was the assortment of "pics" left on her IPhone. "If you could have heard me," she gushed, "I was the craziest mixture of laughs-and-tears you've ever heard." Then she said it for all who listen---or read: "What a treasure!"

Her reference, of course, was to the memory bank of crazy pictures she had stored and saved, preserved especially for her grieving heart and family, in her Smart Phone. Of course, these were "pics" to which at the time of their taking she never gave a thought that one day she would have her "pics" but she would no longer have her daughter---except in her IPhone **memory bank**.

In contrast, Sam would never be classified as a "social media" man: 6' 4", a rugged, trim 240, pounds that is, usually in casual "garb", always "dressy casual" at more formal events. Sam loves life, is always on the go, busy with his business, busy giving time to his family, busy helping others. Sam takes seriously the job of being a husband. By his own accounting, Sam probably has never taken more than a few pictures with his Smart Phone. Sally, his wife, was in charge of family picture-taking.

Yet six months before the auto accident that took his son's life, Sam, in a moment of fatherly joy, after his son's success in a local community event, just happened to **remember** his phone was in his car. Sam grabbed his phone, and in an instant, touched the "photo" button, yielding the photo preserved images of Sam's son receiving his community honor. At graveside, Sam and several of his good friends checked the Smart Phone pictures again, as they laughed, cried and grieved together.

For Sharon, it was an altogether different experience. She had everything you could think of for "connection" and "reminders" of her beloved husband. Yet the "treasure" she treasures most is a one-line text she saved, sent a year before her husband's death: "You are the love of my life." The quote, plus his love, goes everywhere she goes.

"I wish people would..." Second Thoughts about Grief Texts

After the positive, celebrative, even healing effect, of the grief text examples mentioned previously and the high impact example that follows, we must remind ourselves---even warn ourselves---about the potential damage and negative impacts of our texts, tweets and emails. A whole series of "I wish people would..." comments come to mind, illustrating our need to be aware of inflicting pain, even emotional damage, in critical moments.

"I wish people would..."

- "think about my privacy---even if they aren't concerned about theirs."
- "be more thoughtful and in less of a hurry."
- "think before they tweet. A tweet should be a soft touch not a hard slap."

- "put themselves in the 'grief chair' and think about what they're saying---before they say it."

"One Family's Journey Thru Sorrow to Joy"

Candi Pearson-Shelton is a worship leader, songwriter, and independent artist – known for her involvement with the Passion worship movement and her album "Glory Revealed". In her 2010 book *Desperate Hope: When Faith in God Overcame My Despair*, she documents the grief-related social media traffic relative to the illness and death of just one individual, her younger brother.[152]

In an Appendix Candi calls "A Community of Faith", she "packages" the blog, email, text, and social media examples of "personal communications" sent and received during a month of life and grief leading up to and including the memorial service and celebration of her younger brother's life.

"A publishing first"

This may be a publishing first, reproducing several weeks of social media messaging for inclusion in a memoir slash theme title in the Christian tradition.

Candi Pearson-Shelton also introduces a new grief practice I predict will be the wave of our grief future. In the appendix cited above, Candi describes how she picked "the day after" the hustle and bustle, the tears and grief of the "visitation", the graveside service and memorial service celebrating her brother's life.

She intended to read through the blogs, texts and emails that "chronicled our unwanted adventure". She wanted to review "what transpired during those forty days, to relive the collection of communications." (Did you note the 40 days? Think about the significance of "40" in the life of Israel and of Jesus: Noah and the 40 days and nights of rain; Israel and the 40 years of wilderness wandering; Jesus' wilderness temptation as he fasted 40 days.)

Candi perched herself in her living room, her computer in her lap, and an endless supply of tissues within reach. She "read the highly emotional words of countless people who walked through this experience with us."

"A new grief tradition"

"This 'day' of reliving turned into three," for Candi, and because of the editing and inclusion of this on-line human experience in her subsequent book, a new grief tradition has been birthed. Witness this new beginning. I am confident we will see more and more examples of this grief practice of reviewing grief texts and emails following the days of family bereavement.

> "There was no way I could find to effectively read through every word in a twenty-four hour period without a break, some coffee, and a mindless hour of television. I needed to decompress after such an emotional time. The funny thing is, it wasn't so much a time of my emotions being fully committed to remembering Rick and feeling the hurt of losing him; it was more a combination of this with actually feeling the hundreds of people hurting with me."[153]

The Chapter "Take-Away"

Notice how she "felt" the "hundreds of people hurting with me." This is precisely what happens on the other side of our texts, tweets, emails, cards and notes. Listen, as she continues.

> "I found it simply breathtaking at moments, reading words that were clearly typed through tears, some from friends, some from complete strangers. I was able to read these words and slightly detach myself from my own feelings to get a picture, albeit a fuzzy one, of what it felt like for people who became engrossed in what God was doing with this man in the hospital and his family members who were with him and what it must have been like to not be there, right in the thick of it – to feel what it must have been like to hang on to every press of the Enter button to find the latest news and know how to pray next. It struck me so deeply that so many people were doing just this – gathering around computer screens, feeling helpless to do anything else but pray according to the words they were reading from us. They could not be there physically, but they offered what they could. I don't think they knew, or can know even now, exactly how much they did offer. After three days of a swollen face and tear-soaked T-shirts, I had finished my editing. I read every word, absorbed every ounce of emotion and spirit and courage that was to be found in those pages, and I sat astounded by **what God had accomplished in forty days**. He had written a story in blog form (a funny but somehow appropriate thing for Him to do!), one that was to point every finger and toe toward His countenance and give voice to **a cyberfamily of strangers**, all ultimately shouting, 'Holy is the Lord God Almighty – see, look what He has done.' This was hope at its best."[154]

PART 3 - CHAPTER 23

In the Name of the Father, the Son, and the Holy Spirit...All One in the Holy One...

Your grief partner and texting friend,

Fran Buhler

A Grief PS: What about your own grief button?

1. As you post online via social media about the grief journey of your life, ask for wisdom and God's help. Be sensitive to the grief, known and unknown, of others.

2. Before your grief texts become part of a larger online conversation---be alert to the possible impact of your words on others. Be helpful, stay faithful.

3. Text your grief only to someone you trust. Grief texts to the universe at large are not a good idea.

CHAPTER 24

REDEMPTIVE STEPS FOR GRIEVING FAMILIES

Dear Reader and Grief Partner,

Even though death and grief have been prominent in my professional life, the following data slipped up on me. I'm guessing you may have "been there" in your grief experience.

"If you're over age 40", according to the Harvard Medical School Family Health Guide, "there's a 1-in-3 chance that a close relative or friend of yours died in the last year. Or you may be among the 1 million Americans who lost a spouse this past year."

Why This Matters

Chapter 24 suggests four strategic steps any family can take to cope with grief in the family. You don't have to be a Bible scholar or grief professional to put these suggestions in motion.

You will also find five redemptive family actions for your family to help God help you.

Four Strategic Steps for Grieving Families

Following the death of a loved one or friend as survivors, as family, or as colleagues, we begin living with something we can't change---the death of a loved one. We cannot bring our loved one or our friend back to this life. Yet there are several strategic steps we can take as a family to deal with family grief. Consider four suggestions:

1. Circle the Family Wagons

Schedule intentional times for family gatherings and make an extra effort to find a time when everyone can be there.

I've heard of families who "stopped getting together" because a key family member died. If at all possible, don't ever allow a death to trigger such a response.

Family "get-togethers" may be a bit awkward initially. After all it is a new family experience. Make each "together time" a memorable occasion to build a sense of blessing, an opportunity to recall your loved one with appreciation and even laughter.

Use these "together" occasions to help bridge the giant hole in the family after a key family member death occurs. Make it a priority practice in the family to use the deceased person's name in conversation. Allow the family member his or her rightful place in the family. Don't talk and act as if the person or persons never existed. Such behavior only generates more thoughtless pain.

2. Grieve and laugh together

Until we come together as family, we don't know how to grieve as family... with family.

At scheduled family grief "get-togethers", be honest, when you talk about your grief. Be open about what you miss most, what you grieve the hardest, and what has helped you.

Crying together and laughing together as you "recall" a person's memory "together" is a positive, inexpensive form of family therapy. And it works!

Why keep our grief to ourselves? The Holy One knows our grief. Why not give our grief to God, share our grief among family, and move forward by His grace, growing in His strength? God gave us the ability to laugh. It's in our design, in our DNA. And, when it happens naturally, laughter ought to be a part of our grief.

3. Let the "Giver of Life" give Hope

Remember, as a family, the God who gave us life is able to give us hope. Make hope a very practical thing.

Start with appreciation. Appreciation comes about because we knew the one for whom we grieve. We remember things we appreciate about that special person.

Then, in time, move from appreciation into hope. We have great appreciation because we knew and loved someone, and this person's life touched our life. Move from appreciation for the one you grieve to appreciation for the Most High God who gave life to your loved one.

THE GRIEF LETTER

Remind yourself the God who gives us life also gives us hope.

Play a "fill-in-the-paragraph" game about each family member, including the deceased. "The thing I remember about so-and-so is _____."

Why not extend the game to the experience of faith? With a round of: "The thing I've learned about God is _____"?

4. Pray together. Pull forward together.

God knows our grief but do we know God? Do we ask for help? Do we trust the resources of His grace? Do we allow God's healing to have access in our lives?

A Verse for the Valley: "The peace of God, which surpasses all understanding, will guard your hearts and minds through Christ Jesus." (Philippians 4:7).

Bill represents many of us when he said: "I thought, I just need to 'gut' this one out. I learned 'gutting it out' isn't nearly as effective as praying it out. I'm no saint but even I could pray. Most days it's no more than 'God, help me' – but that's enough." Make it a family prayer: "God help us."

Five Redemptive Family Actions

As we grieve the death of a loved one or friend, there are five redemptive family actions we may take within our own ability to help God help us.

1. We can give our anger to God.

He can handle it. He understands it. We may always trust God with our anger.

A father whose son was killed in a hunting accident said to me: "His accident was over 20 years ago, and I'm just now giving my anger to God. Tell people not to make the mistake I made. I carried a burden and a bitterness that could have been lifted long ago – if I had trusted God with my anger the way I do now."

2. We can give our questions to God.

He welcomes them. We may not receive the answers we wish, but why limit God to what we want, what we think is best?

PART 3 - CHAPTER 24

I had just finished the celebration service for a young man who died an untimely death in a terrible accident. His Mother greeted everyone, expressing genuine appreciation for their presence. As I walked her to the hearse, she touched my arm as she said, "I gave all my 'whys' to God, all my questions. I don't want to spend the rest of my life asking unanswerable questions."

3. We can ask God to give us healing from our grief pain.

Cynthia confessed to me, years after her Father's death, "My healing could have begun long ago, if I had been open to it." Then she added: "For me, that was a big 'if'."

Seek His healing. Be open to God's healing. Allow God to begin the healing process.

4. We can allow God to give us His comfort and peace.

God never wants us to be left alone. But we must seek His Comfort and Peace. Almost two years after his wife's death, Charlie told me, "For the longest I never thought about praying for comfort and peace. I never thought about praying at all. For some strange reason, I viewed Karen's death as God's punishment, as His displeasure with me.

"Honestly, I don't know what triggered the change," he said, "but one day in worship it dawned upon me that I could ask God for a sense of comfort and peace about her death and about my actions leading up to her death. At that point in time I began to experience God's Comfort and Peace. That was ten years ago, and today I'm totally at peace about Karen's death. I miss her. I will always miss her. But my grief is not a struggle any more. I'm thankful for the years I had with Karen. I'm at peace."

Are Charlie's words and experience applicable to us? God will never forsake us. God will never leave us "alone" if we seek His Presence.

5. We can grieve with Purpose, in the First Person, as Family.

Q. How do we grieve with purpose?

A. By intending to grieve for a reason. By grieving for the reason we want to move forward with our lives, giving thanks for the one who is gone but not forgotten. We grieve, appreciating the past, but living for tomorrow.

THE GRIEF LETTER

Always grieve in the First Person.

First Person Singular (I): I embrace my grief – grieving because I love and I care. I express as much grief as I feel. I don't allow grief to become a paralyzing bondage. I feel my way through the darkness of my grief. I do not allow my sorrow to slay my soul.

I refuse to become a prisoner of grief. I meet "overwhelming grief" head on. I grieve the grief of love and family. I grieve the grief of friendship. I accept the fact private sorrow may lead to public grief. I trust in the grace and forgiveness of God to heal my grief.

First Person Plural for Couples and Families (We): We embrace our grief – grieving because we love and we care. We express as much grief as we feel. We don't allow grief to become a paralyzing bondage. We feel our way through the darkness of our grief. We do not allow our sorrow to slay our soul.

We refuse to become prisoners of grief. We meet "overwhelming grief" head on. We grieve the grief of love and family. We grieve the grief of human friendship. We accept the fact private sorrow may lead to public grief. We trust in the grace and forgiveness of God to heal our grief.

Jesus and Max Lucado on Grief

As Max Lucado, one of America's most widely read authors and pastors, reminds us, Jesus was no "cavalier Christ". Jesus, in what Lucado describes as "a tsunami of sorrow" and "a monsoon of tears", weeps with Mary and Martha in John 11:33 and 35.

"He weeps with them", says Lucado, for emphasis. Not about them, not away from them, but "with them". And Jesus' tears, says Lucado, "give you permission to shed your own."[155]

In his book, *Next Door Savior*, Lucado states the grief perspective of *The Grief Letter*:

> "Grief does not mean you don't trust; it simply means you can't stand the thought of another day without the Jacob or Lazarus of your life. If Jesus gave the love, he understands the tears. So grieve, but don't grieve like those who don't know the rest of this story."[156]

PART 3 - CHAPTER 24

Forgiven: Something We may have Forgotten!

Growing up in Tennessee, I heard about a cemetery headstone engraved with a single word: "Forgiven." Forgiveness is often interlinked with our grief. And, indeed, we are "forgiven"---each of us. Yet we need not purchase such a stone for our forgiveness to be true. When we confess our sin and trust the Holy One, we **are** forgiven. We who are "forgiven" should grieve more effectively and grieve more purposefully than others. Not that we are better, more capable, or stronger, but because, in our grief and sorrow, we are blessed and lifted by the Most High God who "forgives". What greater comfort could there be when we mourn than to know God forgives **and** comforts all who mourn?

"Forgiveness Frees the Forgiven" is a truth long enjoyed and celebrated by those experiencing forgiveness. Yet there is another variation on this truth that is also true!

Forgiveness Frees the Forgiver

"Forgiveness frees the forgiver" is a phrase I never heard until I was in Dr. Balmer Kelly's "Biblical Theology" course in 1964, at Union Theological Seminary in Richmond, Virginia. Years later I saw the phrase on a fence post sign in rural South Carolina with the subscript: "Source unknown" Because of Dr. Kelly's class I was tempted to stop and write on the bottom of the sign: "Source: 'The God of Abraham, Isaac and Jacob.'"

This corollary truth should be quickly affirmed and not ignored. In my experience, "forgiveness frees the forgiver", the one extending forgiveness.

For example:

Bill and Donna had an attitude; and their attitude – to use a "down South" metaphor – was like having "a deer in the headlights". Bill and Donna's attitude was directed toward John and Louise.

Long ago, John and Louise had been out of town and missed the funeral of Bill and Donna's only child. Bill and Donna were extremely hurt and upset because they felt John and Louise took an optional trip that could have easily been rescheduled. To make matters worse, John and Louise never gave any explanation as to why they missed the funeral other than to say, "We are so sorry we had to be out of town."

The relationship between Bill and Donna and John and Louise became so strained it actually fractured. Without ever discussing the matter, each couple went separate ways, avoiding each other in the neighborhood, at the supermarket, even at church. For more than 15 years, a "wall" separated these two couples who were once friends; until one day when Bill and Donna met a new neighbor, Shirley, a single mom.

Shirley asked Bill and Donna if they knew John and Louise down the street. When they answered yes, Shirley began telling the story of how John and Louise had come to her aid several years ago during a very difficult time in her life. Her husband died when she was nine months pregnant. When her child was born, John and Louise took off from work, came and helped her for a week, until she had strength to carry on.

When Bill and Donna asked the birthdate of Shirley's child, it was the day before their own child's funeral. A simple discovery triggered forgiveness all around, freeing the "forgiven" and freeing the "forgiver".

When you are grieving and praying, first forgive anyone you are holding a grudge against.

Become a Grief Catalyst in Your Family

Anger eats us up inside. Bitterness binds our spirit. Forgiveness frees us! In short, a revengeful spirit gets in the way of healing.

We don't forgive someone because they deserve it. We forgive people because God forgives us, and we don't deserve it.

As a minister I am always open to a request for counsel. I have had opportunity to witness the "freeing up" that follows forgiveness, both the liberation of the forgiven benefactor **and** the liberating experience for the "forgiver".

Over and over again in the grief context of every day human relationships, we see those times and places and people in which simple acts of forgiveness would repair or avert the causes of tremendous amounts of grief, anger and bitterness. When a loved one dies, our emotions may range from simple disbelief to sudden shock or cumulative sorrow. We need a combination of comfort and encouragement to help us endure the pain and begin to heal.

Yes, the circumstances of death may be a factor between our reaction to a loved one's gradual decline over several years versus an unexpected death that hits suddenly, like a sledge hammer blow, and never stops hurting. However death arrives, we experience a possible range of emotions geared to a variety of circumstances, such as loneliness, regret, worry, or even anger or fear.

When we feel the octopus squeeze, grief becomes complicated in a hurry. Every family needs a grief catalyst.

The Chapter "Take-Away"

Everyone needs a better opportunity to grieve honestly, openly, and successfully. We need a culture in which more and more grievers become winners. That's how "The Grief Letter" began, with this redemptive recipe, helping individual grievers become grief catalysts in encouraging and achieving healthy grief experiences for grieving families.

As you think about your grief, think about the grievers within your family, in your neighborhood, at your workplace, in your place of worship, who could use some help. You may be exactly the human presence they need as you come along side their lives. Your own experience with redemptive steps for your grieving family may become an encouragement to other families in their time of grief.

Your grief buddy and forgiven friend,

Fran Buhler

A Grief PS: Forgiveness and grief go together. When we forgive, the grief seems to get better…

1. Choose one strategic, redemptive step you will try with your family.

2. If applicable, what redemptive family action will you try first?

3. Accept the challenge: Become a grief catalyst in your family.

THE GRIEF LETTER

CHAPTER 25

THE "WOE-IS-ME" DISEASE

Dear Reader and Partner in Grief,

I learned a lot from my maternal grandfather. When someone was unnaturally focused on self, exclusively fixed on their own problems, their own pains, their own pity-party, my granddad used to say that person was afflicted with the "Woe is me" disease.

If we have grieved honestly, every one of us has been to this place called "Woe is me!" It's a universal grief-stop everyone makes.

If you have been there – if you find yourself there right now – don't feel badly. It's a sign you are right on schedule in your grief.

Why This Matters

Personally, I believe it is almost impossible to experience the death of someone close and dear to us and not have such feelings. "Why me?" "Why now?" "I don't deserve this!" "This is so unfair!"

Yet to think of a self-centered orbit as applying to ourselves – under any circumstance – is sure to sting. I do not wish to point a finger of accusation, especially at a time when your world may have come crashing down following the death of your loved one or close friend. I've experienced this self-centered orbit first hand myself. When I speak of "woe is me" self-centeredness, I write from personal experience. I have experienced and exhibited the "woe is me" disease. None of us is immune.

I write, therefore, as one who has done battle with the "self-centered orbit". I know what it's like to have a case of "woe is me!" In fact, I've had "woe is me" more than once!

Look upon this chapter as an opportunity to choose life, embrace the possibility of future joy, and move forward in your grief.

1. "Woe is me" is a human reaction

"Woe is me" is clearly a self-centered grief reaction, the tragic example of how we may easily begin to orbit around ourselves. A self-centered grief response is routinely human, but it blocks our healing. In the orbit of "woe is me", the question becomes: "Why did this happen to me?" "Why did God do this to me?" "I am angry because this happened to me." "This is so unfair to me."

I have seen firsthand how our hostility may spill over into anger toward the deceased, the doctor, perhaps another family member, toward life itself, or even toward God.

Such hostile, aggressive, self-centered, "woe is me" feelings actually abuse others. Specific examples come to mind. A grieving widow screams at her children. A grieving widower, a father now functioning in unknown territory, in a fury of frustration and hostility, abuses his children. Another father ignores his children because in his grief he has lost his parental focus, as if the children are not important any more. Great loss often has the human impact of creating pronounced examples of self-centeredness.

2. A "woe is me" life outlook is unhealthy.

"Woe is me" becomes a self-centered orbit in which we do not grieve in healthy ways.

Self-centered grief is a profoundly unhealthy grief. For example: My grief vision becomes twisted and skewed because I have inverted the universe. Instead of the earth revolving around the sun, I now expect the sun to orbit around me. I expect the sun to be my moon. It's a grief melody I call, "self-pity-itis".

Experience with grief helps us understand that normal grief has its challenges, including denial, withdrawal, guilt, self-pity, even hostility, as we have mentioned. However, grief expressions within the range of "normal" include characteristic examples. Consider these healthy and unhealthy contrasts:

Denial – Comes naturally in early grief stages. The challenge is not to become stuck there.

Withdrawal – Some withdrawal from activity may be quite normal, and healthy. A minister friend of mine took a month off following his daughter's death after a lengthy battle with leukemia, a healthy, perfectly normal response, in my opinion.

In contrast, an unhealthy grief response would be withdrawing from work, family or other responsibilities by turning to alcohol or drugs.

Guilt – Feeling guilty following a loved one's death is not unusual, even normal, under ordinary circumstances. But if your sense of personal guilt begins to control or dominate your decisions and your behavior, that's a different story.

In my grief ministry experience, perspective is always the key.

I knew a man who in the advanced stages of a fatal disease, said verbally he wanted his wife to die to spare her the pain and suffering. Then when she died, he was overwhelmed with guilt, a common reaction. He initially had difficulty seeing that his love for his wife caused him to wish for her death---to make it easier on her. His guilt was pronounced and controlled his grief, as he punished himself until he was able to see that his love for his wife had been his controlling wish and his strong desire was her release from pain.

Self-pity – When we hurt, we must give attention to our hurt and the cause of our hurt. Grief always hurts. Under normal circumstances, we take care of our emotional hurts.

"Self-pity-itis" emerges when months after a loved-one's death, I still recite my list of all the bad things that have happened to me. So much so, that I become blinded to the good things in life I have experienced – but now ignore. "Woe is me" is ill-equipped to deal with "self-pity-itis". Unless I recognize this twisted reality, I am unable to take a healthy approach to my grief.

3. "Woe is me" prohibits true healing.

"Woe is me" has a focus on self that gets in the way of genuine grief.

How so?

"Woe is me" places all the focus on "me", ignores the Holy One as the true source of help, and embraces a "moan and groan" grief style.

"Woe is me" simply gets in the way of healthy grief, putting my grief focus in the wrong place, on the wrong thing, for all the wrong reasons.

4. **"Woe is me" leads to a lost life opportunity.**

Instead of grieving in human, healthy ways, I'm asking an uninterested world to give me what I need. The world isn't organized that way. The world isn't waiting to see what my needs are today. Waiting on the world will lead to a lost life opportunity.

5. **"Woe is me" leads ultimately to a deeply felt bitterness.**

The self-centered orbit doesn't work, does not offer relief, does not bring any respite from my soul-deep pain. So I hurt and hurt, and, as my grief dials downward, "woe is me" is the way I sink into bitterness as I blame the world, blame life, blame God, blame whatever and whoever becomes a convenient target.

6. **"Woe is me" leaves me stuck where I am.**

My "woe is me" outlook takes me to a point of bereavement, cemented and tethered in self-centeredness, and even bitterness. "Woe is me" lacks faith.

7. **"Woe is me" does not always respond to kind words and kind deeds.**

Yet kind words and deeds, plus sensitive relational patience, have the God-given power to penetrate over time.

The answer to "woe is me" is not anger, but love and purpose bolstered by huge amounts of patience.

The answer to "woe is me" is the fruit of the Spirit – "love, joy, peace, patience, kindness, goodness, faithfulness, gentleness, self-control." (Galatians 5:22-23)

8. **God can handle your "Woe is me" feelings**

Consider the "What if?" questions. What if...

I'm a bad person? I'm not a church goer? I've never become a Christian? I'm not sure there is a god! I don't know whether I believe or not. I want to, but life is hard.

I'll say it again. God can handle your feelings. Look at all the cantankerous individuals in the Bible God had to deal with! He accepts all of with open arms.

Someone asked: "I feel like I have been in Hell for a year. Can God handle that?"

Yes, God can handle any feelings you may have – spoken or unspoken.

Get it out. Put your feelings into play. Trust God with your feelings, even your bitterness. God can handle anything you may be feeling.

9. "Woe is me" will not change until I change.

I will not change until I choose to change.

"Woe is me" does not have to be a permanent address. I can move anytime I wish.

10. "Woe is me" is an OK reaction if I don't become stuck there.

Getting stuck in "woe is me" is one of the easier human conditions to acquire if we allow ourselves. It can happen in a hurry. Be alert, don't let it happen

Life is too short – and too precious – to live in a "woe is me" mode day after day after day. Get out of your "woe is me" orbit. Kiss your "self-pity-itis" good bye! The sooner you do so, the better.

Examples of what the Bible Says

Many people want the counsel and the comfort of knowing what the Bible says about grief. We focus now on meaningful texts from both the Old and New Testament. Do not limit yourself to the following examples. Explore the Bible on your own. Some of your best texts will come from your own reading, from your own adventure and discovery. Please do not allow my examples below – which have special meaning for me – to deter you from your own journey into the meaning of special Bible texts for you.

The Reality of Grief (regardless of the translation)

Jeremiah 8:18

> "My sorrow is beyond healing, my heart is faint within me!" (KJV)
> "My joy is gone, grief is upon me, my heart is sick." (ESV)

"My sorrow is beyond healing, my heart is faint within me!" (NAS)
"O my Comforter in sorrow, my heart is faint within me." (NIV)

No matter the translation, the Bible speaks to the reality of grief in a personal way.

Comfort for those who mourn

Most any day our world is full of tears, disappointment, and pain. Burdens and trials abound. Humanity everywhere weeps its losses. The tears of grief teach us what's important.

The Psalmist experienced days of tears and testing in his life, and according to Psalm 30:5, he knew that in the nights of trial and the midnights of life, God gives the assurance that "joy comes in the morning." God uses the tears of our night of grief to prepare us for the joy of the morning. Isaiah says to Israel, "For the Lord has called you like a wife forsaken and grieved in spirit" (Isaiah 54:6) If you really want to know how God relates to our grief, consider the following.

A Verse for the Valley: "God is near to the broken-hearted, and delivers the crushed in spirit," (Psalm 34:18).

In Isaiah 61, we find words that speak of what has been called "the exaltation of the afflicted."

"The Spirit of the Lord GOD is upon me, Because the LORD has anointed me to bring good news to the afflicted; He has sent me to bind up the brokenhearted, to proclaim liberty to captives and freedom to prisoners; to proclaim the favorable year of the LORD and the day of vengeance of our God; to comfort all who mourn, to grant those who mourn in Zion, giving them a garland instead of ashes, the oil of gladness instead of mourning, the mantle of praise instead of a spirit of fainting. So they will be called oaks of righteousness, the planting of the LORD, that He may be glorified." (Isaiah 61:1-3)

"Is there any consolation?"

I must be honest and faithful to my personal experience in life as I have known it to be in reality. There will be times in your life when you will need to…

"Pour out your heart like water before the presence of the Lord…"

as we read in Lamentations 2:19b.

"The Lamentations of Jeremiah" in the Old Testament were inspired and written to aid the people of Israel in their extended collective grief and suffering following the capture of Jerusalem in 586 BC.

Jerusalem's afflictions under Nebuchadnezzar offer a grief glimpse of our personal encounter with what may seem initially an inconsolable grief of agony and anguish following the unexpected death of a loved one. The writer wonders, for example, "if there is any pain like my pain," (Lamentations 1:12b) a familiar thought to any of us who have walked the trail of grief while weeping bitterly.

We have known heart-broken cries like those of Jerusalem. Even though Lamentations was obviously not written to provide a personal grief manual for us today, its words and expressions do track and link in a powerful way to our personal experience of grief when a loved one dies.

Historical "grief-work" in Lamentations

As Dr. Norman K. Gottwald of New York Theological Seminary expresses it in his Harper's Bible Commentary on Lamentations, "in its original setting, Lamentations performed a basic task of historical 'grief work'."[157]

In places like Lamentations 3, we find declaration of God's transcendence and mystery. Personally, I find words that speak to my heart and soul now, even though I know rationally and historically these are words written in another time and place for an altogether different audience and purpose. Yet like the heart-broken people of Jerusalem, I find myself in my grief seeking the same hope of relief in God's tender Mercy.

"Remember my affliction and my wandering... Surely my soul remembers and is bowed down within me. This I recall to my mind, therefore I have hope. The LORD'S loving kindnesses indeed never cease, for His compassions never fail. They are new every morning; great is Your faithfulness. "The LORD is my portion," says my soul, "Therefore I have hope in Him. The LORD is good to those who wait for Him, to the person who seeks Him. It is good that he waits silently for the salvation of the LORD" (Lamentations 3:19-26).

A Psalm with "Lamps for Grief's Journey"

As the psalmist writes in Psalm 31:9, "My eye is wasted from grief," or as we might say, "I cried my eyes out".

"I am forgotten," says the psalmist in verse 12," as a dead man out of mind…"

Clearly this is not a brief or superficial matter for the psalmist in his personal grief. "My life is spent with sorrow, and my years with sighing," he declares in verse 10.

Can this be the same person who wrote in Psalm 31:6-8, "but I trust in the Lord. I will rejoice and be glad for your steadfast love…"? The psalmist thanks God for not delivering him into the hand of the enemy, for setting his feet in a broad place, that is, a safe place.

In the midst of grief, most of us would say grief seems perpetual. "For my life is spent with grief," says the psalmist in verse 10. The days and weeks following the death of someone close to us seem "heavy-laden", and any thought of happy times belongs to a distant memory of another life.

Verse 12: "I have passed out of mind like one who is dead…" gives us the tell-tale feel of what J.R.P. Sclater called "overwhelming grief". We easily become "a prisoner of grief", shut off from human interaction, if we aren't alert to our condition. How easy it is to become what Sclater called "a numbed, silent mourner who dwells apart, desiring no company but his own thoughts."[158]

Overwhelming grief even has its paranoia, suggests verse 13, as we hear the whispering of man on every side. A competent psychiatrist would view this outcome as neurotic grief.

"Recovery is Possible"

According to the psalmist in verse 14, recovery is possible and "But I trust" is the important first step. Trusting requires the engagement of the will, especially when trusting emerges from the Black Hole of sorrow.

We all grow impatient with a family member or friend who appears immersed permanently in perpetual grief. Typically, we actually discard such gloomy grievers.

Consider verses 14 – 18: The one who trusts in God, the great Grief Lifter, powered and guided by trust, refuses to allow grief's sorrow to slay the soul.

To escape the grip of overpowering grief, eventually we confess "my times are in Your hand," verse 15, the key to the door marked "Recovery".

For a psalm that begins in verse one with a search for refuge and a strong fortress, this Psalm 31 delivers big time meaning and encouragement, providing lamps for Grief's Journey.

"Into Thy hands…"

Who among us could overlook or underestimate the redeeming value of verse 5: "Into Thy hand I commit my spirit"? Verse 5 gives us Jesus' seventh and final word from the cross. Verse 5 contains the dying words of three giants of faith: Luther, Knox, and Huss. In addition to the three called "the reformers" because of their role and association with the Protestant Reformation, others said to have had verse 5 on their lips at life's end include: Polycarp, Bernard, Henry V, Jerome of Prague, and Melanchthon. Jesus, of course, added "Father" at the beginning: "Father, into Thy hands…" As the psalmist committed himself to God in life, so Jesus committed himself to God in death.

The Chapter "Take-Away"

There is no better alternative in this life. The best light for Grief's Journey is trust in God, complete, total, all powerful trust in God.

For after all, in the context of verse 5, when we say "into Thy hand I commit my spirit," we are trusting the "faithful God" in the b part of verse 5: "O Lord, faithful God." He is an ever constant Presence in the psalms, the God we may trust in the darkness of grief, the God we may count on in the confusion of grief. Should not the God who redeems us from sin also have the purpose and the power to redeem us from the overwhelming sorrow of Grief? The God who is a lamp to our feet and a light to our path also lights our Grief Journey.

The best way out of "Woe is me" is to follow the psalm lamps for grief's journey. Instead of focusing on "me", focus on "Him" – the Great God of all Space and Time.

Your grief partner and listening friend,

Fran Buhler

A Grief PS: Self-examination is a tough cookie to swallow. Show your courage…

1. Talk to yourself about three examples in which you have been in the "woe is me" stage.

2. Explore your Bible for some specific Psalm lamps and some "anywhere" scripture lamps for your grief journey. Push yourself to find at least two you did not know.

3. Challenge yourself by honestly asking: Do I focus on "me" or "the Most High"?

THE GRIEF LETTER

CHAPTER 26

"ARE GRIEF AND FAITH ENEMIES OR FRIENDS?"

Dear Reader and Partner in Grief,

Please excuse my bluntness. The matter we are about to discuss is important. We shouldn't skip it.

Death in our culture has become a "Fire Alarm" fear. We know death is out there, waiting for us, and waiting for those we love. Someday, we know, the alarm will sound for us. Yet we assume "our" death will come on some distant day after we have completed a long and happy life.

Why This Matters

Because of our pervasive fear of death, we also have a hidden dislike for grief. Our grief for someone else is a huge reminder that death will also one day come for us.

Why? Because we know we cannot escape death.

"Death is the most inevitable fact of life", writes Dr. Ira Byock, Director of Palliative Medicine at Dartmouth-Hitchcock Medical Center in Lebanon, New Hampshire, and a professor at Dartmouth Medical School.[159]

After someone has died, grief is the most essential part of dealing with that death, especially someone close and dear to us. We naturally associate grief with **death**.

Grieving, as Essential as Breathing

What if we associated grief with life? What if we came to understand grieving is as essential to life as breathing? Then we might begin to see that how we grieve is as important as how we breathe.

Death and grief are part of life. Shouldn't we give grief the attention and time it deserves?

This is how "the grief letter" started, born of a simple conviction that grief should be recognized, acknowledged and supported. "The Grief Letter" as a book acknowledges the pervasive reality of grief and expresses the profound potential for grief to become transformative.

Grief is not the enemy

Sooner or later we must make this stop and begin the sorting out process.

Grief is not the enemy our culture often makes it out to be. Grief, by its very nature, is often burdensome – can be very heavy. Yet grief is never our opponent.

Think about grief as a form of faith, a personal aspect of faith that serves us well. Warm up to grief as a friend. Jump right in. You'll do fine. Faith can partner with grief anytime.

Consider the following on Grief and Faith:

1. Grief that questions God and grief that embraces God can co-exist in the same person as part of the same grief experience. The grieving heart may hate God in one moment and love God in another moment. And there's no predicting how strong or how long either moment will last.

The grieving heart may settle into one mode of embracing or rejecting God. Yet that same broken heart may also vacillate, cursing God one day and turning to God the next. The grieving heart may totally and firmly reject or embrace the life of faith. Grief always involves personal choices.

2. Pain and grief following a personal loss are spiritual matters. You can grieve in isolation. You may grieve in your stubbornness, repelling all attempts to comfort you in your grief. You may grieve in retreats of unbelief or in a permanent allegiance to atheism. You can even grieve by screaming to high heaven and telling the world where to go!

Writing about grief is like writing about pain. You can't capture it, you can't stop it. You must feel it first, then describe it and cope with it as best you can.

How you grieve is your choice, totally your choice and in your control. Even so, your grief is still a spiritual matter. So think about your grief reaction. What does it mean to you... spiritually?

3. Grief that heals usually has spiritual help. A grief that hurts and screams for release yet finds a path to healing, finds the spiritual journey of faith a help – not a hindrance.

Grief has to make room for faith, give itself to faith, then give faith a chance – give it time. Grief has to see faith as a helping friend.

4. Grief often runs away from faith, avoids faith. Grief says "I can handle this myself." Grief can be "stiff-necked" in its resistance to faith, to the extent that it never experiences the healing processes that are released and replenished by faith. "Run-away" grief leads to stubborn grief.

5. Faith is a friend to grief – not an enemy. Faith enters the house of grief to comfort those who mourn, to say simply, yet powerfully, by one's presence: "I care". Faith does not smother grief with words. Faith says what it says best simply by "being there". By making the time, by accepting the inconvenience, faith makes the most powerful demonstration of either family or friendship: Faith cares enough to be present. Faith gives the extra effort to be there.

6. Faith learns that grief is not an illness – it's worse. How can grief be worse than an illness? An illness offers the prospect of near term restoration. Grief is for the end of someone who cannot be restored, renewed, or replaced.

Illness is often temporary. Grief never is. Your grief may never go away completely. Just like your memory of the one you love and miss never goes away. Aren't you glad?

7. Is there such a thing as good grief? If we went to a funeral of someone we did not know personally and did not know anything at all about the person, most likely we would not grieve. We would be sympathetic. We might even feel very sorry for the family in their collective grief. But if the deceased is someone we do not know, someone with whom we have no connection, then the absence of grief would not be at all surprising. We may feel sympathy for those who grieve. We may feel sorry for those who have had to "give up" a loved one. But without an emotional connection to the deceased, we do not grieve.

Good grief is healthy and helpful.

Good grief is a safety valve to keep us from exploding, a hurting feeling with a positive benefit. Good grief gives perspective, plants seeds of recovery, lives by faith, dares to trust God for a healthy outcome, joins faith as "grief faith" to offer healing and hope.

8. **Bad grief and bad religion often hang out together, reinforce one another, and make good grief very difficult to experience.** Bad grief says: "I don't need help." "I don't need anyone else." "I am capable of handling this all by myself."

Bad religion often plays the blame game. "I hate God for taking my loved one." "For giving me cancer, for _____" (fill in the blank). "How could a loving God do such a thing?" Bad religion leads to bad grief and blames God for everything.

Bonus Insight: One of ten pre-publication "readers", asked to read TGL and offer evaluation and comment, said of # 8: "This is a tough one. If God is capable of healing my personal grief, why is He not capable of healing my loved one's cancer?"

"If He refuses to heal my loved one's cancer, could He not refuse to heal my grief?"

Yes, He could refuse to heal your grief. Still, I believe we have the choice to trust or not to trust. I choose to believe God, and trust Him, even if (and when) He does not heal me or my loved one's cancer. In my experience, He has healed my grief and allowed many of my relatives to die due to a variety of causes. I cannot explain God. But I trust Him.

9. **Good faith can slide into bad faith and produce bad grief.** Bad grief may emerge from the twisted belief that God owes me certain things. The death of a loved one is viewed as if God was going back on his word to bless us and keep us. We may feel God isn't keeping His promise to us as His faithful followers.

10. **Even when good faith prevails, grief is a challenge to manage.** Grief management is like waste management — somebody has to collect the trash, the throw-away stuff, and recycle what's recoverable and reusable.

11. **When we approach grief as a personal matter and treat grief as a friend, then faith guides our grief.** We aren't sure what to do with grief in public, especially when we may feel the dread of "Oh, here comes my grief, spilling out in front of God and everybody!" The universal language of grief is heart-sobs, broken sentences, and broken hearts.

Make grief a personal matter. Allow grief to flow in both words and tears. Receive grief graciously, as a friend. Make room for grief. Let your faith guide you.

12. Grief penetrates us, regardless of the strength of our faith. Grief, therefore, is not an indicator of weakness in our faith.

Just the opposite, grief, the willingness to grieve and the ability to grieve, are personal strengths, born of faith, guided by faith and sustained by faith. Persons of strong faith will grieve because grief is a soul-deep need, part of God's creation – just like faith.

13. Grief is the inevitable price we pay for love. Grief is a caring quotient, a measure of how much we love and care.

Live without ever loving anyone, without ever caring for or about anyone, and you won't know grief. You will have no more feeling than a fence post. And your life will be about as exciting. "Oh, isn't it wonderful to be part of this great fence? Yes, I heard several posts in the south fence were destroyed. So what. There will be more posts where we came from. Not to worry. It's no skin off my post."

Grief is an extraordinary human response to personal and family loss, the price we pay for loving and caring.

14. Grief colors life, tinting everything around us. Grief subdues our soul, quells our spirit, and inhibits our desire to move forward. Worthy tears leave grief stains. The tinting, the inhibiting, are an important part of grief. Grief is a hurting of the heart, an affliction of the mind, and a deep struggle of the soul. We shouldn't run from it.

Grief colors everything, but would we want the alternative – a life without love, without care, in order to have a life without grief?

15. We have researched grief, have volumes of information about grief. We've even charted grief. We know its stages. And… we have a growing body of opinion that rejects the rigidity of grief stages and chooses an alternative view of grief.

We've discovered grief is a "process". Yet we recognize grief in others before we sense it in ourselves. We need books like this one, to walk with us, talk with us, and help us back to a life of joy and caring. So it comes down to grief and faith: Are they enemies or friends? They can be either one. It all depends on how we choose to use them.

"Grief-faith" will see us through.

When we grieve in healthy ways, when we faith through our grief and grieve through our faith, we help ourselves.

When we grieve in unhealthy ways without faith, we hinder the process. We hijack our healing. Don't hijack your healing! Don't dump your faith.

A Verse for the Valley: "I am the resurrection and the life. He who believes in Me, though he may die, he shall live." (John 11:25).

Grief-faith always remembers the resurrected Lord who is our hope. Grief-faith claims the hope that death represents not the end of life but actually its beginning!

"the strength and splendor of belief"

In 1972, Fred Pratt Green gifted the faith community with a rousing, encouraging text that reminds me of the tag line in 1 Thessalonians 4:13: "Do not grieve as those who have no hope..."

> "How blessed are they who trust in Christ
>   when we and those we love must part;
> we yield them up, for go they must,
>   but do not lose them from our heart.
> "In Christ, who tasted death for us,
>   we rise above our natural grief
> and witness to a grieving world
>   the strength and splendor of belief."[160]

The Reality of Grief, Doubt, and Faith

Many times in my role as "pastor," I have witnessed death and doubt even as I have observed death and faith. Real life examples follow.

Real Life Example #1 – One father to another: "I don't know why God takes fine young men like your son," referring to a military death in Iraq.

Real Life Example #2 – "I doubt seriously God had anything to do with this," the mournful father said, following the combat death of his son.

Real Life Example #3 – "She was always a doubter," her mother told me, "and she knew that I knew she had lots of questions. I'm sure that's why she left the note. She did not want to add to my grief and pain."

The daughter took her own life. Yet to avoid inflicting unknown and unintended pain, the daughter wrote in part: "But I'm confident God's Heaven will be big enough for my doubts as well as my faith. See you when you get there. I love you more than I can ever say…"

Real Life Example #4 – "I can't think of anything that will make you doubt everything you've read and been taught about God more than the death of a two-week old child. Where, pray tell, is the Providential Care in all of that?" These were the words of a heart-broken father, following the death of his child.

Within the next six years, this same "father" and his wife had two beautiful children which both the mother and the father described as, "gifts from God." I have heard this father give thanks for the blessing of his children.

A Grief, Doubt and Faith Response

There is a strange sort of comfort in the sheer universality of grief and sorrow.

Religion expresses human doubt as well as human faith. "Doubt is not the opposite of faith;" writes Dr. Edwin M. Poteat, "it is collateral to it." Just as Psalm 77 is a poem about doubt, Poteat suggests, it is "the sort of doubt that has always been the stout ally of religious faith."[161]

"The just shall live by faith", Hebrews 20:38 tells us, and strong faith has no fear of doubt, because faith has room for both doubt and grief.

In Psalm 77:19, we read: "Your path led through the sea… though your footprints were not seen." (NIV) There you have it again – the reality of grief, doubt, and faith!

"Healing Begins"

In his book *Living the Promises of God*, Paul Keller writes about the process of how healing begins. Read Keller's words slowly, let them enter your brain and penetrate your grief.

> "In the midst of our deepest grief the process of our healing begins, slowly but surely. Slowly but surely God's grace comes into focus. Slowly but surely we sense that God is at work in our lives to bring

about our recovery from loss, sorrow, and grief. Slowly but surely we come to trust the faithfulness of the Lord to be with us always. Slowly but surely the helplessness of our sorrow lessens; the deep shadows lighten; lost energy is regained; and hope is restored. Slowly but surely we become astounded by the healing wonders of God at work in our lives."[162]

The Chapter "Take-Away"

Don't live with a "Fire Alarm Fear". Face every day with a "Fire Alarm Faith". Be thankful for your grief. Consider what it means. Be strong in your faith. Consider what it does.

God's nature is to be present with us in our grief and in our doubt – to stay as long as we need Him. Yes, that's a statement of faith – grief faith.

Grief faith is a spring board, providing what we need. Your grief faith will walk with you even when you doubt. Your grief faith will strengthen you, and give you a courageous hope.

Your grief-faith friend,

Fran Buhler

A Grief PS: When our faith and our grief are friends, life just goes better…

1. In your life, does your faith partner with your grief? Consider your answer, then consider, why or why not?

2. Describe for yourself a time in your life when you had a grief-faith experience?

3. Can you think of someone near you who is struggling with grief and could benefit from your grief-faith experience?

CHAPTER 27

GRIEF AND GUILT Q & A: "IS THERE SUCH A THING AS 'GUILT REMOVAL'?"

Dear Reader and Partner in Grief,

I don't mean to invade your privacy, so don't shy away from reading this chapter. It may have been written just for you. Grief and guilt are universal challenges. They go together like life and death.

Why This Matters

Each of us grieve whether we want to or not, whether we acknowledge it or not. And at one time or another, we each find ourselves in the sticky goo of guilt.

Grief is often messy when guilt is involved. "Grief guilt" is like a carpet jelly-spill ---a mess impossible to hide and very difficult to clean up. "Grief guilt" has its own triggers, its own time-table, and it defies our efforts to hide it. Let's jump in and deal with it.

Q and A about Grief and Guilt Where Death is the Prompter

1. What about grief and guilt?

Grief is:
- Anguish, bereavement, sorrow.
- Sadness, heartache and heartbreak.
- Heaviness of heart, a heightened sense of loss, soul-deep tribulation.
- What we feel when someone we love or for whom we have high regard, dies.

Guilt is:
- Remorse, regret, contrition.
- The result of misconduct, bad behavior, personal mistakes and failures.
- The feeling of deep regret we have when we fail, when we say the wrong thing or fail to say the right thing, when we do the wrong

thing or fail to do the right thing, when we are at fault, when we are wrong, and when we are conscience-stricken.

2. Isn't each situation different?

Every grief situation, every feeling of guilt, is unique, different, one of a kind.

Each experience of grief, each feeling of guilt, has its own soul-print. If we honestly confess our grief and guilt, we have the opportunity to move beyond the log-jam.

Different people grieve differently. Each of us experiences guilt in personal ways.

I may know why you grieve but I probably won't know about your deep sense of guilt.

The grief prompt may be the death of a distant cousin or the death of your soul-mate. Each grief has some commonality yet there is really no comparison because we experience each grief with very different grief levels and grief consequences.

The guilt prompt may be something you said or something you failed to do. "He died and everything happened so fast I never had a chance to tell him I loved him."

3. What are the main causes of our guilt?

Our choices, our decisions and our actions.

Our choices may stir up guilt. Our actions may generate gobs of guilt. Don't expect to toss your guilt aside. We have to deal with our guilt-producing choices and actions just as we have to deal with a flat tire.

We can't move forward with either one.

4. Is there any way to unravel the two?

Consider this: Grief results from big losses. Guilt results from deep regrets.

Grief won't go away just because we want it to. Guilt won't wash away, won't subside, just because we wish it to. In order to deal with our grief or our guilt, we have to go as deep as the grief and the guilt go. We have to revisit the choices and the actions that brought on the guilt.

5. Does that mean it is hopeless?

Not at all. Guilt often occurs or results from four things. What we do or what we say. What we do not do or do not say. Either way… guilt is a self-indictment, and it is doubly hard to negotiate with ourselves. That's why guilt is so strong and lasts so long.

It is even harder to forgive ourselves. Yet we often need to, indeed, we must.

We often choose to live with the pain of guilt because it is so messy to address our guilt and attempt to deal with our guilt.

6. Is there such a thing as guilt removal?

Yes, there is. Guilt removal is called "forgiveness".

Guilt removal occurs when God forgives us, when someone else forgives us, and when we forgive ourselves. Guilt removal also occurs when we forgive someone else.

Guilt removal, the profound act of forgiveness, is one of the greatest things we can ever experience or extend. Each of us should be in the guilt removal business.

But remember, the personal guilt we experience drags along with us because we do not or have not asked the other party to forgive us. So if you are beset with guilt, your guilty feeling probably means there is one person or maybe more to whom you need to go and ask forgiveness.

If you really want to make this world a better place, actively forgive your own guilt and freely forgive the guilt of others. Forgive the words, the actions, the inactions that give rise to guilt.

7. Can you forgive someone even when they don't ask for forgiveness?

Absolutely.

A Verse for the Valley: "Forgive us our debts, as we forgive our debtors."

Jesus' words from the model prayer in Matthew 6:12.

Make forgiveness a habit. Forgive and live. Forgive and forget. Forgive and feel good — because you will live longer. The Golden Rule footnote is: Forgive others before they even ask for forgiveness.

8. So… if I forgive and ask forgiveness, will my grief and guilt go away?

Your grief may not go away completely because your grief is independent of your forgiveness of another, or someone's forgiveness of you. But extending forgiveness to another human being and receiving forgiveness from another will do wonders for your guilt.

We can process our grief and thereby ease our grief. We can live with our grief in ways that nurture and address our grief, but none of that addresses our guilt.

We have to meet our guilt head on and deal with it, or we live with it.

9. What should I do about my guilt?

Work your way back to the root cause. Address the action or decision that prompted your guilt.

Our tendency is to run from our guilt. Yet a life of guilt flight doesn't reduce or remove our guilt.

Instead of running away from your guilt, a better strategy is to run to your guilt. Run to it and deal with it. Whatever the action or inaction, the deed or misdeed, the comment or the silence, revisit it, address it, acknowledge it, and, if called for, ask forgiveness for it. You will be surprised. You will feel better immediately. And after that, you will always feel better.

10. Help me understand what you've said. Walk me through it.

Two examples: A good Old Testament background read on forgiveness via the "guilt offering" may be found in Leviticus 6:1-7. In the New Testament, Jesus' classic act of forgiveness was while he was nailed to the cross, in Luke 23:34: "But Jesus was saying, 'Father, forgive them; for they do not know what they are doing'."

Now do the following. Work your way back to the root cause of your guilt:

your mistake, your wrong action, your wrong statement, your wrong-whatever-it-was, and own it, period.

Address the action that prompted your guilt: Speak to the other party in person, by phone, or a personal note. Revisit your personal mistake, your regretful comment or action by acknowledging it, and asking forgiveness for the hurt, damage or confusion you have caused. You will feel better immediately. The effort required will be worth it.

Chapter "Take-Away"

Grief is universal. So is guilt!

I am a member of the Club. Perhaps you are too.

Every one of us stands in need of "forgiveness". And most of us, at one time or another, need to forgive others. Either way, you will discover forgiveness is the best "guilt removal" you will ever find.

Your grief-guilt partner and forgiven friend,

Fran Buhler

A Grief PS: The experience of being "forgiven" comes before the challenge to "forgive". In a civilized world, Q & A about "guilt removal" should be a required course...

1. Name any feelings of guilt you may have about the way in which you handled your grief or the manner in which you responded to someone else's grief?

2. Have you personally experienced in your life the release of "guilt removal"?

3. Have you or could you be the agent who would help someone else experience the release and joy of "guilt removal"?

CHAPTER 28

"HOW DO I KNOW I'M GETTING BETTER?"

Dear Reader and Partner in Grief,

Grief will change you. No question. **But is it possible for grief to change you for the better?**

Yes, I believe it is possible! Let me tell you...

Why This Matters

When the storms of life come near and take a loved one home.
Be still and trust the Father's love so in our grief we're not alone.
For grief will always call our tears and leave us in our grief to bear
the weight of life's together years because of all the love's we share.
There is no future in our fear that death will claim tomorrow.
We live one long and faithful life with God's sure help in sorrow.

In Bob Deits "Growing Through Loss" conferences, he speaks to this transformational grief possibility. Deits wants his conference participants to be able to say the following with confidence:

"The loss I experienced is a major event in my life. Perhaps it is the worst thing that will ever happen to me. But it is not the end of my life. I can still have a full and rewarding life. Grief has taught me much, and I will use it to be a better person than I was before my loss."[163]

How we use our grief to become better persons than we were before our loss is up to each of us. Here is the larger life benefit. Because we find God's sure help in sorrow, we find a renewed energy and enthusiasm for life. As Deits points out, we will begin "to adapt to a new life that does not revolve around our experience of grief". In time, we even laugh again!

What Grief has Taught Us

When we mourn a death, it is always a mix of public grief and private sorrow, a glimpse of our human side made public as well as our genuine and poignant sorrow kept private.

THE GRIEF LETTER

At the outset grief may seem perpetual. I have heard many speak of "overwhelming grief". Others say I am "a prisoner of grief". John Ashley called grief "the parching thirst of death".

Many grievers adopt a "grief prayer." A friend of mine uses Psalm 30:10, for example: "Hear, O Lord, and have mercy upon me; Lord, be my helper."

Helen Fitzgerald knows it is possible for grief to change you for the better. And she can help you know for yourself. When Helen's husband died, she was left a widow with four children. That was when she began to devote herself professionally to the need of those who suffer the death of a loved one.

Today Dr. Fitzgerald coordinates the first grief program in the nation established in a community mental health center, the Mt. Vernon Center for Community Mental Health in Springfield, Virginia. She is a certified death educator and lectures on the subject.

Compassionate Advice: 27 Grief Clues

In *The Mourning Handbook*, Dr. Fitzgerald offers compassionate advice on coping with death and grief. She also offers 27 clues to help you see you are beginning to work through your grief.

The best part, besides how comprehensive she is, is the simple practicality of the list. Scan the list. Read through it two or three times.

See which clue or cluster of clues relate specifically to you and to your grief experience. You know you are getting better...

1. "When you are in touch with the finality of death."
2. "When you can review both pleasant and unpleasant memories."
3. "When you can enjoy time alone."
4. "When you can drive somewhere by yourself without crying the whole time."
5. "When you realize the painful comments by family or friends are in ignorance."
6. "When you can look forward to holidays."
7. "When you can reach out to help someone else in a similar situation."
8. "When the music your loved one listened to is no longer painful to you."

9. "When you can sit through a religious service without crying."
10. "When some time passes in which you have not thought of your loved one."
11. "When you can enjoy a good joke."
12. "When your eating, sleeping, and exercise patterns return to what they were before the death."
13. "When you no longer feel tired all the time."
14. "When you have developed a routine to your daily life."
15. "When you can concentrate on a book or a favorite television program."
16. "When you no longer have to make daily or weekly trips to the cemetery."
17. "When you can find something to be thankful for."
18. "When you can establish new and healthy relationships."
19. "When you feel confident again."
20. "When you can organize and plan your future."
21. "When you can accept things as they are and not keep trying to return to what they were."
22. "When you have patience with yourself through 'grief attacks'."
23. "When you look forward to getting up in the morning."
24. "When you can stop to smell the flowers along the way and enjoy experiences in life that are meant to be enjoyed."
25. "When the vacated roles that your loved one filled in your life are now being filled by yourself or others."
26. "When you can take the energy and time spent on the deceased and put those energies elsewhere, perhaps on helping others in similar situations or making concrete plans with your own life."
27. "When you can acknowledge your new life and even discover personal growth from your grief."

You may not agree with all of the above. Yet each is a viable indicator of our grief progress. Review the list from time to time. And...give yourself time.[164]

"The voice of human sorrow"

In Genesis 23:1-20 we find the account of the death of Abraham's wife, Sarah. Walter Russell Bowie, the late professor of the Protestant Episcopal Theological Seminary in Virginia, in *The Interpreter's Bible Commentary*, Volume 1, caught my attention in 1962. I was 22, teaching history at Fork Union Military Academy in Virginia, enrolled in seminary for the following fall semester.

"Sarah's death is recounted briefly, but the description of the arrangements for her burial is long. From time immemorial the burial of the dead has had a vast solemnity. Human sorrow has tried to immortalize the names and to perpetuate the memory of those whom it has lost. Witness the pyramids of Egypt. So Abraham, though he could have no great monument for Sarah, is represented here as paying a lavish price for the cave in which to bury her. In the customary formula of Oriental bargaining, Abraham pays four hundred shekels of silver. Abraham does not even attempt to reduce the exaggerated price. He weighs out the silver… and calls all the Hittites who are near to bear witness to the transaction. So the cave of Machpelah belonged irrevocably to him and to his family – the cave in which he himself would ultimately be buried, and Isaac, and Jacob, and others after them; and over which a Mohammaden mosque would rise, to guard to this day what are maintained to be the patriarch's graves. The importance of the record for the people of Israel was that the land to which Abraham had come was thus certified forever as belonging sacredly to them."[165]

Walter Russell Bowie calls the sentences with which Chapter 23 opens "personal and poignant". Bowie says:

"Here is the voice of human sorrow which is as old as the world, and as new as the most recent heart-break. Abraham came to mourn for Sarah, and to weep for her."[166]

What May We Learn from Abraham's Grief?

As I continue quoting Walter Russell Bowie, I am altering the usual quotation format in order to give special emphasis to his narrative:

"As Genesis portrays her, Sarah had been a person whose passing, like the fall of some tall tree, must leave an empty space against the sky."

"As Abraham's wife and comrade she had gone through many experiences with him, and always in fidelity."

"She, with him, had made the choice to leave the rich civilization of UR of the Chaldeans, and to go out to the long adventure of the spirit."

"She, with him, had known the uncertain life of Canaan, sojourning 'in a foreign land, living in tents' (Hebrew 11:9)."

"She, with him, had lived through the wistful and sometimes bitter disappointment of the years of childlessness."

"She, with him, had shared the joy and pride of Isaac's birth. According to the portrayal of Genesis, she was very beautiful. She had her obvious faults, but she had character and great distinction – a woman who could be jealous, but who had passionate devotion to those she loved…"

"She was dead now, and Abraham mourned, and wept for her. Then he stood up from before his dead, i.e., he had to go out and meet the world and its sad responsibilities. In every age human beings have had to do that. There is the everlasting poignancy of human pain, bereavement, and then the fact that one must go on in loneliness to face what life requires…"

"It may be either a cold heart, or one unnaturally frozen by some inhibition, that does not at some time like Abraham mourn and weep. Yet there is another truth which Abraham also represented. It is not right that grief should be allowed to become a paralyzing bondage."

Guess what happens?

In the process, as we enjoy God's sure help in sorrow, we begin to sense we are getting better! We begin to own our grief, just as Abraham owned his grief for Sarah. Grief ownership provides a definite marker: We are "getting better". We are moving forward.[167]

"Help me understand what I've just read about Abraham's grief."

One of the most important lessons we learn through our grief is: We don't have to walk the hard road of grief alone. Abraham learned the most merciful God walks with us. In the words of Robert Hamilton, "sorrow can be both our companion and our teacher". And in the words of sacred scripture, God comforts all who mourn.

"A Wideness in God's Mercy"

In the never-ending human yearning for hope and comfort following the death of someone dear, the words of Frederick W. Faber, penned in 1854 on the eve of the US Civil War, provide a standard of grief excellence in hard times.

This is a standard much ignored during and after the Civil War itself, and today.

THE GRIEF LETTER

For the sake of truth and goodness, and for your own sake, stop and review these words. Allow their meaning to soak into your soul.

> "There's a wideness in God's mercy,
> like the wideness of the sea:
> there's a kindness in His justice,
> which is more than liberty.
> "But we make His love too narrow
> by false limits of our own;
> and we magnify His strictness
> with a zeal He will not own."[168]

In our grief and in the grief of others, remember Gods merciful "wideness". Let us commit to conduct ourselves with a decisive "wideness in our mercy". May we refrain from our judgmental nature, an outlook that slices humanity into impersonal chunks of life.

Remember, the heart of the Eternal is wonderfully kind.

Reflect the wonderful kindness of the Holy One. Act and grieve with love, showing kindness in your grief, giving "wideness" in your merciful grief help.

Experience the "Wideness": "God will meet you anywhere"

Hear these words of Shelly Ramsey from Grief: A Mama's Unwanted Journey, describing His "merciful wideness", and apply them to your circumstance:

> "My experience is that God will meet us anywhere. Grieving badly and under the covers? He's there. Sitting at the cemetery, wishing it were you? You're not alone. Siting on your child's bedroom floor still in your nightgown in the middle of the afternoon? He's holding you up. God will meet you anywhere."[169]

In our times of grief, heartache, pain and difficulty, the Most High God stands ready to help. He will meet us anywhere! Such truth encourages us to embrace today and tomorrow with confidence and hope.

Verses for the Valley: 1 Thessalonians 4, verse 13c: "Do not sorrow and grieve as those who have no hope." Verse 14: "For if we believe that Jesus died and rose again, even so God will bring with Him those who have fallen asleep in Jesus." Verse 18: "Therefore, comfort one another with these words."

The Chapter "Take-Away"

As we near the end of Part 3 of "The Grief Letter", I hope the time together has been beneficial. I hope "The Grief Letter", "Grief Adventure Is a Life Choice" and "The Ten Commandments of Grief" have each helped you:

- Grieve in life-enriching and transformative ways
- Move forward in your grief so you aren't captive of your pain and sorrow
- Process your grief for a transformative grief experience, and
- Improve and expand your grief support capability with others

At several points in our lives we must turn in the Book of Life to the chapter called, "Grief". We cannot turn passive in our grief and wait for someone else to do our grieving and our grief-processing. Grieving is neither a sign of sin nor evidence of personal weakness.

Grief done right is a strength, a sign of personal substance and courage, evidence of an essential life capacity. But without God's help, grief is an impossible gulf to span with mere human capability. Grief responds to love better than logic. Grief runs better on simple faith than fierce determination. Grief will always be helped by those four words that never fail, words my wife, Nancy, brought to the grief challenge: "I hurt with you."

"When Sorrow walked with me"

"I walked a mile with Pleasure;
She chatted all the way;
But left me none the wiser
For all she had to say.
"I walked a mile with Sorrow,
And ne'er a word said she;
But, oh! The things I learned from her
When sorrow walked with me."[170]

Yes, grief can change you. Grief can even change you for the better as grief, your teacher, becomes a transformative energy in your life. Grief requires your involvement and your participation to do so.

THE GRIEF LETTER

As your grief becomes a partner in your life journey, your "grief walk" has the potential to become transformational. I believe Augustine anticipated transformational grief when he wrote "a greater joy is preceded by a greater suffering", a sign we are getting better.

Your grief partner and friend,

Fran Buhler

A Grief PS:

1. From the list of 27 grief clues, choose three reasons why you know you are getting better. If possible, for your own benefit, count the number of clues which apply to you.

2. If that is not possible, choose four clues you want to work on and work toward, next.

3. What did you learn from Abraham's grief? Ask yourself: How am I using my grief…to become a better person, to help others in their grief?

Give thanks to God who walks with us in our sorrow, gives hope in our grief and provides strength for the journey ahead---the life that is ours to live and celebrate until God calls us home.

PART 3 - CHAPTER 28

PART 4

WHAT TO SAY AND DO WHEN SOMEONE DIES

Part 4: What to Say (and Do) When Someone Dies!

Dear Reader and Partner in Helping Those Who Mourn,

When you first open "The Grief Letter", especially if you are still heart-deep in raw, tear-saturated grief, Part 4 may not interest you.

There is no magic formula about when to read the five chapters of Part 4. You will know. Your grief and your personal prayer life will help you sense when the time is right.

However, I must be honest and straight with you.

In my personal experience, God has often called me to comfort another grieving heart long before I thought I was ready. In fact, discerning the right time is more of a personal discipleship and a spiritual issue than a personal "I feel this is the right time" matter. Whatever our personal faith and our tendencies may be, the call to comfort those who mourn is not a purely optional matter. **Someone comforted us in our grief. Shouldn't we be alert to comfort others in their grief?**

Why This Matters

Stop and recall those caring persons who interrupted their lives to come along side when your grief wagon was loaded. Remember what their presence and their condolence meant to you? Be honest, you can still name those who cared, those who came, in your time of sorrow. When you were hurting at a soul-deep level, someone cared. Someone came. Someone reached out to you in your grief. Now, it is your turn to care, to care enough to be there, to do the comforting for someone else in their time of sorrow.

What This Means

Death in someone else's life always comes at a busy time in our lives, always. There is not a convenient time to care for someone in sorrow. There is only now. And three questions as to what this means:

- "Do I?"
- "Am I?"
- "Will I?"

"Do I love the Lord?"

"Am I serious about my responsibilities as a human being?"

"Will I go, will I make time, will I adjust my schedule, will I make it happen, will I evidence my personal care and demonstrate the power of reaching out to one in grief?"

Verses to Focus Us When We Walk with Someone in their Valley:
Solomon's Song of Songs 8:6b-7a: "…for love is as strong as death… It burns like a blazing fire, like a mighty flame. Many waters cannot quench love; rivers cannot wash it away."(NIV)

The power of love covers us when we walk with someone who mourns a death.

"Love one another", Jesus said. "As I have loved you, so you must love one another," was the new command Jesus gave in John 13:34. In verse 35, Jesus asserted what the Christian "brand" is supposed to look like, when he said: "By this all will know that you are my disciples, if you love one another."

Clearly, this command applies when someone we know is hurting in sorrow, grieving in heartache and suffering in the pain of personal loss.

Part 4 Chapters

Chapter 29 asks the age old question: "What do I say when someone dies?"

Chapter 30 addresses "The Eleventh Commandment of Grief".

Chapter 31 tackles "Helping a Child with the Challenge of Grief".

Chapter 32 celebrates "The Best Part of Grieving…is Believing", if you can believe it?

Chapter 33, "The Adventure of Listening to Those Who Mourn", addresses the world's best available grief therapy! We should listen more than we talk.

Happy reading! Happy listening!

Your partner in comforting those who mourn,

Fran Buhler

PART 4

A Grief PS:

1. The best way to approach Part 4 is to remember how help came to us.

2. As we comfort others, we discover the good feeling of helping someone in grief.

3. Responding to the grief of another, we rediscover the high calling of giving comfort by listening!

PPS: Remember, you are now focusing on self and your grief needs, but eventually you will reach the stage of grief recovery in which you will begin focusing on someone else and their grief need.

1. You now, by your own personal choice, move from focusing on your own grief to focusing on the grief of others. Ask yourself: Am I staying focused on the other person's grief?

2. Here's a good self-check. What we talk about indicates where our brain is focused. When you are with a grieving person, is your conversation to the person grieving or about yourself and your own personal grief? Are you thinking you are helping the grieving person when you are mostly talking about yourself and your own grief?

3. Monitor the subject of your sentences. Is your language speaking of yourself and your needs, or of the needs of others?

CHAPTER 29

"WHAT DO I SAY WHEN SOMEONE DIES?"

Dear Reader and Partner in Consolation,

You may not want to talk about this topic. But when someone dies, all of us want to say the right thing. **All of us experience "consolation frustration", even "consolation anxiety", and take our turn being uncomfortable with the challenges of comforting those who mourn.**

We may not even think about the challenge until death visits our family, a neighbor or friend. Yet, at some point in every life, what to say when someone dies becomes an immediate challenge, an urgent personal concern. Do we know what to say? Are we coaching and teaching our children and families what to say and do?

What This Means

"The death of a loved one," writes Carol Staudacher in *A Time To Grieve*, is the most profound emotional experience we will ever have to endure." Then she adds: "Dealing with the deep and prolonged grief that follows such a loss may well be the most painful and disturbing challenge of our lives."[171]

We must be aware this is the situation we enter when we decide to comfort someone who mourns. Any time someone dies and we decide to go to the "Visitation Time", we need to remember there is not another situation like it anywhere in life. We meet the challenge or we blow the opportunity to comfort someone who is definitely grieving and hurting.

Grief Help in "a whirling sea of grief"

Following the memorial service for her husband, the grieving wife described her life as "a whirling sea of grief." Then she added, "And would you believe all two of my friends wanted to talk about was the weather!"

When we are with grieving people in our culture, our conversations too often circumvent their grief and sorrow. We talk about the past, the future, what we've been doing, where we're going, what's happening at the office, what's going on in our community. We talk about anything and sometimes everything before we get around to the universal phrase: "Now, if there is any-thing-at-all-you-need, don't-hesitate-to-call". With this "one-size-fits-all" comment, we feel we have done our duty and the bereaved should appreciate all the effort to which we've gone to acknowledge their sorrow. Have we given a thoughtful, meaningful condolence? Not really. Have we extended a helping hand?

Hardly.

"Don't hesitate to call" puts the entire burden on the one grieving, while we go our merry way. So our mindset is: Because they never call, we assume we met and answered their every need. When what we have done is the classic example of how we too often leave another human drowning in "a whirling sea of grief".

Why This Matters # 1

After a life-time in churches and funeral homes, in "visitations" and at "gravesides", I must say those who grieve deserve better. We who wish to comfort and support others in their grief need to get our act together. When we comfort those who mourn, we should extend extra effort to be Christ-like and helpful---genuinely helpful. Part of being kind and helpful is giving specific detail, sharing an example. "I remember a time she kept our children when Roy was in the hospital." "He was the first neighbor to offer clean-up help after the storm in 2010…"

Why This Matters # 2

Grief is about the one grieving, the one whose heart is broken, whose soul throbs with a never-ceasing ache. Yet it is also about the "grief helper". In living our faith, we have a responsibility---and an opportunity---to prepare ourselves, to coach ourselves, in effective ways to comfort those who mourn. One thing is certain. We do not help others in their grief when we continue to spout the grief clichés of the past. If we care, we owe it to the God we say we follow and serve, to sensitize ourselves, to prepare ourselves, to help others on their grief journey.

Positive Suggestions

I credit my wife, Nancy, for my favorite "condolence of choice". Hundreds of times I have borrowed her classic condolence, a simple but strong expression from the heart: "We hurt with you". Many words will do their "comforting work" if we really mean them, such as: "I am very sorry". "My heart goes out to you." "I don't pretend to know your feelings. I just know it's one of our deepest hurts ever!" The key, the spiritual magic, is to put words together, creating an emotional connection, communicating "I care".

When I enter a situation where the grief is heightened by the circumstances of death, sometimes I feel words actually get in the way. Examples come to mind: 1. A spouse, family member, or friend has been killed in a storm, murdered, or died an accidental death. 2. A child dies before or during birth or soon thereafter. 3. A loved one dies during or after surgery. 4. A long multi-year decline in health leads to death. 5. A military representative came to the front door to deliver the news.

When Silence Speaks

For the one grieving, a time of pronounced "alone-ness", such as funeral-home silence, at-home-by-yourself silence, or in-the-middle-of-a-crowd silence, can be heavy, crushing and overwhelming. Introduce a human presence in those stretches of silence and it speaks a comforting word to all who grieve, saying: "I'm here. I care." Grieving persons with whom I have been present in funeral home, graveside, and sanctuary memorial services sum it well, expressing the typical griever attitude and point of view.

Grief Example # 1: "The people who helped me the most were the ones who didn't smother me with words. They were with me. Their presence said, 'I care'."

Grief Example # 2: "I had a friend stand with me. He let me know he cared by the way he stood with me."

Grief Example # 3: "She called my name, and said, simply, 'I am so sorry.' She didn't need to say anything else."

The "I Care Test"

The "I Care" Test begins with the following evidence:

1. Have I been thoughtful and faithful, praying for the one or ones who are grieving?

2. Have I thought thru what I want to say? Am I prepared to express myself in a few words?

3. Will I keep the focus on the one "grieving", not on myself or the weather

or who won the game or what's in the news or what's happening at work?

4. Do I believe in what I am doing and what I am going to say?

Express and communicate "I care" to the grieving ones for whom you are concerned. Speak from your heart because you care. Believe me, this challenge really matters.

"But what if I struggle with what to say?"

In a moment of honesty, Jeannie expressed herself sincerely: "I don't know what to say when someone is grieving." Shaking her head in frustration, she added: "I always dread visitation times. People are really hurting and I feel so verbally clumsy every time I open my mouth."

If she expresses your feeling of frustration, what she describes is not limited to you. Most of us have had this experience of awkwardness. This is the most frequent frustration I have heard from persons who genuinely want to bring comfort to a grieving loved one or friend.

Every death situation is unique, different. There is no single phrase or expression that works automatically in every situation. I have found only one universal rule. "Thoughtfulness requires preparation." Consider your relationship with the one who died and with the one grieving. Choose your words intentionally. You will be glad you did.

Choose your words in the context of your relationship. For example:
- Death of a father and you are a friend of the son:
  "Ron, I'm sorry about your Dad." "I have always had great respect for him." "I was short of help for our big fund-raiser, and he recruited six friends to help us reach our goal." "Your Father was really kind to me and I won't ever forget it."
- Death of a coworker, the wife of a friend:
  "Jim, we're hurting with you. In our office, Jane was the person people looked to for help and guidance. We had great respect and appreciation for her leadership." "She worked late for a week one time to cover for several employees who were ill."
- Death of your neighbor's husband:
  "Susan, I'm so sorry. My heart goes out to you. He was such a good friend and neighbor." "When we had to be away for my father's illness, he offered to look after our place."

THE GRIEF LETTER

Here's a Good Three-Fold Personal Test You may Use: 1. Am I speaking from my heart? 2. Am I offering true "comfort" for the one who mourns? 3. Or am I just spouting words? If we really want to say something meaningful and helpful and we take time to think about it, we will.

When I have been the one grieving, I have found the following self-questions helpful: What words, what gestures from others, have meant the most to me? What do I remember from condolences I have received that I really appreciate? Or want to avoid? This thought process has helped me craft what I am going to say in a given situation.

A Verse to Think About... When Walking with Someone Through Their Valley: "The Lord's love never ends; His mercies never stop. They are new every morning." (Lamentations 3:22-23). I have never said the words of this verse to one in grief. I have said it to myself, for my benefit, to give me focus as I comfort someone who mourns. Reminding myself of God's merciful blessing prepares me to reach out to someone in grief.

Remember: The Question Is Still: "How do I express and communicate "I care"?

First. Decide you want to live and act with honesty about death by acting with sensitivity toward those who are dealing with death in their family or community.

Second. Get the death information accurate. Hearing untrue, incorrect info compounds the grief. Who cares if your information is 60 percent correct? It's the 40 percent that was incorrect and emotionally hurtful that a grieving family will remember.

Third. Give advance thought to what you want to say and how you want to express yourself before you are with the one in grief.

Fourth. Write a personal note. Don't limit yourself to oral words of sympathy. Don't buy a card to do your talking for you, unless you have read the card carefully, slowly, asking yourself: How would I react if the death was in my family and I received these words? When you choose a card, add something from your own heart to the card. Make it personal. Keep it thoughtful. Express your condolence on a "feeling" level. Make it a note that expresses you care, if your relationship and your actions support that expression.

Fifth. This one is critical! Never say: "I know what you're going through…" We know what our grief experience was but we do not know what their grief experience is, has been or will be.

Sixth. Use your faith faithfully and appropriately. Never use faith as a club, nor in a manner that builds a wall between you. Don't assume everyone "believes" just the way you do or uses the same words and expressions you use. If something is meaningful or helpful to you, share it, offer it, but don't be a bully with it. Be your best self. Offer your strongest condolence. Allow God to use your outreach to someone in grief to communicate His Presence and yours.

The Big 7 "Best Things We Can Do"

When a family member, a relative, or a friend dies, and we want to bring comfort to those who grieve, the Big 7 cited below offer good opportunities. Understand this is a listing---not a ranking of importance. The "key" to each of the Big 7 is for us to be prayerfully present and personally engaged as we extend our condolence in one or more of the following ways.

1. Speak to the one grieving in person, as a fellow traveler---not as a superior or more experienced griever.

2. Send a card with a personal note. Take a covered dish or meal. This is optional according to your relationship and your ability to produce and deliver such a gift.

3. Call or leave a phone message, if you are out of town, homebound, or physically unable to go in person.

4. Text, if you have a texting relationship, are out of town, can't get off work, or any of # 3.

5. Email or text if you know each other well. Email or text, if you just want to reach out and extend yourself to the one grieving, even though you may not be close friends.

6. On Facebook, you may use the Facebook grief feature to convey your condolence privately, but only if the recipient is Facebook active and receptive.

7. Make contact via a Tweet, Instagram or other social media options, only if the griever is a regular "user" of that particular option and you have

previously communicated in that medium. Media options tend to be "age specific" in some cases by users most likely to be "internet active". But do not assume only young people are online or that internet use is normal for "20, 30, 40, 50 somethings" but not for older generations. Wrong. Many of us older folks are on the internet for at least one powerful reason---that's where our families are. The point is: Grief is not the right time to force someone to use a new or different communication medium. Don't do it! Find and choose the right medium to reach them in their time of sorrow.

Here's the important thing. The best Big 7 option for the one grieving will enable you to be present and personal in someone else's grief in a mode that brings blessing and comfort.

Presence Speaks

To one torn apart by grief, presence speaks, often louder and with more meaning than words. If the intent of our heart is right and we add a bit of intentional thoughtfulness, then our words and actions will probably be appropriate and comforting. Our presence always makes our words more effective. So if you're wondering what to say when someone dies, "being there" speaks. Add a measure of thoughtfulness to what you say and how you say it, and your words will be appropriate and helpful.

Grief follows death as night follows day. Grief also follows love and care. We do not grieve for one we do not know, love or care. Grief is a relational barometer, a measure of what another life meant to our lives. If you grieve a death, recall what that person meant to you. Let your memories guide your grief. An informed grief becomes a healing grief.

The Power of Tears

Grief is an ambassador for the power of tears. When you see evidence of grief, embrace the opportunity to help someone with the biggest, toughest challenge life can throw at us. When death visits, tears lead the way and, with the right touch, help sweeten the bitterness. How is that possible?

There are tears of love and tears of loss, but there are also tears of love and support. We may also experience the tears of a shared life, togetherness, or team dreams. Life includes tears of achievement and victory as well as sorrow. In the same life, where we see tears of disappointment and death, if we are patient and alert, we may see the overlooked tears of family togetherness, marital milestones, the recovery of joy and transformative faith.

PART 4 - CHAPTER 29

Group Grief Support

Grief support language reminds us immediately of someone who gave us grief support when we really needed it. There are times when we may need to act in concert with others rather than all by ourselves to comfort an individual or a family who mourn.

The death happened years ago, in another time and place. A student died in a horrible car accident. As the pastor said the last words of his eulogy, the student population present broke into instant song---beginning ever so softly, gradually increasing the volume with each refrain:

"Lord, listen to Your children praying,

Lord, send Your Spirit in this place.

Lord, listen to your children praying,

Send us love, send us power, send us grace."

Years later the student's Mother sent a note: "There is nothing better in my grief experience," she wrote, "than children praying---especially when they were childhood friends of your child!"

Then she added: "And they're praying for you."

The Chapter "Take-Away"

An intentional grief connection with a personal "I care" touch really matters to the one in grief. The impact a death has on an individual or a family reflects a variety of ways in which another life may be interwoven with theirs. Having been through experiences of the death of someone near and dear to me, someone significant and important in my life, I know what it means and how it feels when someone reaches out because he or she cares enough to do so.

Take my word, when you take the time and put forth the effort to communicate "I care" to someone in grief and sorrow, you will be forever glad you did. You will be doubly thankful for the sense of God's provisional Presence with you in your "I care" endeavor.

One proven way to reach out to those in grief is via the "GriefShare" network of thousands of grief recovery support groups meeting around the world, including your community most likely. Your church or another church in your city may be offering "GriefShare" multiple times a year. I have participated in my own church. "GriefShare: Your Journey from Mourning to Joy" teaches participants "how to walk the journey of grief and be supported on the way. It is a place where grieving people find healing and hope." I highly recommend "GriefShare" as a strong resource.

Your friend in the adventure of thoughtful grief help,

Fran Buhler

A Grief PS: We communicate we care when our actions support our words, when the "grief helper" really helps!

1. What we say, what we do, in someone else's grief can make a difference, a huge difference.

2. Ask for help from the Holy One. God stands ready to help us help others.

3. Do something simple, thoughtful, helpful. You will be glad you did!

When it comes to grief-helping, a personal motivation and encouragement for me has long been a reminder in the Epistle of Jude, the next to the last book in the Bible, verse 21a. In Christian tradition, Jude is thought to be the brother of Jesus (Matthew 13:55). Jude became a believer after Jesus' resurrection (John 7:5; Acts 1:14).

Jude 1:21a: "...keep yourselves in the love of God, "

CHAPTER 30

THE ELEVENTH COMMANDMENT OF GRIEF

Dear Reader and Partner in Grief Help,

No, in this chapter I'm not targeting you. I'm aiming at all of us. If there was an Eleventh Commandment of Grief, it would surely be: **"Thou shalt be sensitive and helpful with others in their grief."** And it would be so, I believe, because without even giving it a thought we easily slip into negative grief behavior.

What This Means

We wouldn't admit it in a hundred years but this usually means we are often impatient with the grief of others, especially we men.

Our wives are often good, even gifted, at doing things for those who mourn; so in general, we males have some catching up to do.

All of us, both men and women, need to double check our behavior and our grief helping attitude if we are really intent on taking seriously the Bible mandate to "comfort those who mourn". We also have the opportunity to learn from and to coach our own children.

Why This Matters

Whether we realize it or not, our personal reaction to someone's grief, is important.

People never hurt quite like the ship-wreck hurt of grief when someone close to them dies. Our thoughtful help at such times is more than helpful.

From their perspective, we helped when we didn't have to.

We put their need before our own, and that kind of help touches people deeply.

Kids---of all ages---often "get it"

I have seen middle school kids and high school and college students become ambassadors of comfort and support when death enters the life of a classmate or friend. I witnessed our son, Jeff, in the role of class comforter when he was in elementary school and later in his life in the roll of corporate leadership when as an adult he led a volunteer contingent of his company to fulfill his company's commitment to enhance the long-term care and maintenance of Arlington National Cemetery in Washington, D C- --a focal point for the grief of our nation's military families.

Our son, Chip, at the death of his close friend's father, moved into the role of comforter, honoring the memory of a father who quarterbacked a winning Rose Bowl team and treated Chip as part of the family.

Our son, John, who earns his living in a Silicon Valley enterprise with world-wide presence, as the volunteer head of a state-wide prayer ministry, has comforted those who mourn with his gentle presence on numerous occasions.

We often do not get to see or fail to notice the experiences of our own children in the self-selected role of grief comforters. Yet this phenomenon is more likely to happen when we are parental models and encouragers. Our sons learned these comforting skills from their Mother.

"Make the Most of Your Time"

For followers of Jesus Christ, Ephesians 5:16 lays down the "every day" formula for a lifetime challenge of "making the most of your time". Clearly from a faith perspective, making the most of our time involves the strength of our resolve to follow Christ in our everyday lives as well as our sensitivity toward the life needs of those around us. Shouldn't this also include their grief needs? If we really want to "make the most" of our time, we will give attention to the grief need of others. This is the key to grief help.

Grief is a time-taker, a time-user and a potential life-taker. Is there a better use of our time than in reaching out to those who mourn? Is there a more important way to make the most of our time?

If we trust God with our grief, the same way we trust our car to start, the sun to rise or the moon to shine, then our grief-faith will lead us into the grief-adventure of new life. Our grief-faith will also help us become sensitive to the grief of others. We may become one of God's deployed grief helpers.

Here's the truth about this matter of grief helping. If we are willing and ready, we are deployed in the grace and power of God. I have been fortunate to serve in a church with dozens and dozens of Christ-followers who comfort those who mourn. In faith and in service, they are Ephesians 5:16 Christians, "imitators of God" (verse 1) who "walk in love" (verse 2) "just as Christ…gave Himself up for us, an offering and a sacrifice to God" (verse 2).

Yet in all fairness and, in the interest of objectivity, we must note another reaction and viewpoint that is certainly real. As a gentleman asked me, in all sincerity…

"How can I know this faith stuff is for real?"

I can only know "this faith stuff is for real" when I believe the Holy One is for real. This is my opinion and belief, my faith. One way we know He is for real is because we live through those moments, days, weeks, months when, in spite of the thickness and the heaviness of our grief, we experience the lift of His comfort as we mourn.

While no one can fully explain it, we may each experience it for ourselves. There is only one way to know: try it, test it and see.

Sorrow's weakness emerges when it confronts the power of God. There is no human experience of sorrow that we do not in the grace of God---if we are open to it---experience His power to move through and move beyond. It requires faith, only a seed-size faith, and it surely requires time---but not forever.

Sorrow's future depends to some extent upon us.

Sorrow is an invading guest. Some might call it an intruder. And the more hospitality we offer, the longer sorrow will stay. Sorrow's life depends upon the time and space we give it. Sorrow is always a life-jolting experience we live through and beyond. We need to give sorrow an appropriate amount of attention and even appreciation. But we do not have to set up camp and stay within sorrow's borders. We can, in the grace and power of God, and even in genuine sorrow, adventure forward in our lives. A church member friend of mine asked…

"How can we win the grief battle?"

The honest truth is we cannot win the grief battle. Not in our human power.

THE GRIEF LETTER

But God can. The Holy One can enable us over time and in His Grace to win the grief battle!

Have you ever noticed how Isaiah 9:2 connects throughout the Bible? For the record: "The people who walk in darkness will see a great light; those who live in a dark land, the light will shine on them." This reference is to the darkness of bondage in Egypt for the children of Israel, as well as to the universal darkness of sin. Could it also be a metaphor for the darkness of death and grief? Matthew 4:16 quotes Isaiah 9:2 and Luke 1:79 makes reference to Isaiah 9:2.

Ephesians 5:2 urges us to "walk in love" and 5:8 counsels "you are light in the Lord, walk as children of the light."

A Verse for the Valley: Yet in my faith journey I had never asked: How will this come about? What reason do I have to believe? Preparing for a memorial service one evening, I found the reason, in verse 7e of Ephesians 5: "The zeal of the Lord of hosts will accomplish this." I found this verse of assurance and hope for all our grief valleys. What a break-through for grief-faith and hope!

How will I get through my grief?

"The zeal of the Lord" will help me, of that I am confident.

The Chapter "Take-Away"

So we have the standard question. Where do I draw strength and direction to move through and beyond my grief?

Look to the only source with a power stronger than grief itself: "The zeal of the Lord...."

In this life, how will I claim the future God has for me?

I will do it by getting my grief act together, opening myself to His "amazing grace" and believing with all my heart the powerful truth: "The...Lord...will accomplish this."

How will I cope with this massive hole in my life where my loved one used to be? How will I deal with my grief and live thru it?

By giving the matter my honest, best effort and confessing, believing: The

PART 4 - CHAPTER 30

Most High God will accomplish this!

In the Name of the Father, the Son and the Holy Spirit, Amen

Your grief partner and friend,

Fran Buhler

A Grief PS: Make what I've called the "Eleventh Commandment" real in your life, and remember:

1. It has no expiration date, no time limit.

2. It does require participation: Don't ever allow yourself to get so busy or self-absorbed that you can't practice it!

3. Life is short. Grief is long. Kindness is forever.

CHAPTER 31

HELPING A CHILD WITH THE CHALLENGE OF GRIEF

Dear Friend and "Wanna-Be" Grief Helper,

When we are young, we go to school to prepare for life. So where do we go to prepare for the grief we experience when someone dies?

Have you ever heard anyone say, "I'm preparing my child for grief"? And where, pray tell, does a child go whose family may not be prepared or inclined to help with the challenge of grief?

No one prepared me for grief. I doubt if anyone prepared you for your grief challenges. **For the most part, we have little if any preparation for the death of family and friends.**

What This Means

We need to follow Jesus' example. We have to challenge our culture---maybe even our own family---to recognize and value the children in our midst. In Matthew 19, when children were brought to Jesus, the disciples did not want him to be bothered with the children. "But Jesus said, 'Let the children come to me, and don't prevent them. For of such is the Kingdom of Heaven'." Jesus welcomed the children, touching the children and blessing them.

Why This Matters

Most children face the octopus of grief for the first time without any prior preparation or experience. This is an opportunity for parents to touch a child the Jesus way.

What should be a parental priority in every family often goes undone because of our personal grief. I was eight or nine when an uncle died, introducing me to family grief.

I was in high school when my first grandparent died, my paternal grandfather. Other family deaths followed during my college years. In both high school and college I grieved the deaths of two teammates. Each died in car accidents. Team member deaths meant team grief! We had to go to class, write term papers, go to practice, play our game schedule. When could we grieve?

Because of these and other experiences, here are my best thoughts on helping a child through the experience of grief.

Our Adult "Grief Attitudes" Help Children with Grief

1. The best way to help a child is to be open and honest about our own feelings of grief. Being transparent about our own feelings is a tall order. For most of us, this does not come naturally.

My wife, Nancy, is good at helping children with grief, our own sons as well as grieving students in her fourth grade classes over the years. I've seen her coach kids to give "hugs" to a grieving friend and to say "I really miss Johnnie" to a grieving parent.

2. We cannot---and should not---hide our adult grief. We should be straight forward about it. A child may go to his or her room to cry, may even close the door. Kids need to cry too. And sometimes they want their privacy. A child can be helped by adult tears; we shouldn't hide them. As parents, we should be open to the truth grief can become a teaching opportunity. Is there really any need to hide our tears?

3. The next best thing is to avoid becoming so self-absorbed we ignore the needs of the child. As parents, we sometimes must grieve with a dual focus. We must give attention to our own need and, at the same time, give priority to the child's needs. We can grieve, giving attention to our grief needs, and still offer our personal attention and sensitivity to help the child.

4. If needed, find appropriate professional grief help for the child. Possible sources include school guidance counselors, private counseling services and trained grief specialists. Churches, community and religious centers in metro areas often provide staff counseling specialists. Licensed counselors offer help with grief, such as the following telephone "Yellow Pages" ad for clinical services available in my city:

"Licensed Counselor for Adults, Teens, College students
Relationship Issues – Depression – Anxiety
Abuse Recovery – Grief – Eating Disorders"

THE GRIEF LETTER

Seven Ways to Help a Grieving Child

1. Don't assume your child will receive grief help from someone else. After my experiences growing up, you would think I would have been prompted to have preparatory talks with each of our three sons, but I don't think I did. Each of them, early in life, experienced the death of a friend. I missed a real opportunity to help our sons be prepared for grief.

2. Be helpful by discussing without lecturing. Make time to discuss death matters with your child. Notice I said "discuss", not lecture. The first time I talked to one of our sons whose classmate died in a school bus accident, I talked nonstop. I talked way too long; that's a lecture. I learned it is better to begin where the child is, with what the child is thinking and feeling, plus the question of what the child is experiencing; for example, how do you feel? Or how is it going at school? What can I help you with? (That's not the best English: but it is good parenting.)

3. Recall your first grief experience. What was it like? How did you feel? Your feeling level will lead to discovery of possible commonalities in your grief "then" and a child's grief "now". How can you use your grief experience to prepare or help your child or someone else in their grief challenge? What part of your experience is relatable or transferable?

4. We each die sometime, and what we do with our lives is important. Sounds grisly now, but it is a life truth every parent should discuss with his or her child. Encourage the child to think about how he or she wants to live life, what they want to do career-wise, the kind of education they will need. Don't skip the importance of being intentional about these matters rather than floating through life waiting to see what happens. Discuss the importance of faith. Be sure and include the truth of how God walks with us in our day-to-day tasks, comforts us in our grief and carries us in our sorrow. Following a death, share a piece of your own childhood experience with grief following the death of a loved one. Be sensitive. Be real.

5. Answer the Tough Questions.

"What happens when we die?" The younger your child when a death occurs the more likely this will be the question. If you dodge the question, the child will remember. The child will want to know where the person went. For preschoolers, answer in a word or two, not a twenty-minute talk. For middle school and high school, match your length to the child's developmental ability and genuine interest. Share your faith openly on a level your child can understand. The following exchange continues the preschool example.

"Where is Uncle Bob?"

"He is in heaven."

"Will his dog get to go with him?" (I include this question because I have actually been asked this question.)

"Where is heaven?"

"Heaven is where God is."

"You mean God is not here with us?"

"God is everywhere; God is here too. God does not have our human limitations."

"Can I go to heaven?"

"Yes, you can. When you die you can go to heaven. We call it 'trusting in God' and we can begin trusting God as soon as we want to."

See how thin this parent-child conversation is? Only 29 seconds in length! Yet it was enough for the preschool questioner. On another day with another question, when the question warrants it, the parent can give a deeper response.

"Death begins a new kind of experience. Grand Dad is with God. He has left this life and started a new existence." That may be enough initially. Or the child may want more. Be sensitive. Don't assume where the child is in his or her understanding. Be helpful, at the child's level of understanding.

6. Remember, the power and meaning of memory are huge grief factors. The one who has been physically removed and is absent from our lives remains with us in memory. A child can understand memory, with a practical example like the memory of what a family pet or a grandparent did last year. As we remember the experiences we had with that special person, because of their significant meaning for us, we grieve the loss of this one we love and appreciate.

7. Death is like a friend at the door. I heard a well-meaning father tell a child "death is like a stranger at the door" and when death comes "we have to go". Later I had to help the child see the death which came for her grandmother came as a friend. I could literally see the fear in the child's eyes turn into thankfulness. With the matter of what to say to a child when someone dies, we had better give it some good thought before we say it. After all, a child's questions are good questions for adults also.

A helpful guideline Nancy taught me is to only go as far in the discussion as the child goes. When ready with another question, the child will broach the matter again with an "I was wondering…" That's a parental cue, to listen. The child needs to know it's ok to come to a parent anytime with a question about death and grief. It's ok to be sad. It's ok to want to talk about a special person in our lives.

When a question arises and we do not have the human ability to give a precise or factual answer, involve the child, allow the child into the thought process, the faith process. It's ok to admit we do not have all the answers. But we should never neglect the answer of faith. We go as far as we can see, then we go as far as we can believe. And we can believe all the way!

Life is an opportunity to live with grace and make life a blessing for others. Death is like a graduation. Our loved one begins a new kind of life, what faith calls "life everlasting." With our loved one's death, we begin a new kind of life experience without the one who is gone from our everyday lives. Yet the one who has been physically removed and is absent from our lives remains with us in memory. As we actively recall the times we had with that person, because of their significant meaning for us, we grieve the loss of this one we love and appreciate.

Give the Child Permission to Grieve.

Doing a funeral in a nearby community, at the request of one of our church member families, I actually had a child tell me his family told him not to cry at the funeral of his grandmother, saying it was inappropriate.

In my opinion, one of the appropriate behaviors at the death of a loved one is grief with tears. To tell a child not to grieve, not to cry, is telling the child not to be human, not to be sensitive, not to feel deeply about the one who is gone from our lives.

Our grief has its seed in our DNA---we are born to grieve. We grieve even if we have not observed the grief example of others. At the same time, some portion of our grief may legitimately be a learned behavior as we find grief encouragement in the grief examples of those around us.

Grief in "Mr. Roger's Neighborhood"

"Father-figure" and television icon, Fred Rogers, knew how to talk to a child about grief. Listen to his wisdom: "Anything that's human is mentionable, and anything that's mentionable is manageable. When we talk about our feelings," says Mr. Rogers, "they become less overwhelming, less upsetting, and less scary." Then Mr. Rogers offers gentle grief help, useful for everyone in the "neighborhood": "The people we trust with that important talk can help us know that we are not alone."

Grieve in the Arms of God

The "Father" reference we often use to refer to the Holy One has special meaning for we who believe in "God, the Father, Almighty, maker of heaven and earth…"

As "believers" we find grief comfort in the presence of God, bringing a sense of security and protection as we feel love and comfort in the proverbial arms of God.

By all means, pray with the child touched by grief. A simple prayer asking God to help us through our grief and our heartbreak may be the most powerful encouragement the child will experience. We should also help the child understand the nature of grief.

Understanding Grief at a Child's Level

A child does not come into this world already knowing about grief. As adults, we should take time to tenderly help a child understand the nature of grief, and why it hurts so much. The following thoughts may encourage and guide your conversation with a child.

1. We grieve for someone because we loved and appreciated that person. Grief is natural and normal, not a weakness. Grief is an extended function of our love. Grief may vary in intensity, yet our grief is usually with us 24/7.

2. When someone dies, that person leaves this life in death but remains in our memory.

3. We grieve whether we want to or not. Grief imposes itself upon us, and upon our lives. Grief does not let up just because we are in public.

4. Grief has no "on" and "off" switches. Grief is triggered by feelings deep inside us.

5. Grief keeps its own schedule. Instead of adjusting to our wishes and our schedule, grief imposes its schedule upon us. A child may feel sad at the school bus stop or cry at school, not waiting until the funeral the next day, or not stopping because the death was six weeks ago.

6. Grief can be awkward, embarrassing, even ugly. Grief isn't always good. Grief can be honest, open, helpful. Grief may also hide. And grief never goes away just because we want it to.

7. Grief moves in and stays, as long as we need to grieve, as long as we want to grieve, until gradually, over time, we adventure beyond our immediate grief experience.

The Chapter "Take-Away"

So…our grief is always evolving. If we pay attention, we may learn from our grief. Be open to what your grief may teach you and how it may lead you to teach your child.

Don't miss "faith" opportunities. Teach a child to grow stronger by growing closer to God.

Our grief is never about our staying power. All of our grief, even our unresolved sorrow, is about the One who comforts us anytime and every time we mourn. A big help to me has been focusing on God's Presence rather than my loved one's absence. A child can understand.

Gently urge the child to practice faith, to trust God. If we believe, if we seek to follow God in our lives, the adventure of grief will find joy again! That is why I write "The Grief Letter".

For our children, grandchildren and generations yet unborn…

In the Name of the Father, the Son, and the Holy Spirit---all One in the Holy One! Amen.

Fran Buhler

A Grief PS: When we grieve, we tend to feel everyone around us is grief-free and would never grieve as hard as we are grieving. This assumption is incorrect. Remember the Preface statistical summary of "Grief in the US Today". If you skipped it, you may read it now.

1. Don't allow your personal or family grief to blind you to the grief of a child or grandchild.

2. Navigating the raw experience of grief is challenging for a child. As a family member or helpful adult, offer tender love, be gentle and sensitive, give the child helpful support.

3. If you want to help a child in grief, remember how help came to you. Don't "preach" as if you're the grief expert. Be a grief "partner" instead. Give love and helpful support. Let your presence, your speech and your behavior, offer support to the child in grief as you point to the comfort of the Holy One!

CHAPTER 32

THE BEST PART OF GRIEVING IS BELIEVING!

Dear Reader and "Wanna-Be" Grief Helper,

If we grieve by faith, then---as we have seen since the topical chapters of Part 2---grief in the grace of the Holy One becomes a true adventure. The best part of grieving is...

- Receiving God's comfort and grace in our grief;
- Having thoughtful loved ones and friends who sincerely support us in our grief;
- Knowing there is a future beyond this life;
- Believing the one for whom we grieve is now in the presence of God.

Yes, the best part of grieving is believing!

Why This Matters

Isaiah 61:2 makes it clear God is in the grief comfort business. This long ago word from the children of Israel in exile becomes a word to each of us in the "exile" of our personal and family grief. When Jesus was called on to read from the sacred scroll, he chose the portion of Isaiah 61 in which verse two is the key, "to comfort all who mourn."

The best part of grieving is the assurance there is One who comforts us when we mourn. The next best part of grieving is to know by faith there is life beyond this life. With resurrection faith, we have eternal hope in the life beyond.

Live your best life. "Faith" your best faith, knowing that "faith" is primarily a verb and secondarily a noun. Grieve your best grief, believing you grieve in the arms of God. Hope beyond earthly hope the Holy One will be true to his promise to comfort all who mourn. Because...

The best part of grieving is believing.

What This Means

Romans 12:2 makes it clear God is in the transformation business, bringing about transformation in our lives as we have our minds renewed in the school of God. His words come to us via Paul in commandment-like language: "And do not be conformed to this world, but be transformed by the renewing of your mind, that you may prove (that is, that you may live) what the will of God is, that which is good and acceptable and perfect."

If the best part of grieving is believing, then the question is: what makes the believing possible?

New Testament scholar A. M. Hunter wrote: "The gospel has two sides---a believing side and a behaving side." When the "believing side" of faith is applied to the "believing side" of grief, we face the fact we cannot handle this storm of sorrow with our own strength and ability. We recognize we cannot handle the sorrow by ourselves, so we choose to believe in the One who comforts those who mourn. And we find it to be a good choice.

In Romans 12:2, as we have seen above, when Paul turns to the behaving side of faith something transformational takes place. The same is true with our experience of grief and sorrow. As we "faith" through our grief a gradual transformation actually takes place in our lives.

Even when we find ourselves submerged in grief and sorrow, the "believing side" of our faith makes possible the "behaving side" of our faith. With God's help, we live transformed lives. Even with our grief---actually in the experience of our grief---we are strengthened by an ever present transformative faith. Because we seek to live transformed lives, we may even experience transformational grief---a grief that eventually leaves us better and stronger than we were before the death of our loved one.[172]

However, not everyone believes or will believe.

Some actually make fun of faith and ridicule those who live by faith.

Like the man who made fun of our attempts to put a person on the moon. When it actually happened, he said it was on a "movie set" in the Arizona desert, a sham, a giant trick. Death and grief, like space travel, involve the hard facts of truth.

Death is real and so is grief.

Faith is real and so is the Holy One.

Some prefer to live without ever enjoying the adventure of faith and the excitement of a future that includes something like resurrection. It is your choice. I urge you to: Believe, hope, and always stand for the truth.

Remember Zephaniah

Zephaniah, remembered as a true prophet of the Lord, called upon the Holy One. In this three-chapter Old Testament book, we find a Chapter 3, verse 18, promise: "I will gather those who grieve..." When we grieve, oh how we want someone to "gather" us.

Whether appeals for repentance or thundering words of judgment fall upon our ears in faith or in rebellion, when times of grief invade our lives we hope for One who has the power and ultimate purpose to gather us in. For in our grief, we have nowhere else to turn.

Verses for the Valleys of Grief and the Mountain Top of Faith: "I will turn their mourning into gladness; I will give them comfort and joy instead of sorrow." (Jeremiah 31:13). "The Lord has done great things for us, and we are filled with joy." (Psalm 126:3). In Psalm 13, the psalmist cries out "How long must I bear pain in my soul and have sorrow in my heart all day long?" His pain about his adversaries is all the more true when the adversary is death itself, when one we love is torn from the book of our lives, like chapters ripped from a favorite book!

In Romans 9, Paul had "great sorrow and unceasing grief" in his heart because the people of Rome were without Christ and, therefore, without life, sentenced to death by their own stubborn, unyielding disbelief.

God and Our Grief: The Bible Story...from Isaiah to Jesus

The image of one who suffers "for us" first appears in Isaiah. In the verses from Isaiah 52:13 thru 53:12, we see the suffering and the exaltation of the Lord's sin-bearing servant.

The passage is one of triumph, a "looking forward" in history to the time when one identified as Jesus of Nazareth would make possible through his humiliation, his ultimate death and his third-day resurrection, the salvation of all who believe in Him and trust the Holy One for a future that lasts beyond this life.

The Chapter "Take-Away"

As James Muilenburg asserted in *The Interpreter's Bible Commentary*, "This is the most influential poem in any literature."[173] Isaiah calls this servant who suffers in our behalf "a man of sorrows acquainted with grief." "Surely he has borne our grief and carried our sorrows", we are told in Isaiah 53:4. What does this mean for each of us, this language of assertion: He bears our grief and carries our sorrows?

Quite simply, yet powerfully, it means: We never walk the path of grief alone, unless we reject the Holy One who walks with us in our grief.

In verse 5, "he was wounded for our transgressions." He bore our sin which meant his death and our eternal life. Verse 6 completes the picture in the poetic images of the following words:

"All we like sheep have gone astray; we have turned everyone to his own way; and the Lord has laid on him the iniquity of us all."

I was first taught these verses in my church when I was in the fifth and sixth grade. At the same time, I learned the words of Psalm 100, known by the faithful as "The Jubilate", meaning "Be joyful!"

Fran, you can't be serious! I'm grieving and you tell me, "Be joyful!" Yes, even as we grieve, we have reason to be joyful and can, in spite of our grief, one day come to know joy again.

"Shout joyfully to the Lord, all the earth. Serve the Lord with gladness; come before Him with joyful singing. Know that the Lord Himself is God; It is He who has made us (hear this language of the potter working with the clay of our lives), and not we ourselves. We are His people and the sheep of His pasture. Enter His gates with thanksgiving, and His courts with praise. Give thanks to Him; bless His name. For the Lord is good; His lovingkindness is everlasting. And His faithfulness to all generations." (Psalm 100:1-5 NAS)

The collective truth of these words amaze me still today, and their provision of comfort speaks to me in my salvation and in every grief I have suffered in this life.

THE GRIEF LETTER

I pray the same for you.

Your grief partner and believing friend,

Fran Buhler

A Grief PS: I shall always be thankful for the opportunity to discover the best part of grieving is believing. What a comfort! A true faith adventure!

1. What's your story? Stop and think about your life. Your experience of salvation. Your first and subsequent experiences with grief. Your gratitude for your salvation. Your thankfulness for God's comfort in your grief. Let's express our thankfulness to God right now.

2. Pray yourself, or use the Prayer below:

"God, our Father, we give thanks for your presence and comfort in our grief. We thank you for the influence and help of those special persons you placed in our lives. We give thanks for the experience of salvation, the journey of faith and the adventure of grief. Help us in the opportunities we have to introduce others to your salvation and the special assignments you give us to comfort those who mourn. In your Holy Name, we pray. Amen"

3. If you have not experienced the salvation that comes from and thru the Holy One, you may invite God into your heart right now, and begin the journey that will become the adventure of your life. Even if you're grieving…make it an opportunity for believing!

CHAPTER 33

THE ADVENTURE OF LISTENING TO THOSE WHO MOURN

Dear Reader and "Wanna-Be" Comforter,

We have made the case in *The Grief Letter* that grief is a venture, even a personal adventure, for those who grieve. And, as we shall see, our adventure does not end here!

Grief also becomes an adventure for those who give comfort by listening, whether as caregivers, grief helpers, grief family members or friends.

Why This Matters

In order to complete the circle or cycle of grief, grief helpers deserve attention and "honorable mention" in "The Grief Letter". Considering the larger scope of grief, they should not be left out.

For some, comforting those who mourn is a "calling". For others, it may be a job description. Yet many of us think of it in terms of our family responsibility. For all of us who are serious about comforting those who mourn, we need to become good listeners.

Over the last half century, especially the last 25 years, we have reached the point where the term "Caregiving" now has a universal meaning in our culture. Caregiving covers all of those personal needs an aging person may have before death. We have a general understanding of what it involves and a widespread respect for its importance.

What This Means

Maybe we need to do the same with the role and function of "grief helping." "Care givers" assume the "care giving" needs of family and friends prior to death. "Grief helpers" care for those in need following a death. Like caregivers, some "grief helpers" are professionals, such as clergy, Hospice staff, social workers, and facility staff. Some are "paid staff", such as long term care positions in assisted living facilities, rest homes, nursing homes, and other institutional settings. In addition, many volunteer their time and service. Others of us may view "grief helping" as an in-home family responsibility we assume ourselves with outside support.

So, in a perfect world, "care givers" would take care of "caregiving" needs prior to death and "grief helpers" would assist with the "grief helping" needs of someone after a death.

When it comes to the challenges of caregiving and of grief helping, nothing is more important than a willingness to listen!

So, what do we know about "grief helping" and "listening"? Hardly enough! Let me explain.

Research We May Not Know, From 1969

Bernadine Kreis and Alice Pattie met as widows. Having dinner one evening, "two lonely widows sharing a check", Kreis writes in their book *Up From Grief*, they talked casually about grief. Soon they were friends, excited and stimulated, exchanging experiences because they shared "one strong bond---grief."[174]

Kreis and Pattie decided to do a survey on "grief". They talked with 500 grievers, their families, friends, "and the pros who work closely with grievers: doctors, psychologists, lawyers, ministers."

"We often abandon people in their grief!"

One of their findings is that "we often abandon people in their grief!"

Read that again. "We often abandon people in their grief!" Remember they were published in 1969; but, personally, I think our typical response to grief remains about the same.

One of the grief "lids" they lifted was one particular griever's "sense of abandonment" with friends. Hear his testimony in his own words, and recall your style of grief comforting.

"Everyone meant well. They came to see me. The women kissed me on the check and whispered, 'I'm sorry.' The men shook my hand and said, 'If there is anything I can do to help, just let me know.' And then they sat around talking about the weather, even politics. They talked around me, but not with me or to me. It was a nightmare."

When asked what he wanted his friends to do, he responded: "Stop pretending it was a social call. My wife was killed in an automobile accident. I wanted to talk about her."

"I'm sure your friends thought it would be too painful", the interviewer said. "How would they know what to say?"

"If they had sat next to me long enough to listen---I would have talked about her. That is how they would know. The tears in my eyes, the look on my face, would have told them."

In his grief, the gentleman gave affirmation to the power of listening.

He wanted---he needed---his friends to listen. Not just be with him, talking; but listening!

In those intense grieving moments, perhaps more than anything else, he needed someone to listen.

The Chapter "Take-Away": My 21-year Observation

The "look" described above is a look I have witnessed with grieving families in a thousand funeral home visitation times. It is a "look" I wish I could place on a giant video screen in every house and temple of worship, regardless of the brand. This "look" is another reason I write "The Grief Letter" because the evidence suggests those who mourn at any point in time represent a much larger population percentage than we might think. (If you skipped the Preface, take a look at **GRIEF IN THE US TODAY** and see the annual numerical scope of grief across the US. Believe me, it will shock you).

What the grieving husband described above really needed, more than anything, was someone to listen. Listen. L-I-S-T-E-N!

Listening is the world's best available grief therapy.

We don't have to have an advanced degree to listen, although such preparation helps us know how to listen, what to listen for and how to make sense out of what we are hearing.

We don't need graduate preparation to listen.

We are born with the ability to listen. The key skill to listening is patience, and putting someone else first. The key is considering their need, instead of focusing on what we need or want.

Whether we listen or not depends on our personal desire and discipline to do so. There is no better way to comfort one in grief than to listen. Such an opportunity is always a pass - fail moment. Using our grief to help others with their grief will free us from the self-centered orbit to which our grief often evolves.

Let's be clear. As Diane Baggett, a professional grief counselor and wife of a Methodist Pastor and author of her own blog wrote on March 23, 2012 at 4:27 pm: "It is a mistake to believe grief can be avoided if we have enough strength of character, or enough faith. When we suffer a loss, whether we are among the strong or weak, whether our faith is small or great," she wrote, "it is natural for us to experience grief. It is not a sign of weakness, but a manifestation of our humanity."[175]

Early in our grief we are rightfully focused on ourselves, our family and our personal grief needs. Eventually we reach the stage of grief recovery in which we begin focusing on others and their grief need. At some point, by choice, we should transition from focusing on our own grief to the time when we can effectively focus on the grief of others.

Here's a good self-check: What we talk about indicates our brain focus. For example, when I am with a grieving person is my conversation focus on the person grieving or is it about myself and my own personal concerns? Am I thinking I am helping the grieving person when I am mostly talking about myself, my battles, my challenges? Monitor your sentence subjects. Is your conversation mostly about you and your grief need or are you appropriately focused on the one whose life is still in grief-shock mode with his or her sorrow?

The Adventure of "heaven-faith"

The adventure of listening to those who mourn reminds me of a companion adventure, the adventure of "heaven-faith". God's Grace is already at work in our grief even before we know it. Grace changes everything---including ourselves, as well as our grieving friend. Grace speaks to our grief in a language even grief understands. Grace responds to faith, even if it is just a "smidgeon" of faith, making us stronger in our faith and more able to move forward in our lives. Because "heaven-faith" is a life-long adventure!

Death is a friend---not something to dread and fear. In our sorrow there is

One we can trust. We may trust the Holy One. Death comes under His jurisdiction.

I have given much thought to death because I have spent a lot of time with grieving families in funeral homes and cemeteries. I have gone there hundreds of times for graveside services and the burial of dear ones loved by family and respected in the community. Always, this is an act of faith---never an empty ritual.

In such moments, we discover "heaven-faith" is for real, offering us strong comfort. I have personally experienced God's comfort in my grief. I believe in the Most High God. I believe in heaven. And I believe we "adventure" faith to a wholly different kind of existence beyond this earthly life.

What "heaven-faith" Teaches Us

"Heaven-faith" teaches us to "wait" upon the Lord. Some grievers understand---they get it---and celebrate God's love. Some, unfortunately, do not.

To wait upon the Lord is to do everything I can to manage my grief in the near term and to trust God for the long term. In our grief, we lose interest in academic or philosophical discussions. With heaven on our minds, we turn to reminder-verses that speak to our grief and sorrow in expressions of simple faith---"heaven-faith". A good bedrock example of "heaven-faith" is the psalmist's prayer for protection and guidance in Psalm 25.

In Psalm 25, verses 1 and 2, note the complete dependence, the singular focus.

Verse 1: "To you, O Lord, I lift up my soul.

Verse 2: "O my God, in You I trust."

In verses 4b and 5a, note the desire for divine direction, a complete dependence.

Verse 4b: "Teach me Your paths.

Verse 5a: "Lead me in Your truth and teach me.

Verse 5b: "...for You are the God of my salvation:"

THE GRIEF LETTER

Verse 5c: "for You I wait all the day."

The soul-yearning of "heaven-faith" also finds expression in Psalm 119:28: "My soul weeps tears because of grief; strengthen me according to Your word." Or Psalm 56:3: "When I am afraid, I will trust in you."

There are no better words for our strengthening than those of Titus, that little known, "hardly-ever-read" New Testament letter of Paul with which we close.

Think of the words below from the book of Titus as describing the philanthropy of God's grace, poured out on each of us. As you conclude *The Grief Letter*, be aware God stands ready to pour out His Grace upon you.

Verses that Leave Us in Awe:

Titus, Chapter 2:

Verse 11: "For the grace of God has appeared, bringing salvation to all people… (verse 12) "instructing us to deny ungodliness and worldly desires and to live sensibly, righteously and godly in the present age, (verse 13) "looking for the blessed hope and the appearing of the glory of our great God and Savior, Christ Jesus; who gave Himself for us…"

New Testament scholar F. F. Bruce called the phrase "who gave Himself for us…" "words of utter simplicity". In the life and death of Jesus Christ, the Holy One gave Himself for each of us.[176] May we in every grief of our lives remember God is the One who makes us one.

Titus, Chapter 3:

Verse 4: "But when the kindness of God our Savior and His love for humankind appeared,

Verse 5: "He saved us, not on the basis of deeds which we have done in righteousness, but according to His mercy, by the washing of regeneration and renewing by the Holy Spirit,

Verse 6: "whom He poured out upon us richly through Jesus Christ our Savior, that being justified by His grace we might be made heirs according to the hope of eternal life."

Did you note the phrase in verse 4? For every grief we experience, for every sorrow we suffer, verse 4 says it all. "...the kindness of God our savior and His love for humankind appeared..." What better way to end "The Grief Letter"!

My Personal "Thank You"

Thank you for buying and reading "The Grief Letter" with "Grief Adventure is a Life Choice", and the "Ten Commandments of Grief" plus "What to Say and Do When Someone Dies!" Thank you for joining me on this grief journey together, an adventure of grief and faith.

May God bless and keep you in your grief and in your laughter, as you live forward in the personal adventure God has for you.

If by chance the book has helped with your personal or family grief and healing, then, **please, gift a copy to someone. Keep "the grief letter" alive!**

Your grief partner and lasting friend,

Fran Buhler

A Grief PS: The words above from the New Testament book of Titus, describing "the philanthropy of God's grace", poured out on each of us, should make us think---and wonder!

1. Do our lives exhibit the kindness of God's grace? In the aftermath of death, in the presence of sorrow and grief, are we faithful, loving and thoughtful?

2. Challenge yourself by honestly asking and answering the following question: When I am with a grieving person, how well do I listen? Do I listen more than I talk?

3. My hope for every reader of "The Grief Letter" is my final Verse for both the Valleys and the Mountains of Life---anytime, anywhere:

> "I am He... Who will sustain you... And I will carry you."
> (Isaiah 46: 4 NIV)

In the Name of the Father, the Son and the Holy Spirit, all One in the Holy One! Amen.

APPENDICES

APPRECIATION FOR PREPUBLICATION READERS AND FOR PERSONAL ASSISTANCE

Appreciation for TGL pre-publication Readers

For a book written for grieving readers, I felt this placement should be in an Afterward so the hurting reader does not have to endure too many preliminaries. Yet I have an "up front" attitude about my appreciation for the generous help of several TGL prepublication readers who provided their personal reaction and professional comment. Two requested anonymity. I sought:

1. A balanced gender mix with a geographical diversity (eight states) and a grief inclusiveness of several specific categories of grief i.e. death of husband, wife, parent, grandparent, a child at birth, child, grandchild, military death, accidental death, suicide;

2. Clergy with advanced theological education and pastoral grief ministry experience; Clergy / clergy wives with personal family grief experience; other professionals likewise;

3. A seminary president / professor and former pastor.

4. Two grief professionals requesting anonymity: Hospice, counseling and psychology.

Pre-publication Readers (listed in the order they were asked):

Ms. Kathryn L. Funchess: Environmental attorney; Florida Department of Environmental Protection; Choir member, First Baptist Church of Tallahassee, Florida.

Dr. Ken Boutwell: Founder, Capital Health Plan; former President & CEO, MGT of America, management consulting firm.

Rev. Thomas Baines: Vietnam veteran, former Pastor, former Director of Missions, currently Interim Pastor, Piney Grove Baptist Church; Harriman, Tennessee.

Mrs. Beverly Baines: Retired, Production Department---classifieds, page layout and special design, *The Carthage Courier*; Pastor's wife; first of my three sisters, representing the Buhlers.

Mrs. Janice Cruce: Teacher-third grade, W.T. Moore Elementary; Pastor's wife; husband before his death was Pastor of Thomasville Road Baptist Church, Tallahassee.

Rev. Joel Hawthorne, Pastor, Montgomery Hills Baptist Church, Silver Spring, Maryland.

Nancy Buhler, former Director of Christian Education, Third Presbyterian Church, Silver Spring, Maryland; Fourth Grade Teacher, W. T. Moore Elementary, Tallahassee.

Dr. Doug Dortch, Ph. D., Pastor, Mtn. Brook Baptist Church, Birmingham, Alabama; my colleague in ministry who gave me the opportunity in 1994 to fulfill my 1958 "call" to pastoral ministry at FBC Tallahassee.

Dr. William D. Shiell, Ph. D, President and Professor of Pastoral Theology and Preaching, Northern Seminary, Lombard, Illinois; who affirmed my "calling" and enabled me to continue serving until retirement.

I was encouraged by this stellar group of prepublication readers, blessed by their support and I am grateful for the valuable assistance of their honest comment. Their review significantly improved the quality of the TGL narrative. Any deficiency is my responsibility.

Appreciation for Personal Assistance / Manuscript Prep / TGL Website

Paula Clayton: Served for 16 years as my secretary and personal assistant. Paula, who experienced the death of an adult daughter, prepared the annual "grief letter" mailings, gave personal reactions to early TGL chapter drafts and prepared the first TGL review drafts.

Josh Carpenter: A Florida State University Ph. D. candidate in Religion, Josh has experienced the death of a special grandmother, given helpful review and comment on the text and prepared the final manuscript documents for online submittal.

John Buhler: TheGriefLetter.com web-site with its strong "connecting" features was designed and built by our eldest son---the Silicon Valley "rep" in the Buhler family---who is with NVIDIA. John is Senior Design / Verification Engineer, located in Huntsville, Alabama.

Chip Buhler: This Pastor-son who has established and pastored churches in Tallahassee Florida and Atlanta Georgia, and has been associated with a dozen new church plants, and also coached his sons to two Georgia Christian High School State Championships, first gave me the confidence to tackle the challenge of my own web-site based on his experience constructing his personal ministry/coaching site.

Jeff Buhler: This MBA son, in several discussions back in 2010 and 2011 gave me assistance and confidence in thinking thru the "business-side" of TGL or else I would have been woefully unprepared for what lies ahead when TGL comes off the press.

Nancy Lou Baker Buhler: Faithful partner in life adventure and ministry, mother of our three sons, "Mom B" to our seven "grand" Buhlers, our daughters-in-law, two sons-in-law and the best thing that ever happened to me. The most valuable player among this group has been my wife, Nancy, without whom my ministry career and the writing of TGL would not have happened. She has been full of grace and patience with my years of research, writing and revisions. Numerous improvements in the TGL narrative reflect her insightful comments.

In her dual professional careers, Nancy has "adventured" her undergraduate double major in Elementary Education and Christian Education into a dynamic, high impact career. Nancy served as Director of Christian Education for Third Presbyterian Church, Richmond, Virginia, before launching her fourth grade teaching career. Nancy received numerous recognitions of her excellence, including "Teacher of the Year" in multiple years, in multiple categories and many other superlatives. In her daily life, Nancy has always been positive and thoughtful. Rooted in the same Tennessee hometown, Lebanon, near Nashville, we began dating as high school juniors and started our marriage in Virginia 55 years ago. She continues to live up to that long ago description of a Richmond, Virginia, service station attendant's weekly greeting: "Here comes Tennessee Sunshine!"

Nancy and I have each mourned the deaths of very special parents and grandparents, a close brother-in-law and nephew, a long list of uncles, aunts and cousins, plus numerous high school, college, and seminary classmates and our many friends "in the faith".

APPRECIATION FOR GRIEFSHARE AND HOSPICE

"GRIEFSHARE" ENDORSEMENT

Throughout the writing of "The Grief Letter", I was aware of an emergent "network of thousands of grief recovery support groups" called "GriefShare". "GriefShare" is a high quality resource for grief and faith. Grieving participants learn "how to walk the journey of grief... a place where grieving people find healing and hope." I have been blessed by a group of faithful "GriefShare" hosts from our church and participants from our community who share the video seminars and group discussions plus a personal workbook for individual grief help.

My participation in three editions of GriefShare in our church came after I had completed early drafts of TGl. I withdrew to finish the tasks of revision, manuscript preparation for a publisher, and a personal web site launch to support TGL. I wanted to write a grief resource to stand alongside GriefShare, adding to the grief help available publically. I did not participate in GriefShare again until I completed TGL and shepherded it through final revisions.

My intent has been to address individual and collective grief needs witnessed in the course of pastoral grief ministry over more than two decades. I felt it inappropriate for me to draw on "GriefShare" for information, quotes and supporting material.

My hope is that TGL will compliment "GriefShare", giving the expanding universe of grief and sorrow yet another faith resource for meaningful and effective grief help. Our world needs "GriefShare", no question. I strongly recommend the series for your personal grief or for your church's grief ministry to your community.

HOSPICE APPRECIATION

On day six of Hospice care, an email from a church member family announced: "This has been very hard. Thank you for thinking of us." And so another family, gathered in grief as a Georgia loved one lived out his life, turned to Hospice for the end-of-life support every family needs. This Hospice story relates to how TGL began.

Like many families, our Buhler family is indebted to Hospice for palliative care and loving assistance with our loved ones. Our family benefited immensely from the availability of Hospice Care in Lebanon (Wilson County), Tennessee. Hospice helped my father, a minister for half a century, come to the point where he could tell his wife, our Mother, it was OK for her to die. My Dad needed time to accept the gentle Hospice prompt that spousal permission was part of their sacred time together, reflecting the Presence of God in matters of life and death. As family, we learned this was a sacred time in which we who survive become part of the process of death. Hospice coached us to continue the process of positive grief, a life-long, life-giving, life-enhancing process.

The advent of the Hospice movement, the Hospice history of palliative care and loving assistance, has been the most significant development in medical care and grief ministry in my adult lifetime. Reading "The Final Act of Living: Reflections of a Longtime Hospice Nurse", by Barbara Karnes, RN, focused on the "dying experience" as the final act of living, first started my thinking about the life- experience of grieving---following the dying experience of several members of our church plus the death of my Mother. The result is "The Grief Letter", let loose in this world to focus on One who will "comfort all who mourn", where the adventure of grief leads to joy again.

THE GRIEF LETTER

CHAPTER NOTES

1. This first endnote addresses why I use "the Holy One" and the "Most High God" along with "God" and "Jesus" when I am referring to the Divine. If I were writing only for myself, I would be ok using only the referents "God" and "Jesus". Yet I have a responsibility to follow the lead practice of the Bible itself and use several references for "God", such as "the Holy One," "the Most High" and "the Most High God". In our world today, what we call or the word we designate for "God" tends to be divisive. Every religion and faith tradition has its preference and practice for references to God, including the Christian faith in which I am a follower of Jesus Christ. I use each of the above references to the Divine to be faithful to the biblical text, to be as accurate as possible and as inclusive as possible throughout "The Grief Letter" (TGL). Early in the story of humanity, many were like Jacob in Genesis 32:29: "Please tell me your name." Examples abound, such as Psalm 71:22, the "Holy One of Israel" or John 6:69, the "Holy One of God". But God does not belong exclusively to Israel, to the United States, to Jews, to Christians, to Muslims; so I often use "the Holy One". I was first influenced by Habakkuk 1:12, "O Lord my God, my Holy One". I am also drawn to Deuteronomy 7:21, "a great and awesome God"; but I gravitated to "the Most High" as we see in Psalm 47:2, because it encompasses "the great and awesome God" of Deuteronomy 7:21 or Nehemiah 1:5, and because it has an inclusive quality, something sorely needed in today's world. If we allow for what Paul wrote in 1 Corinthians 13:12, that in this life "we see but a poor reflection as in a mirror" or "dimly" or "through a glass darkly" as other translations render it, then we of different faiths would do well to come together around what I refer to in TGL as "the banquet table of faith" and let the Most High help us see and live and believe at a level higher than the walls of separation and misunderstanding have allowed us to live. This is my opening, my upfront and my continuing, page 1 prayer.

2. Bill Moyers, A World of Ideas (New York: Doubleday, 1989), 425.

3. The on-line example from which I quote caught my attention early in the writing process. When I returned to glean information for an appropriate endnote credit, it was gone. Or at least I was unable to locate it again. I do not have and have been unable to find the information with which to acknowledge appropriately the gentleman's name and the web source. I thank the gentleman for his wisdom and life perspective. I also deeply apologize I am unable to give the further credit he deserves.

4. Washington Irving, Goodreads online quotes: www.goodreads.com/quotes/44057-there-is-a-sacredness-in-tears.

5. Mary R. Bittner, "Jesus, Walk Beside Me" (Words c 2004 Wayne Leupold Editions, Inc. c 2010 Celebrating Grace, Inc. Macon, Georgia, 2010), 398.

6. Max Lucado, The Lucado Inspirational Reader (Nashville: Thomas Nelson, 2011), 32.

7. Dean Koontz, Odd Hours (New York: Random House, 2008), 252.

8. Meghan O'Rourke, The Long Goodbye (New York: Riverhead Books, 2011), 11.

9. John Claypool, Tracks of a Fellow Struggler: How to Handle Grief (Waco: Word, 1974), 14.

APPENDICES

10. Ibid., 73.

11. Ibid., 76.

12. Ibid., 95.

13. Ibid., 96.

14. Martha W. Hickman, "Introduction" in Healing After Loss (White Plains: Peter Pauper Press, 2012), 1-2.

15. Bob Deits, Life After Loss (Cambridge: Perseus Books Group, 2000), xii.

16. Ibid., xii.

17. Dolores Dahl, "When a Loved One Dies," in Suddenly Alone (Albany: Single Vision, 1987).

18. Diane Baggett, "Why Grief Counseling?" Blogpost 23 Mar. 2012. http://johnfbaggett.com/blog/?p=20.

19. Dr. Britton Wood, "The Experience of Grief: Reluctant Learning and Forced Growth" (publication by Annuity Board of the Southern Baptist Convention, 1997; 1998; 2000; 2001), 1-25.

20. Ibid.

21. Ibid.

22. Earl Grollman , Living When A Loved One Has Died (Boston: Beacon Press, 1977), 8.

23. Kathe Wunnenberg, Grieving the Loss of a Loved One (Grand Rapids: Zondervan, 2000), 57.

24. Anne Graham Lotz, Why? Trusting God When You Don't Understand (Nashville: Thomas Nelson, 2005), 27.

25. Wunnenberg, Grieving, 57.

26. Brian D. McLaren, Naked Spirituality (New York: HarperCollins, 2011), 169.

27. Deits, Life After Loss, 55.

28. Ibid., 55.

29. Missy Buchanan, Living with Purpose in a Worn-out Body (Nashville: Upper Room Books, 2008), 33.

30. Ibid.

31. Kirk H Neely, When Grief Comes: Finding Strength for today and Hope for Tomorrow (Grand Rapids: Baker Books, 2017), 140.

32. Ibid.

33. Ibid.

34. Henry Sloane Coffin, "Exposition of Isaiah 40," in The Interpreter's Bible Commentary (Nashville: Abingdon Press,1956), 446.

35. Ibid.

36. Doris Moreland Jones, And Not One Bird Stopped Singing: Coping with Transition and Loss in Aging (Nashville: Upper Room Books, 1997), 97.

37. Max Lucado, Facing Your Giants (Nashville: W Publishing Group, A Division of Thomas Nelson, 2006), 86.

38. Jones, and not one bird stopped singing, 19.

39. Ibid., 20.

40. Ibid.

41. Ibid.

42. Helen Fitzgerald, The Mourning Handbook (New York: Simon & Schuster, 1994), 85.

43. Hickman, Healing, June 28--Healing is "A Daily Journal for Working Through Grief" (Thus the calendar date instead of page number.)

44. Lucado, Facing Your Giants, 81.

45. George A. Buttrick, The Gospel According To Matthew, In The Interpreter's Bible (Nashville: Abingdon Press, 1951), 579.

46. Ibid.

47. Judy Heath, No Time For Tears: Coping With Grief In A Busy World (Chicago: Chicago Review Press, 2015), 91.

48. Candace McKibben, Chaplin – Big Bend Hospice: Contradictions open hearts to Understanding (Tallahassee, Florida: The Tallahassee Democrat, July 6, 2013) 2B.

49. AARP/The Magazine, "Lost and Found" (October/November 2013), 12.

50. Wil S. Hylton, Vanished: The Sixty-Year Search for the Missing Men of World War II (New York: Riverhead Books, A Division of Penguin Books, 2014), 2.

51. Ibid., 64.

52. Margaret Flanagan Eicher, "Survived by His Wife, a poem," in When I Am an Old Woman, I Shall Wear Purple, ed. Sandra Martz (New York: Papier-Mache Press, 1944), 39.

53. Ibid., 39.

APPENDICES

54. Emily T. Calvo, Marie D. Jones, and Ellen F. Pill, The Right Words to Comfort You (Mishawaka: Better World Books, 2011), 4.

55. O'Rourke, The Long Goodbye, 11.

56. Ronald Klug, When Your Parent Dies (Paris: Parasource, 2001), 10.

57. Ibid., 11.

58. Jessica Lamb-Shapiro, Promise Land: My Journey Through America's Self-Help Culture (article in the New York Times Magazine, January 19, 2014)

59. Infant Loss website, www.griefwatch.com/infant-loss.html

60. Ronald Reagan, Proclamation 5890: "Pregnancy and Infant Loss Awareness Month," October 25, 1988: Office of the Federal Register, October 26, 1988.

61. Angela Thomas Pharr, Do You Know Who I Am? (New York: Simon and Schuster, 2001).

62. Jan Goodwin, "Interviews with grandparents of Sandy Hook Elementary School students murdered in Newtown, Connecticut on December 14, 2012," in AARP/The Magazine December 2013, 18-19.

63. Orlando News-Sentinal of June 13, 2016, quoting a grandparent about the death of a grandson following the June 12, 2014, nightclub killing of 49 persons in a restaurant-entertainment venue enjoyed by the Orlando LGBTQ community.

64. Alexandra Kennedy, Honoring Grief (Oakland: New Harbinger, 2014).

65. Daniel T. Hans, When A Child Dies (Matthews: Desert Ministries, 1998), 1.

66. Lynn Eib, When God & Grief Meet (Carol Stream: Tyndale House Publishers, Inc., 2009), 15.

67. Melody Beattie, The Grief Club (Center City: Hazelden, 2006), 4.

68. Ibid.

69. Ibid., 5.

70. Ibid., 4.

71. Ibid., 8.

72. Ibid., 5.

73. Mary Craig, Blessings (London: Hoddler & Stoughton, 1979), 133-34.

74. Amy Jacobs, "The Stages of Grief and How to Cope," (Collegiate Magazine, Winter 2010-11), 8.

75. Ibid.

76. Ibid.

77. Ibid.

78. Ibid.

79. Ibid.

80. Ibid.

81. Madame De Gasparin, Metastatio: Vicissitudes of Grief (Elon Foster, 6000 Sermon Illustrations: An Omnibus of Classic Sermon Illustrations, Baker Book House: Grand Rapids, Michigan, 1956), 321.

82. Catherine M. Sanders, Surviving Grief…And Learning to Live Again (New York: John Wiley & Sons, Inc., 1992), 193.

83. Ibid.

84. Ibid.

85. Arthur Golden, Memoirs of a Geisha (New York: Doubleday Publishing Group, 2005), 37.

86. Walter Anderson, BrainyQuotes, https:/brainyquotes/quotes/authors/w/walter_anderson.html. Oct. 10, 1885 – Aug. 23, 1962.

87. Gerald Jampolsky, Brainy Quotes, https:/brainyquotes/quotes/authors/w/walter_anderson.html.

88. Charles L. Allen, When You Lose a Loved One (Grand Rapids: Fleming H. Revell Company, 1959, 2002)

89. Verdell Davis, Let Me Grieve but Not Forever (Nashville: Thomas Nelson, 1994, 2004), backcover quote.

90. Heath, No Time For Tears, xv.

91 Sanders, Surviving Grief, 198-205; 210.

92. Elizabeth Kubler-Ross, On Death and Dying (New York: Scribner, A Division of Simon & Schuster, Inc., 1969), 26.

93. Sanders, Surviving Grief, 198-205; 210.

94. Sharon Marshall, Take My Hand: Guiding Your Child Through Grief (Grand Rapids: Zondervan, 2001), 26.

95. Nancy Cobb, In Lieu of Flowers: A Conservation for the Living (New York: Pantheon Books, 2000, 2001), vii.

96. Ibid., ix.

APPENDICES

97. Thomas G. Long, The Good Funeral: Death, Grief, and the Community of Care (Louisville: Westminster John Knox Press, 2013), 7.

98. John Baggett, Finding the Good in Grief: Rediscover Joy After A Life-Changing Loss (Grand Rapids: Kregel Publications, 2013), 17.

99. Ellen Ashdown, Living by The Dead, (Kitsune Books, 2008), 2.

100. Ibid., 29.

101. Deits, Life After Loss, 67- 77.

102. Ibid., 67-70.

103. Ibid., 71-73.

104. Ibid., 74-75.

105. Ibid., 75-76.

106. Therese Tappouni, the gifts of grief: Finding Light In The Darkness Of Loss (San Antonio: Hierphant Publishing, 2013), xvii.

107. Ibid., 159.

108. Thomas J. Davis, God in My Grief: The Music of Grace When Loss Lives On (Valley Forge: Judson Press, 1998), vii.

109. Ibid.

110. Ibid.

111. Ibid., 3.

112. Ibid., 104.

113. Civilla D. Martin, Baptist Hymnal (Nashville: Convention Press, 1956), 274.

114. David Gambrell, "Great God of Every Blessing," Glory to God: the Presbyterian Hymnal (Louisville: Westminster John Knox Press, 2013), Hymn #694

115. Paul F. Keller, How to Grieve (Minneapolis: Kairos, 1984), 8.

116. Carol Staudacher, "Introduction" in A Time to Grieve: Meditations for Healing After the Death of a Loved One (New York: HarperOne, 1994), 2.

117. Ibid.

118. Chonda Pierce, NPR radio interview heard while driving Tallahassee to Tennessee. Other information is not available, either from NPR sources or from Chonda Pierce website.

119. Doug Manning, Don't Take My Grief Away From Me: How to Walk Through Grief an Learn to Live Again (Oklahoma City: In-Sight Books, Inc., 2005), 61.

120. Ibid., 67.

121. Minnie Louise Haskins, The Gate of the Year (A poem from "The Desert", written 1908, published 1912, by M. L. Haskins). Quoted by King George VI in his 1939 Christmas radio broadcast to the British Empire on the eve of World War II.

122. Rebecca Rene Jones, Broken for Good: How Grief Awoke My Greatest Hopes (Nashville: FaithWords; and Midtown Manhattan New York: Hatchette Book Company, 2016), iii.

123. Ibid., iv.

124. Cos Davis, "Moving Forward After the Death of a Loved One" (Nashville: Mature Living: Lifeway Christian Resources, Mar. 2011), 8-9.

125. Ibid.

126. Ibid.

127. Ibid.

128. Sarah Ban Breathnach, Simple Abundance: A Daybook of Comfort and Joy (New York: Warner Books, 1995).

129. Deits, Life After Loss, 151.

130. Ibid., 205.

131. Ibid.

132. Ibid.

133. Granger E. Westberg, Good Grief (Minneapolis: Fortress Press, 1997) 7-8.

134. Baggett, Finding the Good in Grief, 13.

135. Ibid., 143.

136. Ibid.

137. Ibid.

138. Dahl, Suddenly Alone.

139. Fitzgerald, Mourning Handbook, 25.

140. Thomas H. Troeger, View the Present Through the Promise, Celebrating Grace Hymnal (New York: Oxford University Press, Inc., 1986), 99.

141. Stephen P. Starke, "Scatter the Darkness," in Celebrating Grace Hymnal (New York: Oxford University Press, Inc., 2011), 211.

142. Paul Tillich, The Shaking of the Foundations (Wipf & Stock Publishers: Eugene,

APPENDICES

Oregon, 2012), 26. Note: Hitler barred Tillich from teaching in Germany, forcing his emigration to the US in 1933, where he taught in three divinity schools and published eight books.

143. Eugene O'Neill, The Great God Brown (New York, 1926), A play by Eugene O'Neill that is not well known, but produced this pithy quote.

144. Rebecca Turner and Paul Simpson, 2010 Celebrating Grace Hymnal (Celebrating Grace: Macon, Georgia, 2010).

145. O'Rourke, The Long Goodbye, 155.

146. Pope Francis at audience, June 17, 2015-AFP (Vatican Radio Website: Rome, Italy).

147. Harriet Sarnoff Schiff, Living Through Mourning (New York: Viking, 1986), 37

148. James White, Grieving: Our Path Back to Peace (Bethany House: Minneapolis, 1997), 23.

149. Hickman, Healing After Loss.

150. White, Grieving.

151. Long, The Good Funeral, 18.

152. Candi Pearson-Shelton, Desperate Hope: When Faith in God Overcame My Despair (Colorado Springs: David C. Cook, 2010), "Appendix A, A Community of Faith", 179.

153. Ibid., 181.

154. Ibid.

155. Max Lucado, The Lucado Inspirational Reader (Nashville: Thomas Nelson, 2014), 29.

156. Ibid., 30.

157. Norman K. Gottwald, Lamentations, in Harper's Bible Commentary (San Francisco: Harper & Row Publishers, 1988), 648.

158. J. R.P. Schlater, The Book of Psalms, in The Interpreter's Bible (Nashville: Abingdon Press, 1955), 166.

159. Ira Byock, The Best Care Possible (London: The Penguin Group., 2012), 2.

160. Fred Pratt Green, How Blessed Are They Who Trust in Christ (Carol Stream: Hope Publishing Company, 1972).

161. Edward M. Poteat, Psalm 77, in The Interpreter's Bible (Nashville: Abingdon Press, 1952), 410.

162. Paul Keller, Living the Promises of God (Minneapolis: Augsburg Fortress Publishers, 1988), 28.

163. Deits, Life After Loss, 56.

164. Fitzgerald, Mourning Handbook, 249-50.

165. Walter Russell Bowie, Exposition - Genesis 23:1-20, in The Interpreter's Bible (Nashville: Abingdon Press, 1952), 647.

166. Ibid., 648.

167. Ibid., 649.

168. Frederick W. Faber, 1854, "There's a Wideness in God's Mercy," in The Hymnbook / Presbyterian Church in the US; United Presbyterian Church in the US; Reformed Church in America (Richmond, Philadelphia, New York, 1955), 110.

169. Shelly Ramsey, Grief: A Mama's Unwanted Journey (West Bow Press, a Division of Thomas Nelson & Zondervan, 2013).

170. Robert Browning Hamilton, Along the Road (New York and London: G. P. Putnam's Sons, 1913), Source: Goodreads: www.goodreads.com/author/quotes/5758854.Robert_Browing_Hamilton.

171. Staudacher, A Time to Grieve, 2.

172. A. M. Hunter, Introducing the New Testament (London: SCM Press, 1961).

173. James Muilenburg, Isaiah 40-66, in The Interpreter's Bible (Nashville: Abingdon Press, 1956), 614.

174. Bernadine Kreis and Alice Pattie, Up From Grief: Patterns of Recovery (Minneapolis: Winston Press, 1969).

175. Diane Bagget.

176. F. F. Bruce, The International Bible Commentary: Titus (Grand Rapids: Zondervan, 1979), 1495.

TGL BLOG, EVENTS, AND MORE

Please visit us online at www.TheGriefLetter.com or follow us on Facebook @TheGriefLetter for additional resources including TGL Blog, TGL Events, or TGL Contact for more information about "The Grief Letter", related public appearances, or having author Fran Buhler speak in your area.

The Grief Letter (TGL) - Online

www.TheGriefLetter.com
www.Facebook.com/TheGriefLetter

The Grief Letter Blog

www.TheGriefLetter.com/blog

The Dreaded Question

"'How are you doing?' is the dreaded question," says a man whose wife died six months ago.

"What should be the simplest things get so complicated," observes a Mother whose son died before his time.

"I'm doing pretty good," a college student told me, referring to his Father's death, "until someone asks, 'how are you doing?' and then I come completely apart," he said. "From one moment to the next," he added, "you wouldn't know I'm any better than I was a month after he died. And it has been over a year!" he noted in frustration.

There is Sacredness in Tears

"The longer I live the more certain I am Washington Irving got it right when he wrote:

'There is sacredness in tears. They are not the mark of weakness but of power. They speak more eloquently than ten thousand tongues. They are the messengers of overwhelming grief, of deep contrition, and unspeakable love'."

Source – Washington Irving

TGL Author, Fran Buhler

"God does not remember our sin" (Jeremiah 31:34) but He "keeps track of all our sorrows" (Psalm 56:8).

"The prophet Jeremiah captures our grief pain with words we might never expect to find in the Bible, words even a ten year old can understand: 'My joy is gone, grief is upon me, my heart is sick." (Jeremiah 8:18)

"Grief is like putting an octopus to bed while someone sings 'Amazing Grace'."

ABOUT THE AUTHOR

Fran Buhler possesses a unique background and experience which includes a 21- year ministry career, plus a prior 27-year marketing and business development career. From Fran's two decades of grief ministry, conducting 776 funerals and memorial services, came first "the grief letter," and now the full-length book, titled: "The Grief Letter".

He grew up in Lebanon, Tennessee, a preacher's kid. He is a 1962 graduate of Carson Newman University, where he was elected student government president, voted football captain and selected all conference quarterback. In both high school and college, Fran helped teammates and class mates deal with team member and class member deaths.

Seminary Preparation: His education includes biblical theology, psychology of religion and pastoral care. TGL draws on the author's graduate education from both the Union Presbyterian Seminary in Richmond, Virginia, and Southern Baptist Theological Seminary in Louisville, Kentucky, completing his divinity degree in 1966, including Professional Certification in Clinical Pastoral Care.

Pastoral Experience/Church Leadership/All at one Church (FBC of Tallahassee, Florida): Fran has two decades of pastoral leadership and grief ministry experience. Fran's pastoral and ministry duties include: Interim Pastor/Ministry Coordinator 1993-94; Associate Pastor/Director of Ministry 1995-2012; Interim Pastor 2012-13; Associate Pastor/Director of Ministry 2013-14.

First Baptist Church of Tallahassee: Buhler's church averaged three dozen deaths a year. He performed or assisted in 776 funerals and graveside services. His two decades of pastoral grief experience were in a flagship church in its prime, 168 years old, a congregation blessed with multiple demographics in its ministries---Children, Youth, College, Young Adults, Singles, Hearing Impaired, Internationals, Adults and Senior Adults.

Family: Fran is the oldest of six siblings, the father of three children, the grandfather of seven, and is soon to be a great-grandfather. He has been married 55 years to his high school sweetheart.

Made in the USA
Lexington, KY
24 March 2018